Building
Information
Modeling

Other Books in the McGraw-Hill Construction Series

Defect-Free Buildings: A Construction Manual for Quality Control and Conflict Resolution by Robert S. Mann

Building Anatomy: An Illustrated Guide to How Structures Work by Iver Wahl

Construction Safety Engineering Principles: Designing and Managing Safer Job Sites by David V. MacCollum

McGraw-Hill Construction Locator: Building Codes, Construction Standards, Project Specifications, and Government Regulations by Joseph A. MacDonald

Solar Power in Building Design: The Engineer's Complete Design Engineering Resource by Peter Gevorkian

The Engineering Guide to LEED—New Construction: Sustainable Construction for Engineers by Liv Haselbach

Building Information Modeling

Planning and Managing Construction Projects with 4D CAD and Simulations

Willem Kymmell

New York   Chicago   San Francisco   Lisbon   London   Madrid   Mexico City
Milan   New Delhi   San Juan   Seoul   Singapore   Sydney   Toronto

The McGraw·Hill Companies

Library of Congress Cataloging-in-Publication Data

Kymmell, Willem.
  Building information modeling : planning and managing construction projects with 4D CAD and simulations / Willem Kymmell.
      p.   cm.
  Includes bibliographical references and index.
  ISBN 978-0-07-149453-3 (alk. paper)
  1. Building information modeling.   2. Buildings—Computer-aided design.
  3. Building—Computer simulation.   4. Building—Superintendence—Data processing.
  5. Construction industry—Information resources management.   I. Title.
  TH437.K96   2008
  692—dc22

                                                                2008005196

McGraw-Hill books are available at special quantity discounts to use as premiums and sales promotions, or for use in corporate training programs. To contact a special sales representative, please visit the Contact Us page at www.mhprofessional.com.

Building Information Modeling

1 2 3 4 5 6 7 8 9 0 DOC/DOC 0 1 4 3 2 1 0 9 8

ISBN 978- 0-07-149453-3
MHID 0-07-149453-7

Sponsoring Editor	**Proofreader**
Joy Bramble Oehlkers	Pratima Singh
Acquisitions Coordinator	**Indexer**
Rebecca Behrens	Steve Ingle
Editorial Supervisor	**Production Supervisor**
David E. Fogarty	Pamela A. Pelton
Project Manager	**Composition**
Tulika Mukherjee	International Typesetting and Composition
Copy Editor	**Art Director, Cover**
Patti Scott	Jeff Weeks

ABOUT THE AUTHOR

Willem Kymmell is a practicing architect with more than 30 years of experience in the field. He is also an Associate Professor of Construction Management at California State University (Chico), where he teaches building information modeling and construction documentation, construction document analysis, specifications, building code analysis, and architectural history. Mr. Kymmell's private practice includes residential and commercial commissions, consultations, and virtual building software training.

DEDICATION

This book is dedicated to Ken Derucher, Dean of the College of Computer Science, Engineering and Construction Management, and Mike Borzage, Architect and Professor of Construction Management at CSU Chico, for their friendship and continual positive inspiration and support.

Contents

Preface   xi
Acknowledgments   xiii

1 Background   1

Introduction   1
The Setting for BIM   4
Project Management   4
Project Documentation   7
Current Practice   8
Construction Project Delivery Systems   8
*Weaknesses of the Planning and Construction
    Process   11*
Goals for Process Improvement   13
Legal Considerations   17
The Transition to Model-Based Contracts   18
Contractual Incentives to Implement Change   21
References   24

2 Building Information Modeling   25

Introduction   25
BIM Concepts   27
*The Nature of the Building Information Model—
    What Is a BIM?   28*
The Processes of the BIM—How Is a BIM Used?   37
*The Benefits of the BIM—Why Use a
    BIM Process?   46*
BIM Planning   52
Planning the Purpose of the BIM   53
Specifying the Model   65
Planning BIM Implementation   81
BIM Implementation   84
*Selecting the Project Team—Team Information
    Processing   85*
*Developing the BIM Processes—Project
    Information Processing   87*

*Defining and Scheduling the BIM Deliverables—
    The Product   90*
References   92

3 Software Tools   93

Introduction   93
Modeling Tools   95
Non-3D Element Modelers (Process Modeling)   95
Surface Modelers   95
Solid Modelers   100
Model Production   107
Model Analysis   109
Qualitative Analysis   110
Sequential Analysis   113
Quantitative Analysis   113
Specific Software Options   115
Preparing for the Purchase   115
Software Descriptions   118
References   136

4 Learning BIM   137

Introduction   137
Learning Methods   138
Motivation to Learn   138
Obstacles to Learning   139
Recipe for Successful Learning   140
Skill Sets   143
Tool-Related   143
Process-Related   145
Role-Related   147
The Learners   148
Project Owners   149
*BIM Specialists (Managers, Operators, and
    Facilitators)   151*
University Students   152
Incorporating BIM in Existing Classes   166

5 Case Studies 173

Case 1: DPR Construction 173
*A Practitioner's Guide to Virtual Design and
Construction (3D/4D) Tools on Commercial
Projects: Case Study of a Large
Healthcare Project 173*
  References 204
Case 2: RQ Construction 205
*BIM at Yuba City—Sutter Surgical Hospital
North Valley 205*
Case 3: Turner Construction, Seattle,
Washington 214
*Introduction to BIM for Turner Construction,
Seattle, Washington 214*

Case 4: Gregory P. Luth & Assoc.,
Inc. 224
Tekla Capabilities 224
Case 5: Webcor Builders 235
*Implementation of Model-Based
Estimating 235*
Case 6: Turner Construction, Sacramento,
California 245
*Laser Scanning in Medical
Renovation Work 245*

Glossary 249

Index 263

Preface

This book on Building Information Modeling (BIM) was inspired by the observation that interest in the subject is rapidly growing in popularity. It is easy to miss the breadth and potential of this "revolutionary" process due to its inherent nature. Yes, the process is revolutionary in its anticipated effects on the construction industry; yet its concepts have been practiced for centuries in a variety of forms. This book endeavors to present the current "best understanding" of BIM a format that will benefit readers with varying levels of understanding of the subject. Most BIM practitioners have strongly supported this effort and are sincerely interested in helping others become versed in applying these tools and processes, to educate owners and construction colleagues, to encourage early collaboration between designers and constructors, to build better facilities, and to improve the construction business in general. It is not easy, however, to introduce change to the construction industry The ability to sell (show the value of) and encourage use of BIM concepts to owners, construction companies, and project team members (e.g., designers, fabricators) may be of more use than the ability to utilize the processes themselves. Humans resist change and these processes require a great change. In fact, they will result in a "cultural change" in every company that commits itself to their adoption.

The information presented in this book has been a part of "what and how" we teach BIM in the Construction Management Department at California State University Chico. This book represents a snapshot in time of the evolution of the BIM process. Even the meaning of the term "BIM" is a moving target, and rather than spending a lot of energy trying to pin it down, this work simply accepts "BIM" as referring to the broadest and most widely accepted meaning encompassing the processes of this field.

At this moment it looks like there is a potentially insatiable demand for BIM skills developing in the construction industry. All of design and construction education will need to rise to address the needs of the industry immediately; and the professions will also need to educate themselves as soon as possible. This work indicates a direction for the learning process to anyone wishing to add value and be successful in the construction industry with Building Information Modeling. This book is intended to inspire those readers who truly wish to improve our human lot by fostering collaboration.

The fundamental success of the BIM approach lies in its ability to facilitate what already comes naturally. The model helps us to more quickly see what's wrong. Viewing a 3D model thus can turn this characteristic into a strength. Since the 3D model also provides more transparency to the entire process, it can cause a certain level of discomfort; our work in the model can be seen more clearly by all those viewing the model. As humans, we like to see, but only be seen as we wish others to see us; in other words, we like to mask over those areas we have deemed substandard and emphasize the attributes we are proud of. Because BIM does not hide much, it requires a bit of getting used to. BIM

Figure P.1

The California Academy of Sciences. (*Image courtesy Webcor Builders, Chong Partners Architecture and Renzo Piano Building Workshop.*) See also color insert.

demands a lot of collaboration and forces us to relate to each other differently. It is psychologically a very healthy development, but not necessarily an easy transition. The necessary collaboration develops a team spirit and a particular enjoyment in supporting each other with the responsibility for the end product. The team members will more deeply appreciate their similarities, as well as their differences, and take comfort in the ability to cooperate, rather than compete, and take pride in the shared results of the team's efforts.

This book has been an attempt to step back from technology for a moment, to try and see it in the context of the human activity that surrounds it on a larger scale. There is a parallel between what the Internet has done for communication in general, through e-mail and web sites, and what BIM is doing for construction projects. The challenge of any age is to use the circumstances of the age, rather than to be used by them. In this age of technology the challenge is not to loose ourselves in the availability of information, and to manage the useful information properly. Technology may be forcing human interactions to change, but when we consider our cave-decorating ancestors, and see the delight they must have taken in their art, we can only conclude that it is presumptuous to think that technology will change human nature. Thus it is in all of our best interests to understand human nature a little deeper, and use technology to bring out the best in ourselves.

The intention for this work is to provide a conceptual background to Building Information Modeling. The same ideas will be presented in different subjects throughout this book, and to be read from cover to cover in sequential order is not its purpose (although there is nothing wrong with that either). This book may be browsed, or researched by topic, or simply used for reference, or as inspiration; the main purpose is to improve the understanding of the connectedness of all of its components. There is no teacher like experience, so the material herein needs to be put to use in order for it to have the desired effect on the reader. There will not be many "recipes" for action, our applications are generally too unique to rely on such an approach. It is best to understand the ingredients, the principles, and concepts, and then forge our own approach to solving the problems at hand. The case studies will give an idea of the breadth and depth of individual approaches, and hopefully be able to provide some direction.

Acknowledgments

There can be no saints without devils. The saint becomes a saint through the struggles with the devils. So it is with almost anything we wish to accomplish in this world. Anyone who has tried to introduce a new process into an established situation has first-hand experience in this area. Almost all of the people who have helped with the creation of this book have stories to tell about their personal struggles bringing BIM into their work environment; introducing change generally comes with intense struggles. Exactly who plays the saint and who is the devil in many of these struggles is not always clear either; and it really does not matter that much, because it is the struggle that enables us to produce the effort that propels us ahead. Thus, besides all those persons mentioned, numerous individuals have helped more than they could ever have imagined by trying to stop these efforts.

Besides the many contributions from the companies that have been cited in the text, I am above all grateful to the following individuals for their assistance, guidance, support, and generosity: George Zettel, Turner Construction, Sacramento, CA; my colleague Mike Borzage, who has been a partner in almost everything we have accomplished in BIM research and education; my primary mentors Dan Gonzales, Swinerton Builders, San Francisco, CA, and Dean Reed and Atul Khanzode, both with DPR Construction, Redwood City, CA.; Jim Bedrick and Matt Ryan, Webcor Builders; Chris Rippingham, DPR; Mark King, Lease Crutcher Lewis, Seattle; Renzo diFuria, Turner Construction, Seattle; George Rogers, RQ Construction; Frank Peters, McCarthy Construction; Dace Campbell, Mortenson Construction; Greg Luth, GPLA; Sue Yoakum, of Counsel at Donovan Hatem LLP; and William Lichtig, McDonough, Holland and Allen, Sacramento, CA.

Special thanks go to CIFE at Stanford, especially Martin Fischer and Renate Fruchter, who have been very inspirational throughout my acquaintance with them. The research that comes out of CIFE is some of the most creative and interesting in the field and their graduates are truly the fruit of that labor.

Tom Sawyer of *Engineering News-Record* was also very instrumental in this work. When I sent Tom an article about BIM education, he responded by commenting that I should write a book about the subject—so here it is. I would not have had the idea that this could ever have become a reality without his suggestion and encouragement.

Ken Derucher is Dean of the College of Engineering, Computer Science and Construction Management at CSU Chico. His support and encouragement, not only for the book, but for the development of the BIM curriculum in general, and the support from the industry for the program have set this effort apart from all others. I could not imagine any of this would have turned out this well without Ken.

A number of software companies provided information that helped me formulate my impression of the state of the software industry. Despite my sometimes-questioning attitude about certain aspects of some of the companies, I wish to express sincere gratitude for the help that I received from many of the individuals who work for these companies: Don Henrich, Viktor Boullain, Marcel Broekmaat, and Jake Evinger of Vico Software; Dominic Gallello of Graphisoft; Johnathan Widney and JD Sherrill of NavisWorks; Stacy Scopano of Tekla; Ron Kuhfeld of Bentley Systems; and Noah Cole of Autodesk.

I would like to thank the companies that are supporting the BIM curriculum at Chico State: Turner Construction; Webcor; DPR; and Swinerton Builders.

Lastly, I would like to thank Cary Sullivan and Joy Bramble Oehlkers of McGraw-Hill who have (and are) patiently and carefully guiding me through the publication process. Cary provided the emotional support to get off to an inspired start, and Joy has taken over and is covering all the practical aspects of this unfamiliar process. She must be doing well however, I am already beginning to plan the next publication.

Thanks to all.

Willem Kymmell

Building
Information
Modeling

1

Background

INTRODUCTION

Humankind has been interested in building construction for thousands of years. Construction projects, however, are typically too large for any one individual to accomplish alone, so from the very beginning humans have developed approaches to collaborating on such endeavors. Building often has a social context and benefits a number of persons, whose values it symbolizes. These large-scale accomplishments necessarily require collaboration on the part of the participants. Various cultures create social events around such collaborative efforts that are required to build a facility for the community or for an individual of that community. See Fig. 1.1.

Once completed, the structure becomes part of that community, and it can assume an active role, as though it has its own personality within that society. A building in its setting can "tell its story" and thus become an interesting part of the human experience.

Since building projects are often large and complex, to plan, design, construct, and maintain them may require many specialized persons. The need for efficiency and the profitability of owners, designers, and contractors are being challenged as our buildings and business processes become increasingly complex. The cooperation of many individuals with a great variety of skills and interests is required to make construction possible. The organization of this complex array of human interactions required for the construction of building projects is the subject of this book.

It is challenging to be a human on planet Earth. Each person has been given certain tools (our talents, training, and skills) to make the most of life. Specific talents or characteristics may enable a person to accomplish otherwise quite unimaginable tasks. Many people will attract the work that they seem most capable of accomplishing well. It is a little like casting an actor who will play the part in a production well because he or she can understand ("relate to") what is required for that specific role. It is clear, however, that the *understanding* of the part is critical to the success of the performance.

Figure 1.1

Barn raising. A historical example of collaboration in construction. Amish barn raising in Ohio. (*Photograph by Ian Adams.*)

Actors are able to convey the meaning of a play to the extent that they are able to understand their roles in it and communicate that understanding to the audience. Some roles are more natural for some persons than for others; some roles require more work than others; and sometimes it just is not going to happen, because the available tools are simply not the right ones for the job (e.g., a young person rarely plays the role of an old one well).

Assembling a project team can be very similar to casting and producing a play or a musical performance. It is unreasonable to expect the tuba player to take up a violin. Yet, in the construction industry it is not uncommon to forget that most persons' roles are determined by their talent and training. This did not happen by accident—their talent has attracted their training and become a personal experience that created a specific understanding for that role. Yet, it is possible for the tuba player to join the violin section and play in harmony. It is this type of collaboration that needs to be fostered in the performance of construction projects. And while there are always players who claim to be able to perform any role; it is best to verify this before the performance.

Human beings have some interesting characteristics that can both help and hinder the collaboration process. Humans have a wish to understand the nature of their circumstances; and the better the circumstances in which construction collaboration takes place are understood, the better the results of collaboration efforts will be. Thus bringing a collaborative team together will require open discussions and a fairly democratic approach to team management; yet the complexity of the projects makes a strong and reliable team leader essential.

The goals for a construction project will generally reflect the needs and wishes of the *owner*, since most building projects are initiated by an individual, a group of persons (company or organization), or a community. It is the task of the *project team*, the group of individuals working on the project, to understand and interpret these goals for the owner. The primary goal of all construction project team members needs to be project-related and to help the owner achieve her or his goals and business plan, i.e., to improve education, health care, factory productivity, etc. The secondary goals such as improving project quality, increasing construction efficiency (in time or cost of the construction), improving project safety, or reducing construction risks become team goals that can add value to the project for the owner.

The individual and collective goals of project team members need to harmonize, and not conflict with the overall owner's goals; this will require collaboration on the part of all team members and enable the ultimate success of the team. The use of *building information modeling* (BIM) as a tool may help in achieving the team's project goals; the BIM itself, however, should not be the final goal—it really is a tool. This book endeavors to outline the characteristics of the BIM process so that the reader may be better prepared to determine to what extent the BIM may be a useful tool to aid in improving construction projects.

An interesting characteristic of the BIM process is that it tends to make the management process more transparent; i.e., the three-dimensional (3D) model quickly shows what has and has not been achieved in any given area. The weaknesses of the project thus become more easily detectable in the BIM since most of the process revolves on visualization with the 3D model. This is clearly a large benefit of the process, but it can also become an obstacle for the team members who are not used to working in such a transparent environment. The successful use of the BIM process will require a different psychological approach than most of the building design and construction industry is accustomed to. *It is in overcoming the difficulties of the BIM approach that its greatest benefits are to be gained.* The efforts required to implement the building information modeling approach successfully will develop directly into its greatest benefits—those of improving the four basic concepts of human interaction shown in Fig. 1.2. This industry will not merely change because of software and technology alone; the necessity for change is far more fundamental. All the contributors to the planning, design, and construction of a project have to collaborate and work together to be able to produce the desired improvements.

Figure 1.2 illustrates the basic concepts of human action and interaction that directly relate to the subject of this book—visualization, understanding, communication, and collaboration. It is clear that all four of these concepts are interactively connected and both generate and reinforce one another. The diagram also suggests, e.g., that the alternative routes to gain understanding (of a given subject) can be approached through visualization, communication, or collaboration. Each of the four concepts reinforces the other three. The relationship among these conceptual

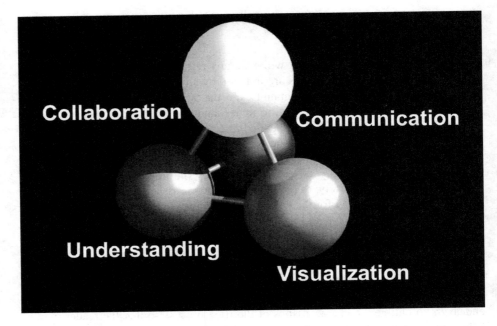

building blocks is similar to that of the carbon atoms in the diamond; the tetrahedron is the simplest and most stable geometric relationship of four elements in three-dimensional space.

An important assumption in this book is that although technology and software tools will continue to change, in the application of building information modeling, the concepts and underlying processes will likely change very little, if at all; and this book primarily addresses these unchanging aspects of BIM.

THE SETTING FOR BIM

Project Management

The three tasks related to building projects—planning, design, and construction—are often considered together, because they all occur in a relatively short time just before the occupancy of a facility. During the middle ages in western Europe, all three of these tasks were managed by the *master builder*—a single person who planned, managed, and executed the project for an owner. This position evolved into the architect's role in later ages. The plans for most projects were communicated from the master builder's mind to the owners and builders by means of scale models as well as direct personal instructions. At that time the entire project team worked on the construction site, and "construction documents," as we know them today, did not exist yet. The master builder would instruct the workers verbally and by demonstration, manage all administrative needs, and guide all aspects of the construction process. Many prototype details were developed as full-scale mock-ups at the construction site. The model with which the master builder had communicated the design intent to the owner became the basis for the *contract for construction* and also could be used to develop and refine the details of the construction process.

This process worked well as long as the master builder with the responsibility also had the authority to run the project as the representative of the owner. It limited the speed, size, and scope of projects to just what the master builder could handle personally; and this also meant that when a master builder needed to be replaced, the project could easily enter a crisis period. The advantage of this method, however, was that there was *one* person to solve problems and address the issues right there on the job, *one* person who had all the information.

As projects became larger and more complex, the master builder required more time to figure things out "in the office." Drawings (two-dimensional representations) began to be used as a means to communicate design intent and detailed construction information to the work force. Following the Renaissance period (around the year 1400CE), more and more construction projects were planned and drawn in an office that was generally removed from the construction site. These drawings became the primary means to communicate the building information to the persons constructing the project in the field. The most significant change was the removal of the master builder from the construction site, and the resulting need for an on-site "superintendent" to run the job from day to day. This split of the master builder's role into two new roles increased the necessity for reliable communication. This change in project management has had a very large impact on the evolution of the construction industry. The person who conceived and developed the plans for the construction project now had to communicate his or her understanding to another individual (the building contractor) whose task it was to ensure that these plans correctly materialized into a project. The traditional single owner—master builder relationship became a more complex threefold relationship among the owner, the architect, and the building contractor.

The evolution of this process resulted in *construction documents*, as we know them today. The drawn representations of projects became more sophisticated, as the role of the designer evolved separately from the role of the building contractor. The instructions for the construction of a building were increasingly communicated by paper documents. This method of communication led to unanswered questions and unanticipated situations in the field, since the person who had developed the project drawings did not work on-site, ready to address these issues. As the architect's role evolved more and more in the design direction, she or he became less "hands on" than during the master builder period. Various specialty fields also developed alongside architecture, i.e., structural, mechanical, and geotechnical engineering. The building contractor organized the entire workforce, acquired all materials, and performed the actual construction.

The increasing scope of construction projects led to the development of the various professional disciplines necessary to handle this complexity. Even though the single master builder soon lost relevance in building construction, the need for a single overall project coordinator became even more important. Traditionally the architect has played this role on the project team. In the last few decades, however, it has become more difficult for any one person to play this role well, and the construction industry is searching for a solution to this dilemma. The architect typically is concerned with the aesthetic and functional issues of the project; while the building contractor focuses on the project cost and construction processes such as schedule, quality, and safety; and the owner attempts to maintain a balance among all concerns.

The essential nature of construction management has not changed all that much over the last few centuries, and this continuity has resulted in a gradual development of improvements to this process. Today there is a choice among various approaches to project delivery methods, in an effort to make construction more efficient. The nature of the problems may not have changed much over these last few hundred years, but the complexity of today's construction projects has exaggerated them to an intolerable degree.

The expense and complexity of contemporary construction projects have brought the problems of the construction industry to the forefront of the owner's mind. The inefficiency of construction as an industry has caused numerous studies and analyses to be published with proposals to address methods to improve construction performance. According to U.S. government statistics, nonfarming manufacturing industries in the United States have doubled their productivity between 1964 and 2000, while the construction industry in 2000 has declined to about 80 percent of its efficiency in 1964. There are of course some very good justifications for this discrepancy (buildings have become much more complex during this time period), but it nevertheless is of concern to the construction industry. See Fig. 1.3.

Figure 1.3

The efficiency of the construction industry (solid line) in relation to all other nonfarm U.S. industries (dashed line). It is clear that the construction industry needs help.

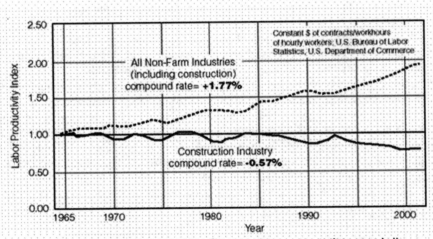

Labor productivity index for U.S. construction industry and all nonfarm industries from 1964 through 2001

Project Documentation

Numerous standards have evolved with the development of construction drawings and specifications over the past few centuries. These two-dimensional (2D) drawings and written instructions, which allow a contractor to build what the owner, architect, and consultants have visualized, are the current "state of the industry." Nevertheless they can also be the source of great misunderstanding, and most persons involved in building construction will agree that the use of only drawings and specifications is an imperfect method of planning and building contemporary complex projects. The use of 2D instructions in a 3D world requires multiple translations, from the original conceptual visualization in the designer's head to all other persons who need to use, add to, or refine the documents. A 2D document (drawing) is used to communicate each exchange of information between persons; this 2D communication results in a 3D visualization with each transaction, and thus each step requires a translation in someone's head, until the resulting instructions finally need to be visualized correctly by the person constructing the project. These transitions between persons may let oversights and errors go undetected until it is too late to address them effectively.

Construction is almost always site-specific and rarely performed by the exact same project team. These variables complicate the preparations for a project and can create substantial challenges for the project team. A certain amount of learning needs to take place among the project team to establish working processes that take into account the specific project and the personal qualities of its team members.

The repetitive nature of the information in a drawing set is another source of errors. The organization of the drawings for large projects can be complex, and as a project develops, it is likely that some of the changes are not "picked up" in all places affected in the documents. That is, a window change may be edited in plan and elevation, but the detail wall section may have been overlooked, thus creating a conflict in the documents. Complex projects generally need to be documented by a large team of drafters and specifiers; they have the daunting task of visualizing and providing construction details for what the designers have in mind, and the builders have to realize. These characteristics of documentation are clearly a challenge to the communication skills of all the project team members.

With the advent of computers, many builders and designers saw their drafting load lightened because repetitive tasks could be automated. The essential nature of documentation did not change, however; the same drawings and specification paragraphs describing the project are still used. A light table (the backlight allows several layers of drawings on transparent paper to be overlaid and analyzed) is also still the primary tool to analyze interference between various building systems, using plan views where height is often difficult to discern. This process still leaves much to chance because it is a challenge to visualize the coordination properly, without the ability to verify it prior to the actual construction. Most construction projects thus have a large quantity of *Requests for Information* (RFIs) about the documents, and a substantial amount of rework before all building components are coordinated during the actual construction. It is difficult with a traditional construction documentation set to completely and accurately represent many of the complex structures built today.

In 2D drawings it is often the transitions between elements that are difficult to represent and easy to forget to design and document. An example is the transition between different cladding systems, particularly where special attention needs to be given to waterproofing. It is often easy to imagine a project is represented completely without knowing what has been neglected, until the builder is ready to assemble it. At that time all that one can hope for is that it will not result in more than an RFI and hopefully be a resolvable issue.

CURRENT PRACTICE

The current condition of the construction industry needs to be understood to formulate specific goals that may lead to improvements. This section addresses the currently popular delivery systems, the weaknesses in these systems, and a list of general goals that address the weaknesses and point to a more efficient way of building.

Construction Project Delivery Systems

A *delivery system* is a contractual method used to realize a construction project. The contracts describe the relationships among all the project team members and their legal and financial responsibilities to the project and to one another.

Stemming from historical experiences, and out of the individual interests and incentives for performance as well as the lack of trust among some project team members, a contract structure has evolved that particularly safeguards the interests of the contract author. Contract authorship primarily begins with the project owner, the person who is responsible for most of the project's financial obligations from start to finish. Contracts generally result in the assignment and transfer of risk from one party to another, and therefore result, in "nonteam" behavior and competition among the project team members.

- *Design-bid-build.* The conventional *design-bid-build* project delivery method is based on an owner having the design prepared by a design team (an architect and consultants) so that several construction companies can bid on the construction of the project after the plans (construction documents) have been completed. The general contractor then builds the project under the watchful eye of the architect, who acts as the owner's professional representative. This process is linear in time, and the construction team is generally not able to be part of the planning process; the lack of early communication between the design and construction teams often leads to oversights and misunderstandings regarding the details of the project.

Due to the many inherent weaknesses in this process, numerous other contractual methods have evolved over the last century. With the contentious nature of the relationship between the architect and contractor, some owners have first hired the contractor and then asked the contractor to consult with an architect regarding the design of the project; or the owner might hire an architect with the stipulation of involving a specific contractor from the early planning stages of the project. In some cases, the owner hires a *construction manager* (CM) and lets the CM contract with both designers and contractors. These various approaches are outlined by the American Institute of Architects (AIA) in conjunction with the Associated General Contractors of America (AGC) in a publication entitled "Primer on Project Delivery" that can be found on the AIA website.* The Construction Management Association of America (CMAA) also publishes "Choosing the Best Delivery Method for Your Project," which can be downloaded from their website.† These methods had already begin to complicate the bid process and were cause for the evolution of some of the following negotiated approaches to building contracts.

- *Design-build.* The design-build contract emerged with either the architect or the builder leading the team. This process is an attempt to involve the design and construction teams in collaboration throughout all phases of the project. This creates new challenges from a contractual standpoint since the project cannot easily be put out to bid in this delivery method. Design-build projects are generally negotiated with a guaranteed maximum price (GMP) so that the entire project team works toward delivering the best product within this GMP.
- *Design-assist.* A design assist approach to construction is a variation on the design-build method. The owner hires a general contractor and specialty subs (subcontractors) who in turn consult with a design team during the planning phases of the project, to provide expertise that will prove practical in the development of the design and the assembly of the construction documents of the project.

Both design-build and design-assist methods encourage the involvement of both the builder and the designer early in the planning process. Either the builder or the designer may play the dominant role on this team, and most of the work is negotiated rather than bid out. These negotiations can occur at different levels of detail; a mechanical systems design-build firm, e.g., can take responsibility for a GMP for its share of the work, but in turn bid it out to subcontractors and/or fabricators who will actually do the construction. This of course eliminates the subcontractor or fabricator level of input from the design and planning phase of the project; however, it is not always possible to negotiate with all entities involved during the planning phases of the construction project.

The term *guaranteed maximum price* that is generally attached to these last two methods has interesting implications; it generates a continuous negotiation throughout the design and construction process between the parties to such an agreement. There is a constant assessment of the risk for the project, and discussion as to who will take responsibility for it. In the end, however, it is the owner who usually is forced to assume the bulk of the risk, by having to accept the financial burden of the cost of that risk to the participants. Therefore these methods work best in an environment where there is a preestablished trust and familiarity among the team members. When the team members can feel confident that they are not assuming certain risks when working with familiar partners, these cost risks may be eliminated from the project.

Contractual responsibilities have to be clear and realistic. There needs to be an incentive in the contract for collaboration rather than litigation. To keep each participant motivated to collaborate, increased efficiencies need to be worthwhile for all members of the project team. These "sharing mechanisms" need to be spelled out in the contractual relationships among all team members.

---

*The AIA website is www.aia.org.
†The CMAA website is www.CMAAnet.org.

In the BIM workshops that Construction Simulation Lab offers to the industry, Michael Borzage, professor of construction management, CSU Chico, has described the weaknesses of current delivery methods and outlined a revised construction management delivery method as developed by GM for its automobile fabrication plant construction:

In the traditional design-bid-build project delivery approach, the design and construction portions are deliberately segregated by means of specific contracts with the Owner, the Architect and the Builder. While the reasons for employing this approach may be debated, there can be little disagreement that the owner loses opportunities for added value, and takes on additional risk in at least three important areas. First, the project budget is established early in the process, and serves as an important constraint in the project program. Scope and quality are tailored to this preliminary cost estimate. Unfortunately, the builder, who best understands true cost, is not included in this process until the completion of construction documents. All too often, the owner is first made aware of the shortcomings of the design-bid-build approach at bid time. This takes the form of "sticker shock," in that the bids sometimes far exceed the proposed budget, thus creating a serious dilemma. The construction documents (CDs) require a tremendous effort that involves an investment of considerable time and resulting fees. Following the bid opening, owners and architects have reason to hope the CDs are salvageable. However, regardless of the strategy employed to identify and to reduce the areas of the project generating excessive costs, the result is damage control at best, and more often than not has disastrous consequences.

The second area of missed opportunity is the optimization of the original design program to maximize the value of the final project. Clearly, it is too late to add square footage or additional stories at bid time. It is then also too late to consider alternative materials, or systems that will already be deeply embedded into the bid documents. Life cycle costing, or market analysis of sales or lease conditions can no longer be considered as influential factors on the project design.

The third opportunity missed by the design-bid-build process is caused by the organization of the design work according to the architectural work phases. The programming/schematic design, design development, and construction document phases become the major project milestones. As a result, large blocks of design time float along over many weeks without focus. There is often little accountability for this time, and it can result in considerable waste of both time and design work that is found to be unusable. This "leap-of-faith" process also results in critical portions of the project not being coordinated with each other, which in turn translates directly into re-work, and extends the project's overall cost and duration.

The owner (and entire project team) will find greatly increased success in an alternative delivery system that utilizes building modeling, and employs a tight coordination between all disciplines throughout the entire project. A design build (or design assist) approach allows the input of the sub-contractors and fabricators to be included during the pre-construction planning phases. These team members bring both construction expertise as well as reliable detailed cost data to the planning stages of the project.

The design process becomes iterative with high frequency cycle periods. The design progresses in small but tightly controlled steps, rather than the large open blocks of time associated with the traditional methods. This work flow is also carefully coordinated with all critical trades before it progresses into a new iteration. Lost time and wasted rework is minimized.

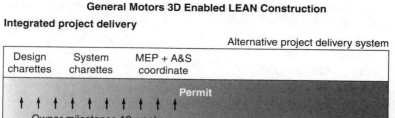

Figure 1.4

General Motors 3D
enabled design-
build lean con-
struction. (*Image
courtesy
Construction
Simulation Lab.*)

Figure 1.4 shows a diagram of the project delivery methodology employed on General Motors highly successful new auto plants.

The illustration of the GM delivery method shows a thorough integration of the planning and design activities of the project. The traditional methods would show linear and disconnected graphics for these activities. A collaborative and iterative planning phase will greatly improve certain aspects of the design quality and construction performance for the project. The challenge for building construction will be to let each project team member do what she or he is best at, and to coordinate the whole into a better result. This collaboration will leave the architect responsible for the functioning and aesthetics of the project, while the contractor will ensure that the design is buildable and affordable; clearly early cooperation will be the key to a successful resolution.

Weaknesses of the Planning and Construction Process

The largest problem in the planning and construction of building projects is the incorrect visualization of the project information ("the devil is in the details"). If it is not fully visualized, understood, and communicated, it cannot be represented correctly in the contract documents and may consequently create problems during construction. Difficulty in visualization begins with the owner's and end users' definition of need and visualization of space. It is critical that the designers and owner/end users understand one another in relation to the project requirements. It is necessary for the designers to understand what constitutes a *defect* in the owner's mind.

Once a design is represented in a series of drawings, the contents of these documents may not be clear to all who use them. The standard method to formally address such questions is to issue the RFI (Request for Information). The RFI is the first indication that communication was inadequate; the information (generally drawings or specifications) is either not understood, or may simply not be there; or the project may actually have an unresolved problem. In any case, the RFI is an indication that a particular issue could actually become a problem, and it will require some special effort to respond to such a request. The RFI is generally at least a symptom of inadequate communication that in turn often stems from an incorrect or incomplete understanding on the part of the person who prepared the documents.

Communication Difficulties

The complexity of construction projects and the involvement of so many individuals can create strenuous demands on the communication between the project team members. Human nature may also be an obstacle to efficient communication. Persons of different character or cultural background often work together. Someone may simply not "like" someone else, or may have difficulty "understanding" that person. There may be difficulty for an individual to have a personal concern as regards to another team member's success with his or her tasks. All these conditions are not conducive to a successful and cooperative team effort.

Most of design and construction-related communication consists of ideas that have been translated back and forth between the 2D representations and the 3D space. The visualization, understanding, and actualization (construction) take place in 3D space, but most communication takes place through 2D diagrams and text (drawings and specifications). Once an idea has been translated back and forth a few times by different individuals, it is not surprising that it may have become unrecognizable. This process has been accepted only because there has been no better alternative. Computer drafting has not made a change in the essential process—the same views and same text are still used as instructions for building complex objects.

Competition among Team Members

Construction project teams often include individuals who place maximization of their personal gain from the project above the project goals and interests. Most contractual documents in place today are written to protect the interest of the team member who is responsible for writing it. A contractor may count on postbid clarifications to add scope to a project in which he feels the documentation is incomplete; this will entice him to be more aggressive with the original bid, as long as he can count on change orders during the course of construction. It may be difficult for a subcontractor to work efficiently after or around other subcontractors, i.e., given issues of proper cleanup, timely removal of equipment and materials, etc. Damage caused by subcontractors to previously completed work may also pose a problem. In other words, contemporary construction teams often do not behave as one team challenging the project, but as competing teams challenging one another.

Risk Shifting

Dissatisfaction with traditional contractual forms has led to the development of alternative delivery methods; essentially most of these variations merely represent the shifting of the risk from one team member to another. In the end, however, the owner, usually bears most of the financial burden for the inefficiency and problems of the project.

Most contractual relationships have no built-in incentives for collaboration. Construction firms are also hesitant to experiment with methods that tend to benefit the owner when they see little chance to create a benefit for themselves from it. This includes risk issues; as long as the owner ultimately bears the risk, there is no incentive for change, except from the owner. At this time most of the contractual and management process changes are still mandated by owners. It is, however, primarily through the removal of risk that it is possible to change the nature of the construction industry.

Project economics are forcing the improvement of construction efficiency, and competition will rearrange the major players in the field.

Litigation

Litigation and construction have been virtually synonymous for too long. Due to the overwhelming complexity of the construction industry, there are too many opportunities for disagreements about the resolution of conflicts, and errors and omissions, generally originating from the planning phase of the project. Project team members are often well advised to build the cost of a certain amount of litigation into their bid proposal. *Litigation happens when there is not enough communication and collaboration among the project team members.* Almost all differences can be worked out in compromise through effective communication. Since the legal industry is the only entity that really benefits from litigation, it is in the team's best interest to collaborate and minimize these avoidable expenses.

Goals for Process Improvement

Goals that are project-related will generally be directly derived from the needs and wishes of the owner and other project team members. The goals will focus on achieving desirable end results for the project, and so they also relate to removing obstacles that might stand in the way of progress toward these results. These goals can thus be seen as reinforcing positive factors as well as removing negative factors.

The weaknesses of the construction process need to be understood to address them effectively. But simply analyzing the symptoms is not enough; the underlying causes of the problems have to be discovered and addressed. The formulation of project goals needs to take the causes of the inherent weaknesses of the construction process into account. These weaknesses may sometimes be part of the process itself, and at other times they may be due to the specific characteristics and limitations of the project's circumstances or project team members.

All the concepts listed below can ultimately be effective in improving the efficiency of a project and will thus either directly or indirectly reduce the cost of the project. For clarity, however, the concepts have been separated into the following five categories: reduce risk, reduce cost, reduce time, improve project quality, and improve life cycle performance.

Reduce Risk

Improve Communication   Unreliable communication is a critical factor in the creation of risk in a construction project. The complexity of construction provides numerous opportunities for things to be misunderstood or missed entirely. Each project team member needs to be responsible for the communication of essential information during the course of the project. Communication channels need to be clearly defined and tested at the beginning of a project.

Collaborate   Team collaboration is also a critical factor to risk reduction. Generally team members prefer to work on their own and not share in either the success or failure with other team members or entities (i.e., the mechanical subcontractor has no interest in the financial success of the electrical sub, but will help in the coordination of the required work as far as it affects the mechanical work).

Collaboration is based on the concept that all team members work on the same project with the same goals, in support of the owner's interests; it is everyone's responsibility to put these goals first and get help from other team members to solve specific problems that affect the ability of the entire team to perform optimally. Good communication and a sound contractual relationship among all project team members are essential aspects of collaboration.

Anticipate Problems   This implies the improvement of predictability of various factors of the planning and construction processes. It is possible to drastically reduce RFIs and change orders by understanding the construction details well enough that all construction information can be documented and communicated completely and accurately in the project planning phases. Methods that facilitate the ability to foresee potential problems and oversights need to be implemented. All aspects of the construction project should be coordinated early, and the overall project has to be better understood to reduce associated risks.

Improve Safety   Safety on the jobsite is high on the priority list for any construction project. A good safety record will also lower insurance rates for the project.

Reduce Cost

Study Parallel Industries   The development of production processes in parallel industries can serve as a model for improvements in the construction industry. The practices of Toyota have already been adapted for use in the construction industry by Greg Howell and Glen Ballard of the Lean Construction Institute (see next paragraph). The use of technology is an important aspect of these improvements. The construction management processes have been lacking in the use of technology in comparison to most of the other industries. The automotive and aircraft industries have been improving the manufacturing processes by virtually prototyping products, since the necessary technology has been available. With a virtual 3D computer model it is now possible to create a "full-scale" simulation of a construction project during the planning stages.

Apply Lean Construction Principles   A significant attempt to address some of the major shortcomings of the construction industry is made by the Lean Construction Institute (LCI) under the guidance of Greg Howell and Glenn Ballard. **Lean construction** principles can have a fundamental effect on the current delivery methods in the industry; these principles were developed in the 1990s and have been gaining in popularity with both owners and construction companies. The core principles of this approach are to minimize waste and add value, and they have their origin in the manufacturing industries.

Lean construction principles are based on the business and manufacturing practices developed by Toyota Motor Company in Japan. Toyota was trying to develop a consistent quality product that could initially supply cars for the Japanese market and ultimately compete in the U.S. market. Having its roots in automatic weaving looms, the company had already developed a system that would shut down the production process whenever a defect was detected, i.e., a thread ran out. This virtually eliminated wasted product due to defects, a problem that had always plagued the U.S. auto industry, i.e., large parking lots with cars from the production line that required some repairs.

Another problem for the Japanese company was the inconsistent demand for the product, which led to the second fundamental principle of the Toyota production system, or TPS, namely, *just-in-time (JIT) delivery*. This meant that there would be minimal inventory of parts, as well as finished automobiles, thus minimizing investment in both the production and the amount of space required for the production process. This second characteristic of TPS also required that the supply chain be carefully managed, so that product could be delivered whenever necessary.

These two principles had far-reaching effects on the manufacturing process for Toyota; they decentralized authority and put the workers in positions of responsibility for product delivery. The cars could have no defects because that would stop the production process and not permit timely delivery. Components could also not be stockpiled in any given area, which made the various production units more dependent on one another, since the entire system can move only as fast as the slowest link in the chain. Thus the whole factory was trying to keep the process moving as quickly as possible; in other words there was built-in incentive for success of the whole process, rather than competition among individual components of the process.

Greg Howell and Glen Ballard have attempted to synthesize the TPS principles into an approach that works within the U.S. building design and construction industry. The equivalent to flow of product is identified as the work that is completed by one team and handed off for the next task. This makes this approach relate directly to construction schedule tasks and thus is more easily understood for a construction project. The construction process planned in this fashion will lead to a reliable work flow for the project teams, which can be achieved only by collaborative planning of all participants for each part of the work. A continual updating of completed work (checking for defects) and commitments will be critical to maintaining the anticipated work flow. Successful implementation of this management technique will result in lower project costs, shorter construction schedules, and better jobsite safety and quality. The Lean Construction Institute calls this system the *Last Planner System* (LPS), and it is the equivalent to just-in-time delivery for manufacturing.

One aspect of lean construction is to refine existing methods to improve productivity or reduce waste. *Waste* can refer to materials, energy, time, money, etc., and often the reduction of waste will result from the refinement of a process, i.e., the way we do something. Simulating a project is a great opportunity to reduce the waste in the project because all the processes through which the project is being realized can be visualized.

Prefabricate   **Prefabrication** is based on the concept that production is more controlled and predictable in a factory than on a construction site. The construction industry is attempting to increase the prefabrication of building components. Prefabricated components require tighter tolerance control in the field, as well as some detailing constraints on the prefabricated units in relation to their use in various applications. By necessity, prefabricated units have a lot in common so that a large number can be fabricated more efficiently; they cannot be custom pieces any longer. That is, there is greater efficiency in the production of a line of generic trusses than in the fabrication of a specific truss order for a particular building.

Reduce Time

Improve Preconstruction Planning   The planning process itself needs to be analyzed through improved scheduling of all the BIM (planning) related activities. It is possible to improve preconstruction scheduling through better collaboration and faster question/answer turnaround time between project team members. This is an area for improvement that is frequently overlooked, but the increased complexity of the planning phase with close collaboration among all project team members necessitates this. The **Center for Integrated Facility Engineering (CIFE)** has done a lot of research for the construction industry in this particular area.

Improve Construction Scheduling   The construction process itself can also be improved through better scheduling of all construction-related activities. The visualization of the construction process is often represented by the schedule, usually a bar chart showing the duration of various construction tasks and their interdependencies. The bar chart can be made more visually clear by representing the tasks and their time lines so that it would be simpler to understand the construction sequence and visualize improvements for it. Construction schedules do not always have a good reputation within the industry; frequently they are not being maintained, and they do not often represent a thorough understanding of the project. Using the schedule to develop a more detailed analysis of all project tasks will result in a better understanding of the project and will allow a tighter (and probably more realistic) time line for all the construction tasks. (See "Project Control" in the Glossary and Index.)

Improve Project Quality

Improve Project Design   There frequently are opportunities to develop ways to improve the design of the building project. Improvements can consist of a functionally better design, enhanced project aesthetics, better use of materials, etc.; and generally these improvements result in increased owner comfort, building functionality, community esteem for the project or the process that created it (i.e., Leadership in Energy and Environmental Design, or LEED, projects), or reduced long-term maintenance costs. Having project user **design charettes** and early schematic design consultations with particular experts is another way to investigate improving the design quality of a project.

Improve Construction Quality   The overall project quality can also be improved by affecting the construction processes of the building project. Improvements can consist of better construction processes (i.e., impact on the site and environment from the construction process), better assembly methods, reduction of project waste, safer building methods, etc.

Improve Life-Cycle Performance

Improve Maintainability of Components   Reducing the life-cycle cost of the project is generally related to looking ahead at the longevity of materials and the performance of the building components over time. LEED ratings for construction projects take many of these issues into account.

Improve Energy Use of the Project   Energy consumption of the project is also addressed by LEED ratings. Both reduction of the energy consumption related to the operation of the project and the reduction of components that require energy in their production can be optimized through the evaluation of alternatives early in the design process.

LEGAL CONSIDERATIONS

The legal aspects of implementing building information modeling have been an area of concern to many owners, A&Es (architects and engineers), general contractors and subcontractors. Issues related to model ownership and responsibility for model accuracy, as well as concerns about the responsibility for the cost of producing and managing the model, top the list of perceived legal obstacles to embracing the BIM process. Current contracts for design and construction services rarely address modeling issues. Current contracts also do not address the sharing of the benefits (or risks) from this additional efficiency (and reduced project risk) among the project team members. It is common for the design consultants, the general contractor, or subcontractors to implement BIM at their own cost and risk. But given that the project is likely to actually cost less (and the fact that so many in the industry are so anxious to implement BIM bears this out), it is often the owner who benefits the most from the improvements due to the BIM process. It would be wise for the industry to develop a contracting method whereby all participants on the project team would share in the benefits from the improvements resulting from the BIM management techniques, thus placing the contract in the position to provide the incentive for collaboration and risk reduction.

In Australia and some European countries, the construction industry is using contracts between the project team members in which litigation is disallowed, except in cases involving criminal or other extreme actions. The team members agree up front that they will work out all project problems by negotiation among themselves, and all will benefit (or suffer) equally from the decisions made by the project team. It is important to remember that the owner is also one of the project team members. It is critical that some methods be developed in which the contract will actually encourage the type of collaboration required to take the best advantage of the BIM process.

In California, Sutter Health is planning a large amount of new construction and has shown an interest in these new contracting approaches. Until recently, most developments in contracting have produced less than satisfactory risk assignment; rarely have new contract methods created incentives for new behavior that would result in a reduction of the overall project risk. With the use of BIM and a collaborative approach (the incentive for new behavior) to solving the project's problems, it may actually become possible to bring about a significant reduction of overall project risk. An attorney will be a powerful ally to the project team, and it is clear that care has to be taken to choose a counselor who is capable of fairly supporting the team's efforts to represent the owner's interests.

The Transition to Model-Based Contracts

Despite many recent developments in project delivery methods, owners are often still dissatisfied with the results of the construction industry; projects still take too long and come in over budget, while the quality frequently is not up to the client's expectations. The irony is that, on a new project, the project teams competing for the work often promise that "this one will be different," while in fact the changes from the last project are so minimal that it is unrealistic to expect a major change in the outcome. The structure of construction contracts is based on their history and reflects the type of contracts required by the industry. The American Institute of Architects and the Associated General Contractors (of America) have each individually developed a series of contracts that address the popular modes of project delivery. Many larger companies will have their own attorneys draft custom contracts reflecting their needs on any given project. Needless to say, these contracts do their best to reflect the interests of the author, and are only as concerned with the interests of the other participants as they are forced to be. Moreover, these contracts are based on more traditional delivery methods, few of which are capable of addressing the collaborative needs of the BIM process.

The current contract structure is often based on separate contracts between the owner (or project manager) and architect for a design and the required construction documents, and between the owner (or project manager) and the construction contractor for the building of the project for a specific sum according to the construction documents. Traditionally the construction contractor has had little or no influence on the work of the architect; this "disconnect" was based on the historical belief that the architect could manage all aspects of a project for the owner, including the construction cost projections and any constructability issues. The changes in the construction industry during the 20th century, in response to the scope and complexity of today's projects, no longer support such an approach. William Lichtig* states that

> Over the past one hundred years, the design and construction industry has become increasingly fragmented. Each specialized participant now tends to work in an isolated silo, with no real integration of the participants' collective wisdom. As construction practitioners, we are familiar with the most common industry responses during the past 30 years. Post-design constructability reviews and value engineering exercises, together with "partnering" and contractual efforts to shift risk, have been the most prevalent. However, these "solutions"

---

*William A. Lichtig from McDonough, Holland, and Allen, Sacramento, California, is an attorney specializing in construction contracts. He is currently working on a new contract structure for Sutter Health in California.

do not attack the problem at its root cause; rather than working to avoid the problem, providing higher value and less waste, these attempts merely try to mitigate the negative impact of the problems.[1]

For the architect the problem is fundamentally related to the difficulty and risk associated with the production of construction documents for a project that is too complex to be coordinated and built from only the architect's drawings and specifications. The architect's concerns about the project delivery method will focus on issues related to the accuracy, coordination, completeness, required preparation time, etc., of the design and documentation of the project; and the architect will also be concerned with the projected budget for the project since she or he is responsible for adapting the documentation to bring it within the budget in case the construction bids are too high. All these responsibilities of the architect are becoming unrealistic in light of the nature of many of today's projects, hence the evolution of various alternative delivery methods that attempt to address the shortcomings of the traditional approach. The major alternatives are a group of delivery methods that are classified as design-build (see "The Setting for BIM" earlier in this chapter); in the design-build approach to project management, the constructor and designer collaborate early in the process, primarily so that the contractor can help the architect with constructability and budget issues. A variety of different contract types are now commonly used for the preconstruction services of a project. Even these new contracts that address the changed relationships among the owner, architect, and contractor describe the project in much the same way that it had traditionally been described. The architect is still responsible for producing the documents so that the constructor can build a specific project within a certain budget. The methods used to achieve the project are left to the discretion of the architect and constructor. The incentives required to address the traditional problems are still missing from the delivery approach.

There is some concern on the part of design consultants regarding liability and responsibility for content and accuracy in the models that are to become the basis for the construction documents. The transition that the industry made from manually drafting the construction documents to preparing them with the computer serves as an example of dealing with the concerns that arise around the use of the tools and the responsibility for the content of the construction documentation. Sue E. Yoakum* advises that the architect's main concern is the product and the associated liabilities. That is, can the architect be held responsible for drawings that may have been changed by others? The answer to this question is the same whether the drawings are prepared by hand, computer-drafted, or computer-modeled: The architect is only responsible for his or her own work, no matter how it comes about; and the architect is responsible for the content in any case. Safeguarding the information is one of the issues, and there are numerous methods that reliably do just that. As soon as someone else changes a drawing, or model, it is no longer the responsibility of the original author. There are very good methods, however, to make both drawings and models "read-only" files. The accuracy and completeness of the content are the other issue, and this too has not changed particularly as a result of the tools used to create the documents. This second area, however, could potentially improve dramatically with the proper use of 3D modeling and early collaboration between the appropriate project team members.

---

*Sue E. Yoakum, Esquire, AIA is of Counsel at Danovan Hatem LLP of Boston. She is attorney specializing in desizr and Construction services Contracts.

Sue Yoakum[2] advises that the design professional's performance is measured by the "standard of care" and that the following standard-of-care contract clause should be in every design professional's contract:

> The Design Professional's services shall be performed in a manner consistent with that degree of skill and care ordinarily exercised by practicing design professionals performing similar services in the same locality, and under the same or similar circumstances and conditions. The Design Professional makes no other representations or warranties, whether expressed or implied, with respect to the services rendered hereunder.

This type of clause will relieve the design professional from some of the imagined unnecessary pressures regarding the expectations of others about the quality of project documentation. It does not, however, change the risk assumed by the design professional for the actual quality of the documents, and it is in everyone's best interest for the quality of contract documents to be improved to the best possible degree. The reluctance to adopt new methods to prepare and manage project information has largely been associated with cost of implementing the new process and fear of new and unknown liabilities. Since it is in the best interest of the entire project team—including the owner—to improve the reliability of the project documents and decrease project risk, the contract should reflect these developments and provide incentives to help the project team toward this goal.

The sudden popularity of the BIM approach to project management has brought a certain amount of misunderstanding with it. Some owners are asking for BIM without specifying exactly what they want, or why; this can lead to unrealistic expectations that could easily escalate into litigation. "When unrealistic marketing promises meet legal performance, the result can typically be disastrous for design professionals, contractors and subcontractors. It is critical that the Owner's "expectations" are realistic regarding the use of BIM and its limitations."[3] Good communication is the best means to begin the initial project meetings among the project team members so that the entire team can agree on a realistic approach for the specific project (see BIM planning in Chap. 2). Sue Yoakum further states:

> A reasonable contingency for change orders will continue to be a valuable risk management tool in projects utilizing BIM. Below is a recommended contract clause for maintaining a contingency:
>
> **Use of a BIM Model on the Project** The Owner and Design Professional acknowledge the Project will be designed using Building Information Modeling (BIM). The Owner acknowledges the use of BIM by the design and construction teams may not result in savings for the Owner. It is anticipated the use of BIM will assist with a better understanding of the design, coordination of documents by the design team, better and earlier understanding of costs and potential construction conflicts prior to the starts of construction. The Owner and the Design Professional acknowledge a reasonable number of change orders may occur during the construction resulting from errors and omissions in the documents prepared by the Design Professional and its consultants. Owner agrees to maintain a reasonable contingency in the estimate and budget to be used for design coordination change orders.[4]

The other aspect of contractual change related to model-based project management is access to the information contained in the BIM. It is part of the BIM planning (see Chap. 2) to establish the protocol regarding copyright and ownership issues connected to the BIM. On this account Sue Yoakum advises: "The parties contributing original information to the BIM model should maintain ownership of their work and copyright, with the owner and the other parties granted an irrevocable nonexclusive license to access the BIM model per the terms and conditions of an electronic data or digital data transfer agreement. There is no reason for any party contributing original information to the BIM model to give up her or his copyright or intellectual property rights because the BIM model can have multiple owners."

The AIA has new contract documents that deal with the use of digital data and can provide assistance when allowing use or transferring a BIM model. The AIA C106-2007 document is the Digital Data Licensing Agreement for use as a stand-alone agreement with any party regarding the transfer and use of digital data. The AIA E201-2007 is the Digital Data Protocol Exhibit for use as an exhibit to an agreement that addresses the transfer and use of digital data. Of note in the AIA E201-2007 document is the chart in article 3 that outlines the data format, transmitting party, transmission method, receiving party, and permitted uses for the data. These are all important issues to address when transferring digital data or a BIM model. In addition, the AIA C106-2007 and E201-2007 documents address other issues important to resolve prior to granting a party access to the BIM model.[5] In any case it is important to have the agreements among all the project team members in place before information sharing can safely begin. It is thus clear that the industry is developing adaptations to the introduction of new technology that will make it seem that "business is pretty much as usual." Is anything actually being fixed by these approaches? What will make the participants on a project team want to bring about improvements? What is required to really reduce risk, increase value, etc.?

It appears that necessity is the mother of invention, and that things will not change until it becomes absolutely necessary. It is the author's belief that the industry will only change when it becomes necessary—either because the owners will demand certain improvements in the planning and construction of new projects or because competition among designers and builders will require these improvements just so that they can stay in business.

Contractual Incentives to Implement Change

The primary incentive for change is the need for a solution to the current construction problems. A secondary incentive will be the benefits achieved through the improvements to the management process (see Chap. 2 on BIM benefits).

The desire on the part of the owner, Sutter Health in California, to address the shortcomings of the construction management process led to the work of William Lichtig, who is developing a contractual combination of "lean project delivery" and an integrated team. This work is particularly interesting for its connection to the BIM processes.

William Lichtig states:

> A study by the Construction Industry Institute exploring the impact of different project delivery systems on cost, schedule, and quality found that
>
> Projects are built by people. Research into successful projects has shown that there are several critical keys to success:
>
> 1. A knowledgeable, trustworthy, and decisive facility owner/developer;
> 2. A team with relevant experience and chemistry assembled as early as possible, but certainly before 25% of the project design is complete; and
> 3. A contract that encourages and rewards organizations for behaving as a team.[6]

These three points do seem like common sense when they are applied to a sports team or a music ensemble; but it seems far-fetched to apply this to the construction industry. The current system is strongly rooted in the history of the professions, and nothing short of a cultural or psychological revolution will likely change this in a significant way. Necessity, however, is forcing the industry into this direction, and it will behoove all the players on a team to acknowledge that they are part of a team and learn to behave accordingly. Coordinated collaborating project teams will be a requirement for survival in the industry in the not too distant future.

The Integrated Agreement developed for Sutter Health incorporates aspects of "the five big ideas" that were developed by the lean project delivery community. These ideas are outlined as follows:

1. Collaborate; really collaborate, throughout design, planning, and execution.
2. Increase relatedness among all project participants.
3. Projects are networks of commitments.
4. Optimize the project, not the pieces.
5. Tightly couple action with learning.[7]

It will become clear from reading Chap. 2 of this book that BIM at least encourages, and in many instances requires, these actions specifically to become successful on a project. It is also through the use of BIM that Sutter Health hopes to achieve its ends, although BIM is not specifically mentioned as a requirement for success in a construction project.

> The Integrated Agreement expressly sets forth the goals of forming an Integrated Project Delivery (IPD) Team:
>
> By forming an Integrated Team, the parties intend to gain the benefit of an open and creative learning environment, where team members are encouraged to share ideas freely in an atmosphere of mutual respect and tolerance. Team Members shall work together, and individually, to achieve transparent and cooperative exchange of information in all matters relating to the Project, and to share ideas for improving Project Delivery as contemplated in the Project Evaluation Criteria. Team members shall actively promote harmony, collaboration and cooperation among all entities performing on the Project.

The parties recognize that each of their opportunities to succeed on the Project is directly tied to the performance of other Project participants. The parties shall therefore work together in the spirit of cooperation, collaboration, and mutual respect for the benefit of the Project, and within the limits of their professional expertise and abilities. Throughout the Project, the parties shall use their best efforts to perform the work in an expeditious and economical manner consistent with the interests of the Project.[8]

The Integrated Agreement furthermore calls for collaboration as follows:

In order to achieve owner's basic value proposition, design of the Project must proceed with informed, accurate information concerning program, quality, cost and schedule. While each IPD Team Member will bring different expertise to each of these issues, all of these issues and the full weight of the entire teams' expertise will need to be integrated throughout the pre-construction process if the value proposition is to be attained. None of the parties can proceed in isolation from the others; there must be deep collaboration and continuous flow of information.[9]

This collaboration includes the development of a *target value design*[10] plan by the group to best serve the owner's value proposition. Target value design makes value, cost, schedule, and constructability (including work structuring) basic design criteria.[11] The collaboration encourages the team to share in the design decisions throughout the process, rather than it being a handoff of documents at the end of a phase. Collaboration continues into the construction phase, where lack of coordination traditionally causes large amounts of rework.[12] The Integrated Agreement calls for a built-in quality plan to be developed by the project team. The success of such a plan will depend on the communication of the designer's expectations to the contractors executing the work. The emphasis is on solving problems before installation and avoiding rework.

The success of an Integrated Agreement heavily depends upon the ability of the project team members to meet their commitments to one another. Open communication is paramount, and personal contact will greatly assist in keeping communication open and forthright. Solving issues verbally and personally will reduce the misunderstandings to a minimum, and again it is clearly of great assistance to have a 3D model as the means to share and visualize ideas. The Integrated Agreement seeks to share risk among the team members, rather than shift it. This will provide incentive to collaborate, and thus improve coordination, and reduce risk. Risk is further shared by creating one IPD team performance contingency for the project, rather than having separate design and construction contingencies. Thus "the success of every team member is directly tied to the performance of all members of the IPD Team."[13] This is further incentive for collaboration and communication. The Integrated Agreement also includes clauses about fees, financial responsibilities, liabilities, etc.; but these are beyond the scope of this discussion. It is interesting to note that a contract of this type will certainly provide the incentive for a new approach to construction planning and management, and that it is so comprehensive that this is not likely to be able to be implemented without the BIM approach.[1] The owner is requiring the project team to sign such a contract, thus paving the way for the change.

REFERENCES

1. Lichtig, William A., "The Integrated Agreement for Lean Project Delivery," *Construction Lawyer*, vol. 26, no. 3, Summer 2006, published by the American Bar Association.
2. Yoakum, Sue E., *Building Information Modeling: New Risks, and Challenges for Design Professionals*, p. 3.
3. Ibid., p. 4.
4. Ibid., p. 5.
5. Ibid., p. 8.
6. Lichtig, William A., quotes Victor E. Sanvido and Mark D. Konchar, Selecting Project Delivery Systems: Comparing Design-Build, Design-Bid-Build and Construction Management at Risk, State College, Project Delivery Institute (1999) p. 3.
7. Ibid., pp. 11, 12.
8. Ibid., p. 15.
9. Ibid., p. 16.
10. Ibid. Target value design is similar to target costing, but may be broadened to encompass additional design criteria beyond cost, including time, work structuring, buildability, and similar issues. For a discussion of target costing see Glenn Ballard and Paul Reiser, "The St. Olaf College Fieldhouse Project: A Case Study in Designing to Target Cost," *Proceedings of the 12th Annual IGLC Conference*, 2004.
11. Ibid., p. 16.
12. Ibid. The Construction Industry Institute's study entitled "Costs of Quality Deviations in Design and Construction," (Pub. 10-1) concluded that the average rework on industrial projects exceeds 12 percent, equating to waste of $17 billion annually. See also Construction Owner's Association of Alberta, Project Rework Reduction Tool available at http://rework.coaa.ab.ca/library/prrt/default.htm.
13. Ibid., p. 21.

2 Building Information Modeling

INTRODUCTION

Various forms of simulations have been used throughout the recorded history. The wooden project models built in the 15th-century Renaissance period were simulations, and so are the diagrams, drawings, and specifications that have been used for hundreds of years as instructions for building. The information contained in these examples is, however, very limited and fragmented (disconnected from other parts of the information). The meaning of the word **simulation** in this book will refer to a single coordinated and integrated entity containing (or linked to) all required information to plan and construct a building project. The **building information model** is a *project* as well as a *process* simulation. The production of simulations should be carefully planned and intentionally implemented. This chapter discusses the basic concepts of the BIM, the **planning**, and the **implementation** processes. The BIM concepts section of this chapter describes the nature and characteristics of the BIM, the **processes** involved with creating and using the BIM, and the benefits of both the BIM's creation as well as its use. The next section of the chapter addresses the planning required to create and use a BIM successfully, including the development of goals for the purpose of the BIM, generating a set of specifications from these goals, and producing a plan for the implementation of the process. The chapter closes with a discussion of the realization of the planning phase, the selection of the **project team**, the **deployment** of the processes, and the specification of the deliverables. Proper care in **understanding**, planning, and realizing the BIM processes is critical for the successful implementation of a building information modeling approach to construction planning and management.

The planning and the realization of the BIM are very similar to the planning and the realization of the actual construction project. The simulation process will actually parallel the process that it is simulating; which is the main reason that the BIM is such an effective tool; the preparation process is in fact a rehearsal for the actual performance. Creating a BIM is labor-intensive and involves many persons on the project team; it is important for the BIM to meet the project team's expectations, and thus it should not be entered into naively. The implementation of this process should not be careless or rushed, as small errors can lead to much larger difficulties when not prevented early through proper planning and procedures. It is not uncommon for a modeler to reach a point where there is a very insistent urge to start over with the model (and this may well be the best course of action). These feelings result from the deepening of the level of understanding of the project and its processes, and suggest that there are numerous ways to improve the BIM. Often at this stage the BIM will already be quite complex and detailed, and frequently editing the existing models may in fact require an effort as great as, if not greater than, that of starting afresh. Continual evaluation is an important part of the BIM development, and will be influential in the actual implementation of the process plan.

Since the understanding of the project develops through the creation of the model, it is possible that at a certain point the simulation (model) no longer accurately reflects that (increasing) understanding. This is the right moment to reevaluate the usefulness of continuing with the current model, or to restart a new one. Generally it will take a fraction of the time that it took to get to the same point of development because all the thinking and planning has now been done and the modeling has been well planned and can be executed efficiently. The result will be a new model that will no longer slow down progress or be inaccurate in the way it represents the project.

A fundamental characteristic of the BIM is its development through an information feedback loop. The evolution of the model and the relevant project information is cyclical (iterative); and as the different project team members develop the project, the available information gradually increases in scope, depth, and relatedness. A coordinated and intelligent project will grow out of the building information that is continually cycled through the BIM at a more and more detailed and coordinated level.

The spheres in Fig. 2.1 represent the project collecting information and developing as more information is connected to the project over time. The white spiral represents time and the flow of information over time. The spheres suggest the milestones in the process where a project passes through critical stages and where evaluation and reflection can take place.

This chapter outlines the nature, development, and use of the building information model. Frequently subtle differences between various concepts will be pointed out to call attention to certain facts, the understanding of which will ultimately help the reader to better implement the BIM approach in construction projects. Human beings generally overestimate their understanding of a specific subject, only to realize at a certain point that "if we had only known . . . , things could have been different." It is easy to confuse knowledge with understanding, this age is information-rich; but gathering knowledge does not equate to developing understanding. Effort is required to generate understanding in any given area, and this effort is frequently made through the accumulation of experience. Once a certain amount of experience has accrued, the understanding will generally have developed to lead to a whole new level of use of that knowledge; it will in fact seem to have "increased" the knowledge, when actually it is the understanding

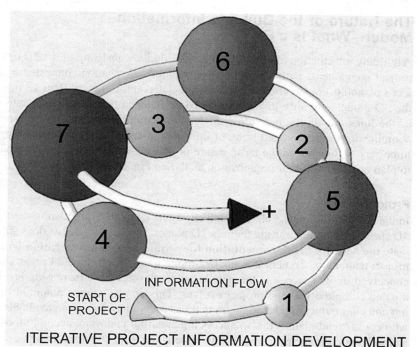

Figure 2.1
Information
feedback loop.

ITERATIVE PROJECT INFORMATION DEVELOPMENT

that has increased. Without knowledge there is little to understand, and without understanding it does not matter what is known.

BIM CONCEPTS

Building information modeling simulates the construction project in a **virtual** environment. A simulation has the advantage of taking place in a computer through the use of a software package. Virtual building implies that it is possible to practice construction, to experiment, and to make adjustments in the project before it is actualized. Virtual mistakes generally do not have serious consequences—provided that they are identified and addressed early enough that they can be avoided "in the **field**" (the actual construction of the project). When a project is planned and built virtually, most of its relevant aspects can be considered and communicated before the instructions for construction are finalized. The use of computer simulations in the building construction field is revolutionary. Various manufacturing industries have been very successfully applying simulation techniques for decades. Many construction companies have now also successfully applied similar techniques to their building projects, even though critics claim that simulations will only benefit repetitive production processes, and that construction is by definition unique. The case studies in this book illustrate some of these projects. *After all, if there is only one opportunity to do it right, it makes a lot of sense to prepare well for that single occasion virtually, and thereby reduce the inherent risks and improve the chances for success and efficiency.*

The Nature of the Building Information Model—What Is a BIM?

A building information model is a project simulation consisting of the 3D models of the project components with links to all the required information connected with the project's planning, construction or operation, and decommissioning. This section describes the 3D models, the information contained or attached to these models, and the nature of the links among the individual models, the components, and the information. The complications of this varied array of information containers can be daunting, and it is important to understand the basic nature of these concepts so that it becomes possible to plan and manage their organization well. See Fig. 2.2.

Project Models

In the last few decades, architects and engineers have begun modeling their projects in 3D space rather than drafting them in 2D planes. In many cases this does still not eliminate the need for 2D **documentation** for permits and **communication** with the other project team members; but it is the beginning of a new approach. Projects can now be conceived in 3D space, and the details can be developed to increasing levels of coordinated complexity as the project evolves. This creates a huge potential for visualizing and communicating information that has previously only been available to persons who could "read plans." It also allows much earlier and more accurate feedback from anyone related to the project who can understand the 3D models and does not have to read plans.

Figure 2.2

A BIM graphic showing various types of information being derived from a 3D model, e.g., plans, sections, etc., and component information. (*Image courtesy of Vico.*)

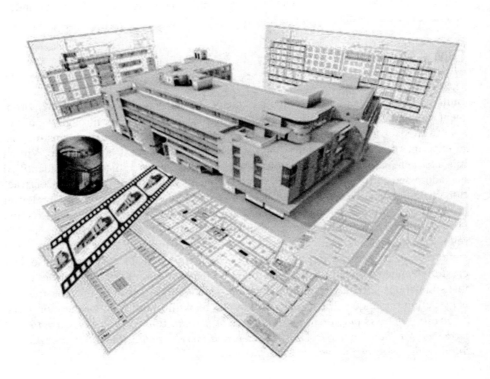

The goal is not simply having a BIM, but it is the project understanding generated through the creation of the BIM, and the benefits of the use of the information that is available through the BIM.

Virtual Models   Virtual models generally fall into two distinct classes: surface models and solid models. Models that are only for **visualization** purposes may be made with *surface modelers.* The components of a surface model only contain information concerning the size, shape, location, etc., which facilitates the study of the visible parameters of a project. Surface modelers cannot create "solid" components, because components consist of "surfaces" only, and will look like a solid, but in fact be hollow; none of the surfaces have thickness or volume characteristics. A surface model is ideal for visual images of the project, and thus well suited for aesthetic design, planning, and marketing purposes. The surface modeling software tools are often simpler to use than other modeling tools and particularly effective for presentation and communication.

Models that contain more information than the surface models are often referred to as *smart models* and are typically generated with solid modelers. Virtual construction techniques primarily employ solid modelers because they allow the simulation of much more than merely the visual aspects of a building project. The nature and handling of building information in a simulation can take on a variety of forms.

A solid model has the additional advantage of having the possibility to generate 2D views that can be developed into conventional construction documentation. This means that a solid model can first be used to develop the project concept and details, after which the views of this virtual project can be turned into the drawings required for the permitting and construction process, as shown in Fig. 2.2. In theory a BIM should be able to communicate all project information so that no 2D drawings will be necessary; but in reality the software tools and permitting processes will have to develop further, before the need for 2D drawings can be eliminated. There are some examples of projects, however, where various aspects of this approach have been successfully implemented; and it clearly looks like the elimination of traditional 2D construction documentation will be commonplace in the (not too distant) future.

The Fort Bliss model in Fig. 2.3 is a surface model made in SketchUp and rendered in NavisWorks to present as a project proposal.

The City Hall model in Fig. 2.4 was made in two parts; the building is a solid model made in Constructor by Vico, and the site model was made in TriForma by Bentley; then the combination of the two models was rendered in NavisWorks. The previous figures show that in a "rendered" image there is no difference between a surface model and a solid model.

Model Intelligence   *Model intelligence* refers to the fact that information may be contained in a 3D virtual model. Some of this information is physical; in other words it will contain information about the nature of an object because it is a simulation of an actual object. This physical information includes the **dimensions** of the object (its size), the location of the object in relation to the location of the other objects in the model, the

Figure 2.3
The Fort Bliss
Headquarters pro-
posal. (*Image
courtesy of RQ
Construction.*)

quantity of objects in the model, and other **parametric** (embedded) information about
the object. *Parametric information* refers to the information that distinguishes one particular component from another one that is similar. This may refer to a wall, all walls
have wall qualities in common, but each actual wall, although made with the same
"wall tool," may have different parametrics; its dimensions, or material makeup (wood
or metal studs, type of sheetrock, etc.), or supplier information, etc., may vary. Each

Figure 2.4
The Victorville City
Hall addition.
(*Image courtesy of
RQ Construction.*)

aspect of this type of information can be programmed into the specific wall object so that it accurately represents what the project requires. Since this information will be contained in each of the model components (or objects), it can also be retrieved and used, and thus constitutes a smart model. Solid modeling with parametric components is also called *object-based modeling*. Some companies in the construction material industry are producing virtual 3D components of their product lines, and these virtual components can then be used in a smart model and carry all the manufacturers' embedded information within them, e.g., a window manufacturer can produce a virtual catalog containing the product line in "3D object model" format, ready for use in a project model. In all cases the **file format** of the objects needs to be taken into account when planning to use such objects in a specific Building Information Model (see Interoperability).

Each of the images in Fig. 2.5 shows the settings for the wall tool; the image on the left is set for feet and inches, while the dialog box on the right shows the metric settings for the wall dimensions. Each of the dialog boxes shows some of the pull-down tabs where the parametric information can be selected; on the left the "Floor plan and section" menu dictates the graphic characteristics of the plan and sections views of the wall in those views of the model, and the Model menu settings determine the look of the materials in the 3D views of the model. Most modeling tools will have similar functionalities. The Estimating tab in the right-hand image shows various Recipes to which the wall entity can be linked to represent itself accurately in a **cost estimate** of the project.

The creation of a *composite model* provides another dimension to model intelligence. Various models of different components of a project can be collected into a composite model that will have the combined information from all the submodels embedded in it. One advantage of a composite model is that different project team members can work on various parts of a project independently and combine their work at specific times to analyze the combined results. The architectural, structural, and MEP models will often be produced by the design consultants or specialty subcontractors who are responsible for their own specific portions of the work, and thus can also be combined into a **composite model** showing the total of the project for **visualization**, **coordination**, and other purposes.

The concrete work in Fig. 2.6 was modeled in Vico's Constructor, the structural steel in Tekla, the utilities in AutoCAD-CadPipe, and the truncated zones of influence for the footing loads in SketchUp. The composite was coordinated (analyzed) and rendered in NavisWorks. The image shows the concrete footings and grade beams with some of the structural steel on top. Below the concrete footings are the truncated pyramids that represent the ground volume that is affected by the footing load and cannot have any utilities located within its volume. The layout of the underground utilities can now be coordinated in this model so that it will meet all the necessary design criteria.

Model Sources   The best possible source for a building model is the in-house staff, someone on the project team who is inside the circle of project influence. The understanding that is gained from the development of the model will benefit, and remain part of, the project team's resources. The modeling experience itself, and the understanding of the project that is thus developed, is in fact one of the main advantages of the BIM

Figure 2.5
Model information. These images show the same dialog box with access to the information that can be programmed into the wall object in Vico's Constructor.

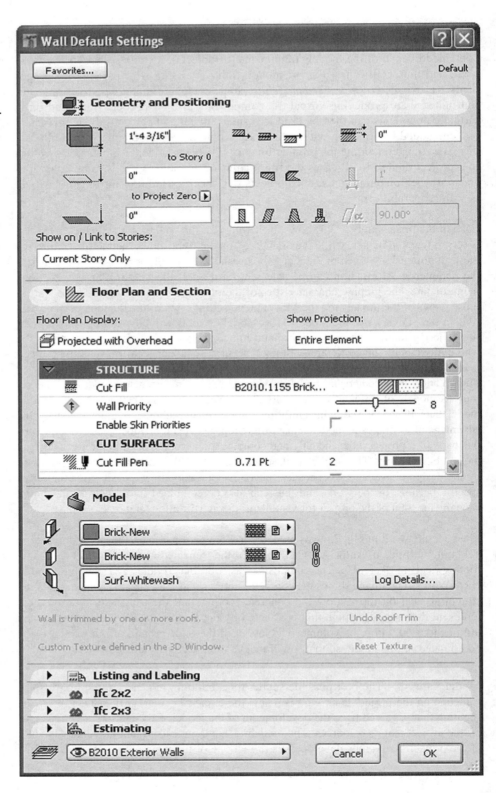

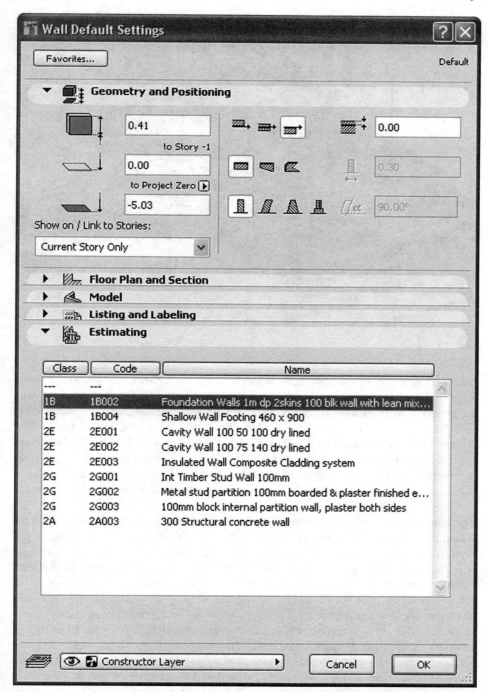

Figure 2.5
(*Continued*)

Figure 2.6
Composite models
for underground
utility coordination.
(*Image courtesy of
RQ Construction.*)
See also color
insert.

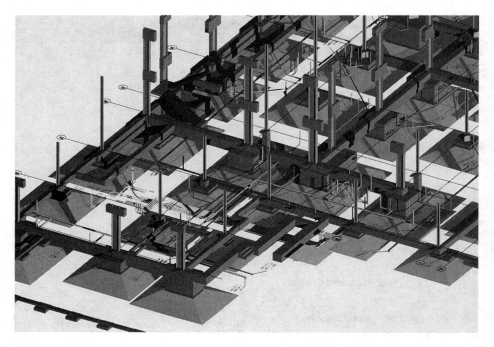

process. There is hardly a comparable opportunity in the construction planning process as far as becoming intimately familiar with the characteristics of the project; modeling the project exposes many issues that may otherwise remain undetected until much later in the planning or construction process. Generally it will be in the project team's best interest to let the structural engineer model the structure, the plumber make the plumbing model, and so on. This will lead to the best form of collaboration among the team members when all these models are combined in a viewer so that the whole team can see the results of all their work in the context of everyone's contribution to the project.

The remaining option for acquiring a model is to outsource it to a modeler who is not on the project team. While this is better than not having a model at all, it is clearly difficult for the project team to benefit from the understanding of the project of someone outside the team. It is useful for the project team to have access to an outsourced model, but it will require a significant amount of time to analyze it enough to recognize the issues that would have been found by the modeler if he or she were aware of the team's concerns. The main challenge for a project team is internal communication and collaboration; adding outside modelers will only increase the difficulty for the team to successfully collaborate. If there is no other alternative, then it will be useful to try to include the modeler as a remote team member and to establish a personal level of commitment to the team's goals and processes on the modeler's behalf. A long-term team membership will also encourage a more responsible approach to the model's accuracy, details, and relevance. The modeler will often be the best person to address various project issues and therefore needs to be actively involved with many of the project planning activities.

Links

Linking is an important concept in virtual construction simulations, and various types of links will be discussed. Linking refers to the interconnection of different sources of information. This information may be part of the 3D model, or it could be contained in another format separate from the model file itself, such as in a **schedule**, a spreadsheet, a database, or as a text document.

Model to Information Link   Parametric object information is information that is part of a specific object in the project model. The nature of the link is **automatic**, it is usually simple to edit the model object to reflect whatever changes are required in the information. Some software tools provide the opportunity to change this type of information from several "locations." That is, a 3D model containing steel trusses will permit the editing of a particular truss in the dialog box for that specific truss object. Entities such as truss length, depths, web pattern, and bearing characteristics may be parametric values for a truss object. In a schedule (parts list) from the model it may also be possible to change the parametric values for certain **elements**, and this change will then also take effect in the model that the schedule is linked to; in other words the model and the schedule are actually just two different views of the same BIM and will thus only need to be addressed in any one of these views to result in an edit to the project model. *Caution:* Not all software tools provide this functionality with all their model elements.

Model-to-Model Link   Another common link in BIM exists in the **interoperability** of various models that may have been created by different software tools. This is a very demanding area, and there is a large effort going into the development of standards to define interoperability between models. The International Alliance for Interoperability (IAI) has created a uniform platform—file format—for software developers; this is called the *international foundation class* (IFC) format. This means that for a model to be able to be compatible with models created by other software tools, it is necessary for all of them to be translatable into a uniform file format, so that all the object's information can be transferred correctly. In most cases it is a challenge for such a translation to retain all the information that the model contained in its original native file format. Software developers will continue to struggle with this issue for some time into the future. *The best **method** of determining interoperability is to try to link several experimental files that contain examples of all the information the project team is concerned about, and put the test file through all the anticipated processes.*

Specific software tools can have a built-in capacity to be able to read and use the file format of other modelers. This is outside of any overall interoperability compliance and generally is dictated by market demands. A number of the larger modeling software companies are now developing suites of modeling and construction-related software tools that are quite interoperable among themselves, similar to the Microsoft Office suite of software tools. (See Chap. 3, "Software Tools.") *Caution:* Most of the "suites" of modeling and peripheral software tools only address interoperability among themselves and not in relation to other manufacturers' products.

Project Information

Successful project management relies on access to information and its proper management. *One of the chief advantages of a BIM is the fact that* all *the information related to a project can now be contained in, or linked to, the BIM.* It is a challenge, however, to manage this complex array of information containers well.

Simulation models allow for a variety of ways in which project data may be available to the user. See the earlier section "Project Models" under the heading "Model Intelligence." The most basic model information is related to physical parameters, such as size, location, and quantity; further information will be embedded in the objects of the model, such as material specifications, model numbers, and suppliers. It is also likely that time-related information may be linked to the model **components**, and this will permit the scheduling of ordering, manufacturing, and installation tasks. Model components may also have links attached which refer to any other type of computer file such as e-mail, purchase order, manufacturers' website, installation specifications, cost information, and project accounting information. Almost all information can be linked to a BIM; a critical question concerns whether linking a particular type of information to the BIM is really how it will be most useful for the goals of the project. Managing information is similar to organizing a desk and a file cabinet. Some things are more efficiently accessed from the desk, others from the file cabinet; and there will probably be files that will spend one-half of the project duration on the desk and the other half in the cabinet. Even though it is theoretically possible to consider the BIM as the single central information source, it may not be practical to create it as such. Bentley systems, producer of TriForma, advocates a federated **database** for larger construction projects. Autodesk, somewhat naively, or perhaps from a marketing standpoint, suggests a central database for all project information. Vico is letting things work themselves out in the industry; after all there is no known construction project of any size that has managed to centralize and manage all its data successfully. *The goal, however, is not to simply have access to the project information, but to be able to use it intelligently.*

Many factors have an effect on the information structure of a BIM. Simulation models may be produced during any of the phases of the project planning or operation, and the information contained by the model will thus also be dependent on the project's phase of development. The nature, and level of detail, and quantity of information dramatically change throughout the planning process; and the nature of the model therefore needs to reflect the requirements of the model in the particular phase of the process. This is the most important reason why it can be so difficult to keep the same model through the various phases of project planning; it may indeed be better to build a new model to the required specifications for the associated phase of the project. Nevertheless, it is very important to carefully plan the collaborated model so that the modeling process will be as efficient as possible, and the utility of the models will be maximized.

Several considerations need to be taken into account in relation to starting over with a model:

- No one generally *wants* to start over, because it seems like a **waste** of time and effort.
- But there must be some reason why it is even being considered. Make sure to find out those reasons and address them effectively. (What is the underlying cause?)

- Use the opportunity to reorganize the entire simulation to reflect the current best understanding of the project. This requires a thorough **analysis** of the approach to the simulation as well as the other project conditions and constraints.

- Do not try to avoid the required efforts; it will both go faster than anticipated and create more benefits than hoped for.

- Do not start over too often. Remember, the process is a tool and does not have to be perfect; but it does have to produce worthwhile results.

The Processes of the BIM—How Is a BIM Used?

The processes related to the project simulation and the virtual 3D models of the project can be separated into several major groups:

- The processes enabling the owner to develop an accurate understanding of the nature and needs of the purpose for the project
- The processes enabling the design, development, and analysis of the project
- The processes enabling the management of the construction of the project
- The processes related to the management of the operations of the project during its actual use

Such processes describe what happens with the information from the building information model to achieve our stated goals. These categories are clearly related to the phases of a construction project and may require a very different type of BIM in each of these phases. There can be a lot of carryover, however, from a BIM used in one phase to the one required for the tasks of the next phase. This discussion now begins to clarify the fact that the BIM is not a single static model of a project. The nature of the components that make up a BIM (3D models and project information) will evolve throughout the developmental phases of the project and result in various major changes in the nature of the character of both the 3D models and the linked information. This observation particularly serves to reinforce the importance of the process, rather than the model itself; building information modeling *is* a dynamic process.

This section has been organized into three parts representing the time phases of the project: preconstruction (the planning and design phase—activities before construction), course of construction (the construction management phase—activities during construction), and postconstruction (the property management phase—activities after construction). There will also be overlap between the activities of these phases due to the various attempts to plan early in this approach; procurement, e.g., will be part of both the first and second phases, while equipment maintenance or decommissioning procedures can be part of both the construction and the postconstruction phases.

Preconstruction Planning

Planning processes generally focus on the development and analysis of ideas. The owner's operation can be analyzed as a value stream map of a business process, and thus results in a spatial needs assessment and specifications for the qualities for those spaces. The model can help with the communication of these concepts, and results in a clear program for the requirements of the project. The planning activities can include a

target value design, e.g., the optimization of the development of its design based on the functional requirements and the project **construction budget**. These are of primary importance in the early phases of a project (preconstruction), and they may also be useful when an already developed plan needs to be analyzed or altered.

Virtual Design and Construction   During the early 1980s several software tools were developed that could build "virtual" projects, i.e., 3D models consisting of components with attached information. These tools immediately showed great potential in their ability to communicate design intent by providing 3D views of these models, which also helped the designer in the development of the project details (through improved visualization). The 3D models facilitate the study of alternative approaches to design solutions ("what if" scenarios can now easily be modeled and compared). The model has a connection to traditional construction documentation, because most of the drawings can be developed from model views (see Fig. 2.7a and b). The connection between model and documents ensures that a change in the project model will be accurately reflected in the linked drawings. Since a set of construction documents will generally show the same building parts in several instances throughout the drawings, the use of a model linked to the construction documents largely addresses the potential risk of failing to update each and every one of the drawings affected by a project change. Thus construction drawings are finally able to be more "intelligent" by connecting the drawing content to its source—the 3D model.

The project's design performance can also be better developed with the help of a model. The improved ability to visualize the design proposals in the early project phases greatly aids in the assessment of the spaces and aesthetic finishes of the project. The intent of the designers is more easily and accurately communicated to the other project team members, and adjustments can be made until the design meets the desired goals.

The creation of a virtual 3D project model often consists of multiple efforts by different team members. Either the consultants or the specialty subcontractors (if the model is to be used for fabrication purposes, thus functioning as the shop drawing) will generally model their area of responsibility in the project, so that these individual models may then be combined to show a more complete model of the project. All the parts of this composite model can be coordinated so that any existing conflicts (multiple objects occupying the same space) can be found and resolved. This process is referred to as *clash detection*. It is a critical task, especially in relation to MEP (mechanical, electrical, and plumbing) and FP (fire protection) design. Systems coordination has conventionally been accomplished by overlaying 2D plan drawings on a light table, to visualize (imagine in our head) the location of the system components in 3D space (see Fig. 2.8). Needless to say, the use of a light table leaves room for many misunderstandings and oversights, and will generally result in potential conflicts that will ultimately be discovered and addressed by the installation crews in the field. Plan drawings do not provide a visual clue about the height of the drawn objects; thus the potential for conflicts has to be visualized from the study of several drawings and written information.

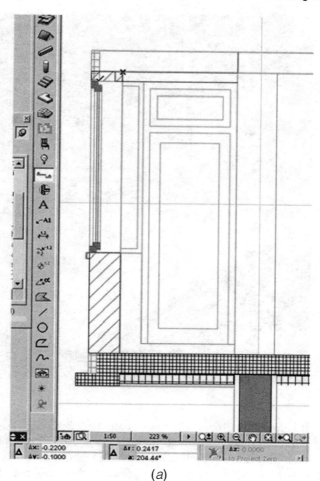

(a)

Figure 2.7
Drawings can be derived from models. (*a*) The **2D** drawing is seen as a specific view (section) (*b*) of the **3D** model. (*Images courtesy of Vico.*)

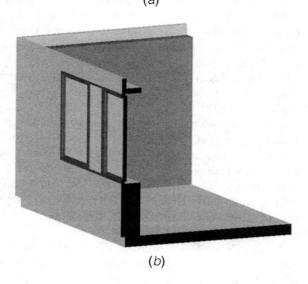

(b)

Figure 2.8

A traditional light table for drawing coordination. (*Image courtesy of F.M. Booth Design Build Co., subcontractor on this project of Turner Construction— Sacramento.*)

It is far more effective to coordinate these building systems using a visual approach with a 3D model, so that the location and relationships of all the components and their potential conflicts can be resolved while still in the planning phases of the project. This method is clearly superior in detecting the clashes; the resolution of the conflicts, however, can still only come from the collaboration of the designers (and/or installers) of the clashing model parts. The 3D model also helps to visualize and develop potential solutions to the conflicts during the coordination process. Clash detection is an iterative process in which all noted project conflicts are addressed and reevaluated (often on a weekly basis) until the desired level of coordination has been achieved. Special model viewing software exists which will find, highlight, and list the clashes of the model components. The coordination of complex project systems is perhaps the most popular application of BIM at this time; it is an ideal process to develop collaboration techniques and a commitment protocol among the team members. This type of cooperation benefits from the **big room** approach, where the critical members share the same work space to improve access to one another. Communication techniques and response times to conflict resolution are important factors in establishing the preconstruction schedule of the project, and can be greatly improved by use of a big room.

In Fig. 2.9 NavisWorks identified the clash between the ductwork and structural steel beam in the center of the image by coloring the duct. The software will locate and identify all clashes found between model elements.

Figure 2.9
Clash detection in NavisWorks between structural and mechanical systems. (*Image courtesy of CSU Chico, CM Dept.*)

A virtual model will enable a variety of construction process simulations; these processes may also focus on design evaluation and can help to determine whether, and to what degree, the actual project is expected to meet its specifications (goals).

With a complete BIM of a virtual 3D project it is possible to visualize **constructability** and construction sequences. Simply seeing the project in 3D space and being able to virtually move through (and around) it will generate a new level of visualization and understanding. The model will enable preparation for the component installation in tight spaces, and the installation sequence of such components can also be simulated in the form of a movie. The layout space for a particular task can be visualized to determine how multiple tasks need to be scheduled, etc. The model thus becomes the source for a visual construction schedule.

Since the model already contains quantitative information in its model parts, it may be linked to a cost database that can produce a cost estimate based on the model quantities. All model parts have information such as material, size, number (count), length, width, height, area, and volume that can be linked to cost data and generate interpreted project costs. For example, if the model contains a slab, that slab will have a volume that can be multiplied by the cost of concrete per cubic yard and will yield a total cost for that model part (project slab); and if the model contains a certain number of specific windows, that number will be multiplied by the cost per window from the database, and will yield a total cost. Thus the cost estimate is directly related to the content of the 3D model and will reflect changes made to the project in the model. Construction cost estimates can be derived from the model quantities throughout the development of the BIM. During the **conceptual** phases the cost can be assessed on a conceptual level, and at a more detailed model level the cost estimate can also become more detailed. This can facilitate the target value design approach that helps to track the project cost in relation to the budget throughout the planning process. The cost data linked to the evolving 3D model provide such cost tracking. The flexibility of the cost data—model link permits a large variety of interpretations that will yield almost any type of cost information from the model.

The dialog box in Fig. 2.10 shows an estimate derived from model quantities that generates costs based on the recipes that have been attached to the model components.

The design intent energy performance of a project can be simulated and evaluated in a BIM, and alternative materials can be studied in a comparative analysis. A building's energy performance can thus be predicted and adjusted in the planning phase of the project. This is ideal for the study of the **life-cycle cost** of a project. In other words it becomes possible to simulate the operation of the building and analyze the cost of using the building over its life expectancy. This tool will aid in the planning of long-term investment strategies. The building lighting can be studied in a similar fashion; the penetration of daylight into a space can be analyzed in the 3D model, and artificial lighting may be specifically designed to complement or mimic it.

Assembly instructions can be part of the information attached to the components of the BIM, so that the visual context of the specific location in the 3D model can help with the communication of such instructions from the designers and manufacturers to the installers. In complicated areas where various building elements are close to one another, it may be useful to study the installation sequence in the planning phase, to ensure that the installer can actually have the necessary access for the proper installation of the components. This is another aspect of systems coordination.

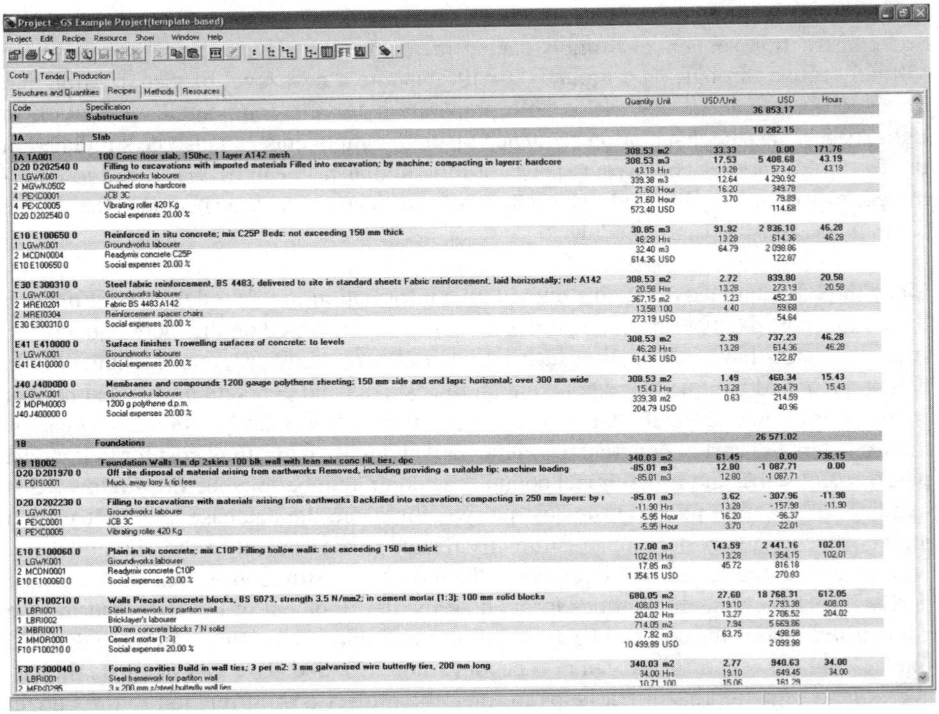

Figure 2.10

This image shows a cost estimate directly derived from model quantities in Vico's Estimator. (*Image courtesy of Vico.*)

Caution: It is important to note that the BIM will not show elements that have been left out; it can only show those that were placed in the model. It is critical to use the model as a visualization tool that will help with the evaluation of the project, and will aid in the remembrance of all aspects of the process; this remembrance can only come from the experience and understanding of the project team members. The making of such models and the coordination of all the components provide many opportunities for the project team to better understand and refine the planning and construction processes for the particular project.

Course of Construction

The construction management phase may already have access to a developed building information model from the planning phase. It is necessary to reevaluate the nature of the BIM for this phase and assess whether it will be able to provide for the necessary information management processes for this stage of the project. Now that the project has been planned in detail and all components have been coordinated, it becomes essential to focus on communication, cost control, and the fabrication and assembly of the building components. To utilize the BIM across these phases of the project, it will have to be well planned ahead of time. See the BIM planning section of this chapter. Just as the model functioned to help with the visualization that resulted in the coordination of the various building systems, the model can again function at regular construction meetings to help with the visualization and coordination of the installation requirements (and field conditions) for the subcontractors. Safety issues can also be analyzed and discussed with the aid of the 3D visualization. A construction sequence analysis (in movie format, or in the real-time 3D model) can provide a "6-week look-ahead" for all the crews working with the project.

The construction sequence in Fig. 2.11 begins with the piles and pile caps, then the placement of the grade beams and steel structure, after which the walls and scaffolding are shown, to be completed with the plaza and landscaping.

It can also be useful to have the model be able to show exactly what has already been installed as a tracking mechanism and communication tool for billing and cost control. The model can contain the information concerning the status of its components in the fabrication, installation, and billing stages. This phase of the project requires the most detail from the BIM, particularly if it is intended for fabrication purposes. It is not uncommon for the mechanical subcontractors to create a 3D model of their work for fabrication; this replaces the shop drawings and is also useful in coordination efforts with the work of other trades. Models with this level of detail can also be used to study installation procedures in tight spaces, i.e., the mechanical and plumbing in an interstitial space of a medical facility or laboratory, where installation access and clearances can be modeled and the sequential order of installation can be simulated (in movie format).

When specific problems arise during the construction phase, it is quite possible that the BIM may be able to help formulate a solution, by aiding in the correct visualization and assessment of that problem. This may lead to the need for a model showing more details in the problem area; it is then appropriate to develop a specific area of one of the BIM

Figure 2.11
A construction sequence of the Student Services Building at CSU Chico, created by the third-semester BIM class.

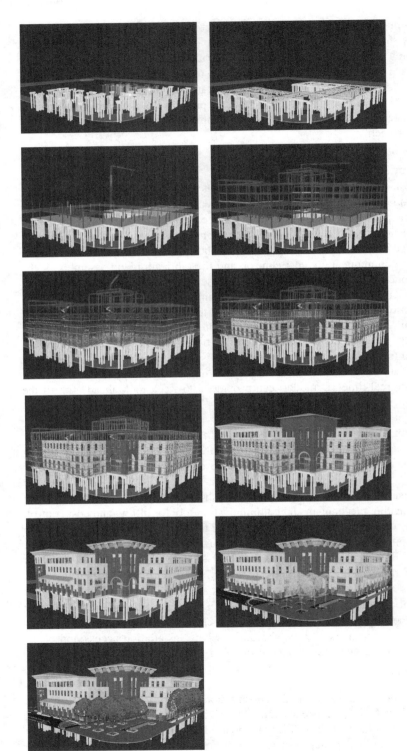

models, or to create a new model simply to serve the purpose of solving that problem. Such a model may be created in a different software tool with its own level of detail, and never be combined with the main BIM of the project. *Generally a modeling effort is worthwhile, if it serves its purpose, whatever that purpose may be.*

Thus in this phase the BIM again becomes the focus of communication and collaboration among all project team members. It will not only enable interaction between the individual members, but also aid in their collective understanding of the project requirements and constraints. One of the valuable potentials of the BIM is the ability to represent the site conditions as they become important in their effect on the construction processes. Issues such as construction site access, lay-down space for materials, temporary structures, site security, etc., can benefit from the visualization aid of a 3D model. See Fig. 2.12.

Postconstruction

In the postconstruction phase of the project, the BIM will be available to the building's managers for operations and maintenance procedures. Once again, the nature of the model and the information may need to be adjusted for these purposes.

The BIM that was used during the construction phase may require some adaptations to accurately represent the "as built" conditions of the project. This can be particularly important in such areas as underground utilities, where the potential excavation at a later date may require research into the accurate location of the specific underground

Figure 2.12
The BIM facilitated coordination meeting. (*Photo courtesy of DPR Construction.*)

lines. In general, if there would have been a desire for as built drawings on a project, it is worthwhile to consider updating the BIM to reflect the actual condition of the project.

Additional modeling in the postconstruction phase may include furniture or other movable assets that may need to be tracked as part of the managing of the activities of the building. The control of some of the building systems, i.e., the mechanical system, or special plumbing systems, and consumption of energy are often of interest to the building managers. Equipment maintenance schedules can also be managed through the use of a model. The instructions for maintenance and tracking of service calls can all be recorded and accessed through a BIM and **links** to databases. It will be possible to solicit the aid of the 3D visuals of the model to help understand and address a situation more quickly and efficiently if repairs or an emergency response should be required. It is not difficult to imagine how security alarm operations could also benefit from the model to indicate where a security breach may have occurred.

The use of the BIM for space utilization can be very visual for the occupants of the project. The model will be able to track the assignment of space and the location of furniture and equipment within those spaces. The Government Services Administration (GSA) has very effectively chosen to require a 3D model (BIM) for the property and space management needs of its projects.

For the remodeling requirements of existing structures for which a model had not previously been developed, it is now feasible to generate a model from a *laser scan* process. This will permit almost any 3D environment to be "mapped" to a "point cloud" that can then be used for the creation of an *intelligent* 3D model of that environment. Special software can be used to place intelligent objects in place of the point cloud objects from the laser scan. This is a 3D version of a similar 2D process whereby bitmap images are traced with vector lines to produce a vectorized drawing. See Case 6 in Chap. 5.

The Benefits of the BIM—Why Use a BIM Process?

Many of the benefits of the BIM will be viewed as direct benefits, although the largest benefits actually are the indirect benefits. Direct benefits are qualities such as the improved visualization and the centralization of (project) building information. The indirect benefits include the necessity for collaboration and the resulting better project understanding, and the reduction of project **risk**.

Simulations allow us to plan and virtually test a design before the actual project is constructed. A model will help to visualize the project, to stimulate thought about the project requirements, and to assist in describing the project in an efficient manner.

The many benefits of this fundamental change in planning and executing **construction projects** will become more apparent throughout the remainder of this book. In a few words, *the BIM process's primary benefit is the reduction of project risks.* Most of the various construction project **delivery methods** that have been developed over the past decades have more successfully shifted construction risks from one project team member to another, rather than accomplished much toward the reduction of that risk; there also still is little progress concerning any of the other fundamental problems plaguing the construction industry. See Chap. 1, "Current Practice."

A project simulation (BIM) actually requires a lot of preparation on behalf of all the project team members. It is unlikely that a complete high-quality simulation can be developed without the collaboration of the entire project team. To whatever degree the project team can manage to produce a simulation, the team will benefit from the collaboration required to achieve that result. Since the underlying principle of the simulation process has the elimination of risk as its focus, it is a primary tool for the implementation of *lean construction* techniques. It is precisely from these changes in the *process* of planning and executing a project that the primary benefits are obtained. *The solution to many of the construction industry's fundamental problems lies in successful collaboration.*

The benefits of a BIM process are inherent in the nature of the process; it will be up to the participant to make proper use of the process and thereby reap the benefits. It is a little like orienting a house properly in relation to the sun. If this is done correctly, the sun will improve the comfort of the house; if not, it will likely increase the level of discomfort.

Visualization, collaboration, and elimination are the three main headings under which the benefits of the BIM are organized. There is in fact much overlap among these categories, but they have been chosen as the main ideas around which all the benefits can be better understood. **Visualization** primarily addresses the benefit to an individual and the improvement in her or his personal understanding as a result of using the BIM. **Collaboration** refers to the cooperative action of several team members as that is encouraged and facilitated by the BIM. **Elimination** addresses mostly project-related benefits, such as reduction of conflicts, **waste**, and **risk**.

Visualization

People often say "I see" when something is understood. This relates to visualization and also points to the close connection to the word *understanding*. The clearest benefit from a 3D model is the improved ability to visualize (understand) what is being represented. Many persons have difficulty understanding 2D drawings; yes, even those who pride themselves in this skill are sometimes surprised when, after studying drawings intently, something suddenly becomes clear. A 3D model, however, clearly represents the project and allows the visualization of many of its features, even with surprisingly few details. The human brain excels in its ability to abstract and to understand through the use of **abstractions**. Symbols are a powerful way to convey a lot of meaning with very minimal information.

Humans have to be able to visualize something (an object or an idea) to communicate it and to understand something to visualize it. The visualization actually is an abstraction of the object or idea; it is not seen or understood in all its intricate detail at once—the significant features seem to be in focus, while the rest appears fuzzy. This implies that each person may focus on slightly different characteristics to compose the visualization of the object or idea; and it is this difference that is most often the cause of misunderstandings between persons attempting to communicate. Humans also have varying ability to learn how to visualize; but even with a lot of ability "a picture is worth a thousand words." And if a picture is worth a thousand words, then how much will a 3D model be worth, or a movie of a timed sequence of events? Thus it helps to develop a visualization (and understanding) through the use of a model that represents far more information and details than can be contained in the visualization (in the mind) of most individuals.

An integral part of visualization is the ability to access the right information in the correct format, so that it can be "seen" in the context of the whole project. The possibility to use the BIM as a central depository (or link) for much of the project information is promising. Just this feature alone could revolutionize information management for a project. The model may enable better access to project information and thus improve project understanding and control, and become a powerful management tool. See Fig. 2.13. The model was made in Vico's Constructor and rendered in NavisWorks.

The nature of almost all relationships between persons is based on communication. The concept of communication is based on a *two-way* exchange of information. Simply providing (sending) information is not communicating; a receiver has to do something (respond) with the information to establish communication. The degree of success can then be assessed depending on the action taken by the receiver of the message. An acknowledgment of reception of the information is a first step in establishing a form of communication; this may also include an indication verifying that the information

Figure 2.13

A simple 3D model of the structural system. The model was made in Vico's Constructor and rendered in NavisWorks. (*Image courtesy of RQ Construction.*)

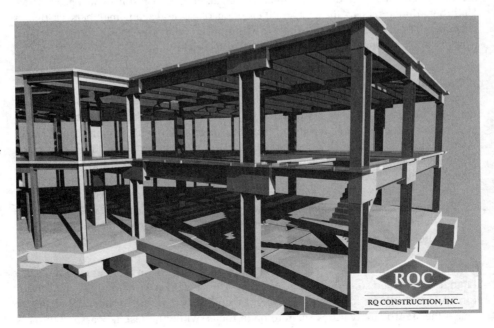

was properly understood. A further step may indicate that a certain action will result from the use of the information. Communication can take on various forms. In construction the most common forms of communication generally revolve on the creation of a common understanding among the participants by visualizing a subject and its issues. This will enable a collaborative effort among the participants to resolve the issues, and this is one of the primary purposes for project simulation. It is useful to have more than one person look at almost any issue, and BIM simulations are by far the most effective way to communicate ideas, forms, concepts, and general approaches in design and construction-related issues.

All aspects of the project must be clear and accessible to all concerned participants. Important aspects of communication are the free access to and flow of information. The BIM is characterized by the availability and connectedness of all information that has become part of the project, such as its **dimensionality—2D, 3D, 4D** (time-related), **5D** (cost-related), and any other type of information. In a centralized model all information can be connected to the model and accessed with embedded **links**. Information should exist only once, rather than be duplicated unnecessarily for convenience of individual access. There is a significant risk in the duplication of information for convenience sake, because it creates difficulty for the user to discern whether that specific information is in fact the latest available. Great care has to be taken to develop a method by which the whole project team supports and has access to the most updated information for the project.

Good communication can result in evaluation; once an idea can be "seen," it becomes possible to evaluate it. An evaluation can result in feedback that will in turn affect the simulation and allow it to evolve further. It is also possible to generate a building (or process) simulation for several variations on a theme that can then be evaluated by comparison, and thus result in a decision for the better alternative, e.g., the consideration of design alternatives, structural systems, finish material choices, or construction process alternatives. In such a case it may not be necessary to adapt an entire model to reflect alternative choices; often a small mock-up in a quick modeling tool will be more practical. The emphasis therefore is on the proper use of the tool, not on the BIM itself. If the goal is to develop a spatial layout for a portion of the building, then a quick model in SketchUp can communicate the proposals to all concerned and will be equally effective and far less work than creating a proposal with the more complex architectural model in a BIM. Then, once all decisions have been made, the actual BIM can be updated to reflect these decisions, and the resulting consequences for other areas (e.g., building systems) can be addressed with the BIM.

The steel and glass components in the model shown in Fig. 2.14 were modeled in Bentley's TriForma and the concrete components in Vico's constructor; the composite was rendered in NavisWorks. The model is a study of the **constructability** of the clerestory. The architectural and structural drawings provided conflicting information, which caused the contractor to build this model to resolve the connection details of the steel and glass. This is a particularly detailed model; it is not always necessary to model to this level of detail unless there is a specific problem to be resolved.

Figure 2.14
Study model of building components. UC Santa Barbara Student Resource Center. (*Image courtesy of RQ Construction.*) See also color insert.

Project coordination is also greatly improved with 3D visualization of a model that represents the critical systems of the project. Model views will allow the participants to share one another's concerns in any given area and communicate with one another about their collaborative approach to the resolution of conflicts. Visualization is at the root of the communication necessary to collaborate and coordinate. See Fig. 2.15.

Figure 2.15
The lab at CSU Chico, with students participating in a coordination meeting with Turner Construction.

Collaboration

The necessity to collaborate to employ simulation techniques in the construction industry is without doubt its greatest benefit. It has been shown repeatedly that early collaboration has large benefits for the planning and construction of a building project; thus the development of a virtual model is one of the best means of ensuring early and in-depth collaboration of the project team on most relevant planning, design, and construction issues. It is inconceivable to have a concert performance where the musicians and conductor do not cooperate as a team; even if individuals have different approaches, they need to harmonize with the orchestra to create a satisfactory performance. It is no different in any endeavor, and lack of respect for this fact is one of the main contributors to the construction industry's performance record. *Behind advocating a process (BIM) that fosters collaboration lies the assumption that most humans, when given the opportunity, value supporting one another, rather than competing with one another.*

If the challenge can be summed up as helping a project team to learn *how* to collaborate, then using the BIM process will be the ideal tool for this. A BIM can be such an amazing device that the participants generally become increasingly positively involved and enjoy using the model as the focus for their discussions, negotiations, and understanding of almost any issue. The management of the team, the BIM, and its linked information are the substance of the challenge. The spirit of teamwork that is produced by the use of the BIM is intriguing; it may be based on the sense of a common understanding of the issues among the participants. The discussions now center on a 3D view of the model, and quickly generate a feeling of mutual understanding, rather than using words to describe what is seen in a 2D drawing. When actual communication takes place, when two persons really listen to each other and are sensitive to each other's responses, conversation and communication are further encouraged, and mutual understanding and respect becomes possible. Real communication is required for true collaboration, for interdependency and mutual support among team members, and to work toward common team goals.

The information feedback loop represents the continual evolution of the information connected with a project. The BIM provides the source for the generation of new information that is fed back into the BIM, and will result in the addition to and refinement of this information, thus resulting in growth of the BIM. The analogy is a tree that absorbs nutrition and grows so that it can take up more nutrition and grow more. See Fig. 2.1 for a diagram depicting this concept.

Elimination

By virtue of the increased ability to visualize, communicate, evaluate, and coordinate through the use of a BIM, it becomes possible to speed up and improve understanding, coordination, material use, etc., in the management of a building project. The BIM process helps to reduce construction conflicts, construction waste, and project risk (and thus likely also project cost).

Conflicts can be identified more easily through the centralization of access to all information regarding the project. Conflicts in location, scheduling, etc., can be detected in the various views of the BIM. It is of course critical that all the sources of information that enable this process be synchronized in space, in time, and in format (see BIM planning).

Location conflicts apply to the components of the models occupying the same space. This refers to, say, the location of items such as ductwork, structural components, and cable trays in the interstitial space, or the alignment of vertical shafts through a series of floor slabs. Scheduling conflicts relate to work being done in the same area by different crews, or a prerequisite part of the work not being ready before the subsequent task is scheduled to begin. A construction sequence analysis of the project will likely reveal such inconsistencies to an experienced observer.

Construction waste reduction is another potential use of model analysis. Lean construction defines *waste* as "that which is unnecessary." In this context, analyzing the construction simulation may help the development of more efficient construction procedures, and could stimulate ideas to improve the efficiency of the use of materials, time, and energy.

By having a deeper understanding through better visualization and more thorough planning, many potential conflicts and unknowns can be removed from the project, and construction risk is reduced. Improved visualization makes the project more definite during the planning stages, e.g., end users will more quickly understand what is intended in the design, eliminating much unnecessary redesign time and providing for shorter meetings; and better coordination of systems installations will significantly improve the possibilities to prefabricate and reduce the quantity of RFIs (and conflicts resulting in required rework).

BIM PLANNING

BIM project planning is based on the fundamental BIM concepts and includes

1. Determining the purpose for the BIM (set project and process goals)
2. Developing BIM specifications (choose processes, tools, and milestones for the work)
3. Developing the implementation plan for the process (develop process strategies, select the team, and develop evaluation and adjustment methods)

The planning of a building information **model** is the preparation for the implementation of the BIM process. The fundamental questions at this stage are as follows:

- What is the nature of the project?
- What is the nature of the project delivery method?
- What are the anticipated benefits of the simulation?
- What are the most critical anticipated difficulties (both project- and process-related)?

It is important to be explicit in defining all anticipated aspects of the project development, and to establish controls and methods for evaluating the results of the process. The answers to these questions will become the basis for the specifications of the simulation; this is a critical and often underestimated aspect of this process!

It is tempting to focus on the more **object**-oriented (3D model), rather than the process-oriented, aspects of the BIM specifications, even though it is ultimately the process that determines the requirements (characteristics) of the model **objects**. For example, if the exact size and location of concrete slab pours in a construction sequence is being studied, the slab sections will need to be modeled exactly as they are anticipated for the concrete pours, so that they can be properly represented in the construction sequence. This may require close collaboration between the modeler and the construction superintendent, and it could take several modeling sessions to optimize the pour sequence for the slab. If a **cost estimate** is desired, a deliberate choice of model components will have to be planned (with the appropriate level of detail) to represent the project in the cost estimate. In other words, it is more important to establish the various processes that need to be addressed first, before becoming distracted with the actual modeling itself. The planning discussion is divided into three parts: first, the analysis of the purpose of the BIM, next, the development of the specifications required to achieve the desired results, and finally the implementation plan for the steps that are necessary to meet the chosen specifications.

Planning the Purpose of the BIM

The goals for the simulation will determine in large part what needs to be modeled and what information needs to be part of the simulation. The phase of the project planning will establish the level of information that is available, which in turn will determine what can be simulated and how the simulation may best be realized.

The purpose of a simulation is closely related to its benefits; i.e., a particular benefit becomes the purpose due to its nature. For example, the benefit of better visualization permitting large improvements in the coordination of building systems leads to the goal to coordinate the building systems with the BIM. This goal, in turn, is affected by the amount of available information about the project systems at various phases of project planning. It is useful to analyze the project goals by phase, since this will make it into a more linear, simpler process. The goals of the owner will be primarily project-related, and the goals of the other team members will also include process-related subjects; a good team will then find a creative balance between all these aims. In the earlier goal to coordinate the building systems it is evident that the owner will be interested because this may lead to cost savings for the project, while the designers and subcontractors will be interested in reducing RFIs and required rework, or perhaps even in prefabricating larger portions of the work to reduce installation costs.

Planning and Design—Planning and Preconstruction Phase

Currently it is not uncommon to find BIM applications in the preconstruction phase of a project. This is in large part due to the fact that simpler models, and less information, associated with the planning phase, will still provide large benefits to the project. The discussion of this phase has been divided into two parts, addressing first the conceptual design and marketing aspects of the project, and then the planning and design during the development of a complete set of instructions for the construction of the project.

Conceptual design and marketing uses will generally require 3D models for visual communication purposes, as well as 5D models to begin developing a **cost analysis** at the conceptual design stage. Even a very simple model can still serve these purposes very well. Although more sophisticated rendered views of a detailed model may be desired, various forms of images can be created from an early design model, and with use of the right software it is also possible to create sophisticated images from relatively simple models. The primary purpose for such images is the communication and the development of design ideas with feedback from the project participants. The associated cost analysis of such a model will necessarily also be based on either square footage costs or large-scale system costs, depending on the level of detail represented in the model at this stage. A *target value design* is very important in establishing the needs of the owner and an associated budget that can be refined during the remainder of the planning process. The creation of a budget that actually reflects the project design at this early stage is in fact revolutionary and could potentially make the design efforts much more efficient and focused. Without cost projections in early design stages, all too commonly high construction bids after the project's design has been completed may require *value engineering*, undesirable compromises, and/or a lot of redesigning and redrawing in an attempt to save the project.

Such simple conceptual models may also be used to presell a project, before construction takes place, to help secure the financing for the project. A sales effort may utilize sophisticated images and/or movies showing the completed virtual project. The **schematic** models for these purposes are often produced with surface modeling software. It is generally simpler to use a surface modeler, and the results are well suited for communication purposes.

The model in Fig. 2.16 was produced in Vico's Constructor and rendered in NavisWorks.

The planning and design activities of the preconstruction phase benefit enormously from a 3D model that has the ability to quickly and reliably communicate and evaluate design intent. It may be appropriate to generate design alternatives at this stage of the project; the model can provide the ability to compare 3D views of the variations side by side, to encourage discussions and facilitate feedback from the project team. The 3D model development, constructability analysis, construction schedule development, and project cost analysis are all aspects of the planning and design discussions that follow.

Figure 2.16

California Academy of Sciences, San Francisco. The model was produced in Vico's Constructor and rendered in NavisWorks. (*Image courtesy of Webcor Builders, Chong Partners Architecture, and Renzo Piano Building Workshop.*)

Development of the 3D Model   This is the essence of the planning and design phase of a project. The information feedback loop through which the model contents are developed is very dependent on the model itself. The model is the focal point for the evolution of the design process, and all project team members primarily communicate through use of the model. The improved 3D enabled visualization is also very helpful for the designers with respect to progress in their own work. Almost all ideas for the project will be reflected in the model in one way or another. At this stage the project is still fairly schematic, and therefore it is generally not difficult to represent the ideas of the project team members in the model. The model becomes a live representation of the work of the group. *It is critical to the success of this stage of the work to adopt a process that will enhance the interaction of the team members and record the comments and feedback from the discussions.* Renate Fruchter's work with PBL at Stanford is described in the "Project Management" section of this chapter under "BIM Planning." Dr. Fruchter's work focuses on the development of communication skills to enable successful project team collaboration.

During this phase the collaboration of the consultants is essential to take advantage of their expertise at the right moment in the development of the design concepts for the project. With an understandable 3D schematic architectural model, it is often simple to get valuable input from structural and MEP consultants, while it is still possible to incorporate their ideas into the project design. During schematic design such developments will generally not create too much additional work for the architectural team. (It is actually shocking to realize how often a good idea is dismissed due to an unwillingness to redo some part of the already completed work.) Design evaluation and communication are thus the primary benefits of the 3D model in this phase of the project. Evaluation often includes the study of alternatives, and it is useful to be able to quickly grasp the essence of an idea and provide meaningful feedback to the designers. The 3D model clearly is also an excellent means to communicate the design decisions to the owner for her or his understanding, feedback, and approval.

The 3D schematic building model will be the basis for the consultants to begin their design work, and it will help them to develop and evaluate potential alternatives. Energy issues can also be addressed at this point, and design alternatives for various building systems (structural, mechanical, building skin, etc.) can be evaluated and coordinated conceptually. This may include an analysis of the project's energy consumption. The model could generate heat gain and loss data, and it could accommodate the assessment of alternative material and design approaches and their effects on the long-term energy use of the building. A more informed selection of heating and air conditioning equipment could result from this analysis. It is also possible to evaluate the *return on investment* for the energy-related components of the building. The same will be possible in relation to the maintenance issues for the project; i.e., the return on investment may be considered with respect to long-term maintenance items so that these options can be optimized with respect to the initial construction costs for the project and reflect the goals of the owner.

The 3D model is an excellent tool to coordinate all the various system components as the project evolves through the design development phase. This can be accomplished with *clash detection* software that analyzes the model for coordination conflicts. The model will contain the location of all the system components, so that the software can show where objects are occupying the same space or are located too close to one another. See "Clash Detection" in BIM processes. This is clearly the ideal time to resolve these conflicts and ensure that the building components are well coordinated and installable without conflicts.

Figure 2.17 shows the model views before and after 3D coordination; notice just left of center of picture, the (sloped) drainage plumbing inside the large rectangular duct

Figure 2.17

MEP coordination for Sutter Surgical Hospital North Valley. (*Image courtesy of RQ Construction.*) See also color insert.

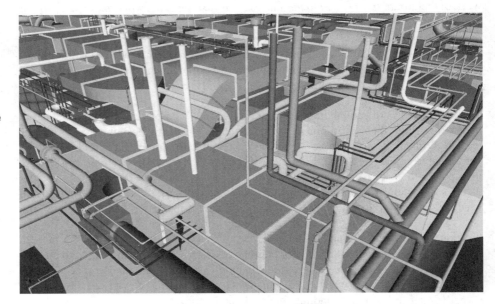

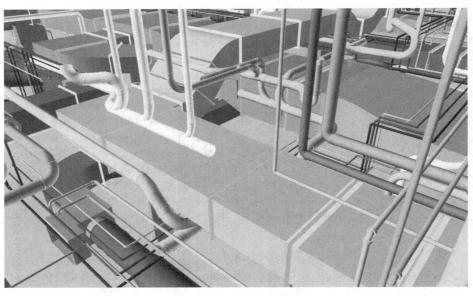

before the coordination, and above and below the duct afterward. See Case 2 in Chap. 5 for more information on this project. The "before" model in this example actually represents the modeling of already light table coordinated MEP drawings. The contractor made the decision to model the project and provided his own model of the MEP systems based on already "coordinated" 2D drawings from the MEP subtrades. The result is clear from the images: The general contractor was fortunate to have created a model, even at this late stage in project planning.

The Constructability Analysis   This is another valuable part of the preconstruction phase that refers to the assessment of the requirements and circumstances of the construction process itself to achieve the desired result (i.e., how can the materials be best assembled?). This will include an evaluation of the use of materials and systems as well as the analysis of the fabrication, assembly, and installation details of all the project parts. Constructability also includes addressing the layout of the construction site, access for supply deliveries, site preparations (including excavations and backfill operations), the job trailer location, etc. Value engineering can be very effectively introduced at this early stage of the project. *Value engineering* in this sense refers to the considerations taken into account to maximize the value of the project design and components. Optimizing the project value can be achieved through brainstorming sessions where the entire project team collaborates, through the 3D model that facilitates visualization and communication among team members.

The final preparations before installation starts also include communications with subcontractors regarding the specifics of the project conditions. It would be ideal if the subcontractors had already been involved during the design phase, so that their input were incorporated into the project design. The model will aid in any case, however, to improve the understanding of exactly what and how things need to happen in the field.

The primary purpose for the modeling of the project shown in Fig. 2.18 was the MEP (mechanical—electrical—plumbing) and FS (fire sprinkler) coordination with structural. The walls have been made transparent in this model so that their context can be seen without hiding the relevant parts for the coordination purpose.

The Construction Schedule   The construction schedule can also be developed with help from the 4D model. If a preliminary schedule is available, a schematic construction **sequence** can be simulated. This will facilitate the visualization of the construction process and allow the consideration of alternative approaches to sequencing, site layout, and crane placement, etc., during the construction process. The model components can also contain production rate information (for all the associated work tasks) that will permit a **lines of balance schedule** analysis; this approach allows the fine-tuning of tasks based on their location in the project and production rates, and helps to eliminate start and stop cycles within tasks. For example, if the framers of interior partitions are a little slower than the sheetrock installers, it will detect this and suggest either speeding up the framers or slowing down the sheetrock workers, so that the overall production is optimized. Improvements to repetitive tasks and production rates can make a significant difference in the efficiency of a large project.

Figure 2.18
Sutter Surgical
Hospital North
Valley. (*Image
courtesy of RQ
Construction.*) See
also color insert.

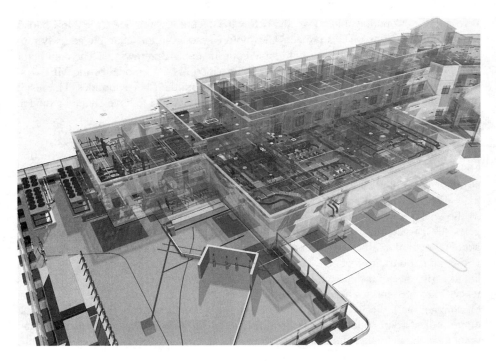

Project Cost   Project cost can be forecasted and tracked with a BIM throughout all phases of project planning. In the early stages of a project it is helpful to establish budget areas; these can be represented as square footage costs in an extremely simple model. A schematic 5D model will provide schematic quantities, and an outline cost estimate can be generated. When the project cost estimate and budget are tracked through use of the model throughout the design phase, it is referred to as a *target value design*. As the models evolve, cost tracking can be refined with the increased level of model detail; and the cost implications of design alternatives can be evaluated at any stage of design development. Most cost analysis will be based on the link between the model components and an external database that contains the actual cost information. The quantities in the model are combined with the linked cost data so that a project cost estimate is generated. The database is editable and can be customized to the users' choice. Many companies will base their cost estimates on historical data and can use already familiar data from a proprietary database. It is also possible to use commercially available cost data.

Project Management—Preconstruction and Construction Phases

The BIM process in the construction phase applies both to project team management (people-related) and to process management. The BIM also continues to be useful for planning purposes that carry over into the construction phase.

The use of a BIM for construction management is only recently beginning to gain popularity. Currently the primary uses of BIM in the construction phase are communication, identification and resolution of coordination issues, planning of construction sequencing, and replacement of fabrication shop drawings by a detailed 3D model. All these uses require a fairly high level of detail in the model components, and they are often implemented with models that a subcontractor may already have produced specifically for these reasons.

The BIM has great potential for optimizing the construction schedule (productivity optimization) with a Line of Balance scheduler, or for tracking cash flow, but currently these applications are not widely used.

Project Team Management   This applies to the guidance of the interactions among the participants in the design and construction processes of the project. It is important to remember that the project team is working for the owner and needs to keep the goals of the owner clearly in mind while establishing the construction management parameters for the project. The project's BIM plan should reflect these goals and be the tool with which the team is realizing its goals. The primary concerns are communication and coordination issues among the project team members.

It is easy to underestimate the depth of change required to implement the BIM process successfully, within the structure of a project team. The collaboration necessary to build an accurate and coordinated simulation of a project forces a different kind of interaction than the project team members are accustomed to in conventionally managed construction projects.

A good place to begin planning communication channels and assigning responsibilities is to address what, when, and how to report project progress to the owner. Reporting protocol may occasionally be specified in the contract, but it will likely be an area that the team will have to define for itself. Updating of the BIM is the second critical area to address early; a system of keeping a central model coordinated and a detailed description of the roles of each of the modelers is important. The BIM will encourage the consideration of many responsibilities of team members and thus open the possibility for developing clear guidelines for the relationships among the project team members. The team will be able to optimize its productivity through well-defined deliverables. *The use of BIM will make the deliverables more transparent to all team members, and thus exercise a certain individual encouragement to compliance with the team's expectations.*

Coordination of the work of the project team members is an extremely valuable aspect of a BIM. A 3D view of a detailed project can quickly and easily reveal many characteristics of the project that may otherwise be difficult to visualize in the conventional 2D drawing format. Such model views also encourage the interaction among the responsible persons to resolve apparent conflicts, or discuss other design or construction-related issues. A discussion between the design consultants and subcontractors based on the 3D models may help in communicating the designer's intent and visualizing the specific construction or installation procedures before they are to take place in the field. Thus the BIM can function as a focal point for the relationships and communication among all construction team members. The model can accommodate the visualization of the regular construction schedule update as well as the look-ahead ideas practiced in Lean Construction.

See the Case Study 1, entitled "A Practitioner's Guide to Using Virtual Design and Construction (3D/4D) Tools on Commercial Projects," by Atul Khanzode and Dean Reed of DPR Inc. in Chap. 5 of this book.

In her paper entitled "Global Teamwork: Cross Disciplinary, Collaborative, Geographically Distributed e-Learning Environment,"[1] Dr. Renate Fruchter, founder of the Project Based Learning Lab (PBL) in the Department of Civil and Environmental Engineering at Stanford University, describes the program she has developed to address the communication and collaboration needs of the architecture, engineering, and construction industry. In her words: "The AEC (architecture, engineering, construction) global teamwork program is based on a PBL pedagogical approach, where PBL stands for Problem-, Project-, Product-, Process-, People-Based Learning. PBL is about teaching and learning teamwork in the information age. PBL is a methodology of teaching and learning that focuses on *problem* based, *project* organized activities that produce a *product* for a client. PBL is based on re-engineered *processes* that bring *people* from multiple disciplines together."[2]

The PBL laboratory program is based on recognition of the fact that more than a building information model is necessary to improve the planning and construction of structures in the 21st century. To prepare students for the tasks that lie ahead in the industry, Dr. Fruchter has set up the PBL lab with its headquarters at Stanford University and its participating students distributed throughout the world. The assignment is for a team of students, who play the roles of an architect, one or two structural engineers, and one or two construction managers, to complete the planning and preparation of a construction project within approximately 5 months. The students come together at the beginning of the period to meet one another personally and to plan their approach to the problem; then they return to their respective home schools and communicate by phone, Internet, etc., and develop their project solution as a team. At the midpoint of the project there is an all team "Fishbowl"[3] design session, hosted by Stanford, but with most students participating virtually from their home schools. In this session the students watch on their computer screens (Internet connection) and listen (via speaker phone) to the mentors address the teams' questions and the various issues critical to the project. Everyone is communicating in **real time** via various media connections. It gives them an opportunity to see some of the practical areas, in which they lack experience, tackled by professionals with experience. It also is an opportunity to pose questions and provide input that may lead to discussions. At the end of the project all teams physically reconvene at Stanford to present their final solutions and receive critique from the mentors and from one another. The teams are advised and coached by the mentors who are professionals from the industry and have the necessary experience to help the students understand the difficult project issues. The projects simulate actual life experiences; thus someone will play the owner's role so that the design team can learn to interact with the owner. The teams have four challenges: cross-disciplinary teamwork, use of advanced collaboration technology, time management and team coordination, and multicultural collaboration. The cross-disciplinary teams give the students valuable experience and understanding of the various aspects important to a building project; it is an opportunity for the participants to develop an appreciation for each team member's contribution to the overall planning, design, and construction processes.

The use of advanced collaboration technology provides the team with the latest tools to communicate and coordinate their work efforts. In most cases these experiences with technology are ahead of the level at which the industry has implemented similar processes, thus preparing the students to help introduce these changes in their future workplace. The focus on time management and team coordination helps the team address realistic problems with realistic methods and resources, thus developing valuable personal skills through this exercise.

Multicultural experiences seem to have become the norm in contemporary business; thus learning to deal with culture, language, and communication issues at this level will be another invaluable dimension to the semester-long project. The persons chosen to participate on the teams can come from a variety of countries around the globe, and they will have a background and professional training that reflects their culture. It is clear that Dr. Fruchter's work is not only valuable for the educational purposes of Stanford University, but also critical for the development of communication and collaboration processes that will benefit the construction industry.*

Construction Process Management Construction process management refers to managing the processes required to enable the construction of building projects. These processes are often related to construction mobilization, procurement, scheduling and sequencing, cost control and cash flow analysis, material ordering and handling, and component fabrication and installation. All these processes have evolved out of a need to handle these activities more effectively, and this could just as well mean eliminating what is unnecessary (waste in the form of time, materials, or resources) as adding what is desired in terms of materials, means, or methods to a project or process.

Schedule and sequence analysis addresses the time required and order (or sequence) in which the components of the project will be assembled. This may have an effect on total project cost by affecting the efficiency of the tasks of the construction schedule. Productivity may be optimized by minimizing the "starts and stops" of a work crew on the project. If the productivity rates of crews are relatively predictable for a given task, it may be possible to schedule the location and surrounding tasks of the project to optimize the productivity of that particular crew's task. Assembly sequence/space studies may also provide useful information for the improvement of the efficiency of particular tasks. Especially in hospital or laboratory projects the installation of MEP can be a demanding and complex job in an extremely tight space; the ability to create virtual installation scenarios can be of great value to the installers, so that they are able to visualize and resolve the anticipated installation difficulties before commencing the work (perhaps even prefabricate portions of the work).

The construction schedule will generally have been developed during the preconstruction phase. During the construction phase, construction progress may be tracked on the schedule; or the schedule may be fine-tuned based on more detailed and updated

---

*Dr. Fruchter can be reached at fruchter@stanford.edu for copies of her articles and further information regarding her work.

information. Ideally the schedule is actively maintained and utilized throughout the construction phase; in reality, however, this often is not the case. The schedule can also function as a shopping list for the project, and can be useful in the scheduling of procurements for the work. The BIM will permit the linking of procurement and installation information to the model elements and thus provide an overview and summary list of the order status of the materials.

Cash flow analysis also becomes possible through the information connected to the BIM components; this tracks the material purchasing and labor costs for the project. The use of "cost buckets" (for budgeting) can benefit from procurement analysis in the BIM, and the amount of money spent in any desired cost area (bucket) can be tracked, so that adjustments may be made as required at any stage of the construction. This process is the equivalent of target value design for the construction phase. See Case Study 1 in Chap. 5.

The BIM can also enable billing controls. It is possible to track and represent work completed in the BIM so that billing quantities can be taken off the model and invoiced accordingly. Financing agencies generally need to see some physical description of work completed to release a draw for the project; this process can be facilitated by the use of the visualization possible with the BIM. Inspectors can also more easily visualize what exactly is supposed to be finished in a project, with the help of the model.

The third and possibly largest area of BIM utilization in construction processes is that of fabrication. A detailed model can take the place of shop drawings and provides numerous additional benefits. Traditionally the systems fabricator plans the fabrication process. The design consultant will submit the design drawings to the architect for approval before they are sent to the fabricator, who will prepare shop drawings from the design submittal. These shop drawings reflect all the required fabrication and installation specifications for the components and need to be approved for production by the architect and/or consultants. This can be a complex process and easily lets errors slip through, especially since another translation from 2D drawings to 3D is required in the checker's mind to try to find the inconsistencies in the drawings of the components. The coordination of a large set of shop drawings can be very tedious and time-consuming. The creation of a 3D model will allow a much deeper understanding of the information required for fabrication, and it will be much easier to find planning errors. Many fabricators already employ manufacturing methods that use a 3D model to provide instructions to the fabrication equipment, thus eliminating the shop drawings entirely. This process is referred to as *DDE*, for direct digital exchange, or *EDI*, for electronic data interchange. The coordination and checking of the fabrication information in a 3D model are far more manageable and reliable. A detailed 3D model allows many subcontractors to prefabricate components, rather than to field-fabricate and to shop-assemble, rather than to field-assemble, thus further increasing installation efficiency.

The images in Fig. 2.19 show a structural steel model and the information connected to each of the steel pieces to generate shop drawings for fabrication. If a steel fabricator is set up properly, the actual shop drawings can be eliminated and fabrication can take place directly from the model; this is referred to as direct digital exchange. It is far more effective to coordinate the fabrication through a 3D model than through conventional shop drawings.

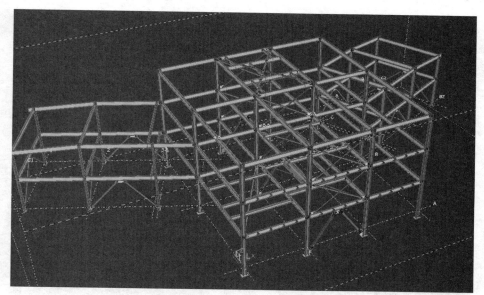

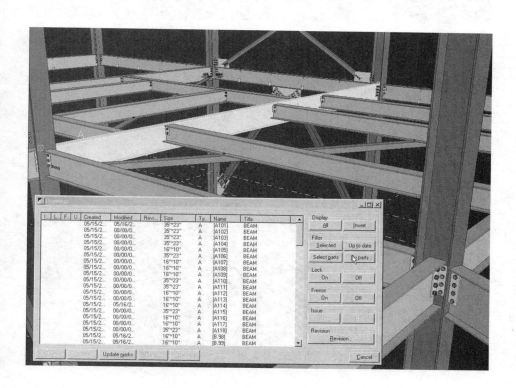

Figure 2.19
Various views of a
Tekla model.
(*Images courtesy
of Tekla.*)

Figure 2.19
(*Continued*)

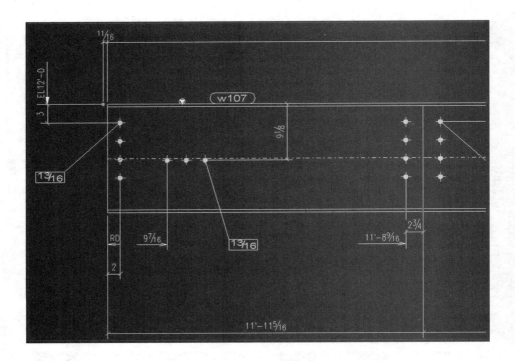

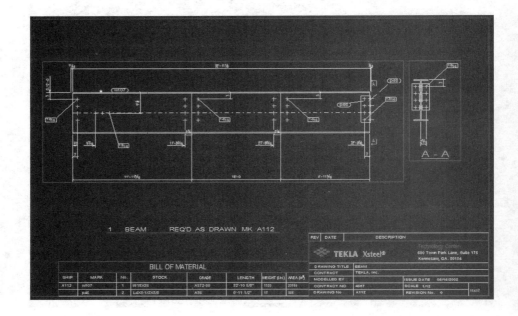

Facilities and Operations Management—Postconstruction Phase

Building information models are rapidly gaining popularity with facilities management (FM) tasks. The BIM's ability to contain vast amounts of visual information has attracted a lot of interest from facilities managers and operations and maintenance units. The benefits are similar to those listed for the other phases of the project. It is often easier to manage tasks visually; using the 3D model, to be able to view certain aspects of management, helps one to visualize it oneself, and to communicate it to others. The focus in this section is on control rather than planning—control of operations, data, and processes.

Operations control refers to the ability to manage, e.g., maintenance for the project. The components of the BIM can show maintenance-related information such as replacement parts ordering information, maintenance scheduling information, past maintenance records, and installation and maintenance instructions.

Other data control may include inventories of furniture, personnel locations, space assignments, energy consumption data, space utilization schedules and data, etc.

Process controls refer to the use of the model to control heating and cooling systems, energy consumption analysis, security system controls, access analysis, and functional applications (manufacturing process or storage analysis) of the project.

For most of these applications, object model-based management is still quite new, and there will undoubtedly be vast improvements in the next few years. If any postconstruction use of the BIM is anticipated, it will be well worthwhile for the project team to take this into consideration in the BIM planning phase so that it can be accomplished effectively.

Specifying the Model

A model is an abstraction of reality—the character and level of detail required to make the model successful will depend on its purpose, and the viewers' level of understanding. In most cases, models are generated to help communicate a particular understanding about the subject. The diagrams in this book can be seen as models of concepts, and each viewer will bring his or her personal level of understanding to them. Over time, a model (or diagram) may gain more meaning due to the increase in the level of understanding of the viewer.

The purpose(s) of the simulation will determine the specifications for the modeling. These purposes will generally be associated to the phase of the project's development. The type and amount of information available about the project are directly derivative from the level of development (phase of the project); and as a project plan evolves, both the available information and the known level of detail will steadily increase.

It is important to take both the model and the linked information into account when considering the level of detail that will be required to see, analyze, and communicate through the use of the BIM. In specifying the BIM, the nature of the components, the nature of the information, and the link between these two need to be planned (and tested) carefully.

The matrices in Fig. 2.20 show a way to consider the required level of detail for various types of models.

Figure 2.20

Level of detail analysis developed by Vico. (*Image courtesy of Vico.*)

Model Progression Specification

Pad Footing	LoD 100	LoD 200	LoD 300 ...
Model	N/A		
Estimating	**Recipe based takeoff** Foundation Conceptual ls or $/ sf	**Model based takeoff** •Formwork •Concrete Reinforcing •4000 psi Concrete	**Model based takeoff** •Formwork # of form uses •Grade of steel •# of rebar mats •Mat bar size •Bar spacing •Accelerator
Scheduling	**Master Task** Foundations	**Master Tasks** •Form Pad Footing •Reinforce Pad Footing •Pour Pad Footing	**Micro Management** •Prep •Set Anchor Bolts/Embeds •Formwork •Reinforcement
Procurement	N/A	Purchase Order Subcontracts	•Place & Finish Purchase Order Subcontracts
Fabrication	N/A	Tolerance	•Formwork design •Anchor bolts and embeds •Reinforcing Steel

VICO SOFTWARE
Integrating Construction

Model Progression Specification

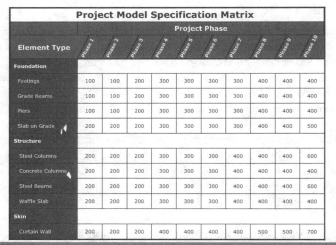

Project Model Specification Matrix										
Project Phase										
Element Type	Phase 1	Phase 2	Phase 3	Phase 4	Phase 5	Phase 6	Phase 7	Phase 8	Phase 9	Phase 10
Foundation										
Footings	100	100	200	300	300	300	300	400	400	400
Grade Beams	100	100	200	300	300	300	300	400	400	400
Piers	100	100	200	300	300	300	300	400	400	400
Slab on Grade	200	200	200	300	300	300	300	400	400	500
Structure										
Steel Columns	200	200	200	300	300	300	400	400	400	600
Concrete Columns	200	200	200	300	300	300	400	400	400	400
Steel Beams	200	200	200	300	300	300	400	400	400	600
Waffle Slab	200	200	200	300	300	300	400	400	400	400
Skin										
Curtain Wall	200	200	200	400	400	400	400	500	500	700

VICO SOFTWARE
Integrating Construction

Only experience will make this matrix more useful. In this context it should simply be seen as a relationship between level of detail and information. The two basic questions that emerge are as follows:

- How much detail needs to be represented in the model and its components?
- How much information needs to be contained in, or attached to, the model?

The nature of the model components addresses primarily what needs to be modeled and how those parts will be represented in the model. This is a description of the physical parameters of the objects. The nature of an object also affects the ability to embed (parametrically) or attach information to it. Both the type of object as well as its level of complexity will need to be specified. Typically all permanent work needs to be modeled; the general guideline is to model all parts that are 1 inch (in) or larger in diameter. This means that $^3/_4$-in pipes are often not modeled, and neither are the pipe hangers, braces, or cable tray concrete inserts. Such an approach, however, clearly limits the use of the model to larger-scale interference detection. The reason that the small items are not modeled is that they can usually be fitted in by the installer in the space that is left after the bigger components are already installed. Modeling small items can also be fairly tedious and time-consuming; *all modeling efforts ultimately have to be worthwhile*. Modeling small objects is clearly very dependent on many factors, and these should be taken into consideration when planning the BIM. The purpose of the model has to be clearly understood to generate a specification so that the desired result is achieved and realistic enough to serve its purpose as a simulation. Besides the nature of the components themselves, the way in which the model file is organized also has a large effect on the possibilities for model analysis. Modeling software organizes the contents by object type, layers, and sometimes stories or zones; this structure is the primary method of organizing and later selecting groups of components for a specific purpose. (See Chap. 3 on software tools.)

The stories of the model file can be used for the physical stories of the project, but they can also contain various other types of information, such as the 2D base drawings upon which the model is built, or the "object construction area" where specialty components can be assembled to serve their purpose in the modeling process. See Fig. 2.21.

The nature of the representation of the model component will be suggested by the function of the actual object in the project. For example, when a wall is modeled, it needs to be decided whether that simulated wall will consist of a simple object to which all necessary information is attached, such as framing information, finish information, etc., or whether it needs to be modeled with individual studs, sheetrock, etc. This decision depends on the ultimate purpose of the model, and if the construction sequence of the individual studs and the sheetrock in realistic detail is required, all these items will need to be modeled separately; this is rare however, and generally a simple wall object that could change color in a more abstracted representation, to indicate the phase of its construction, is adequate for most purposes. *The model specification thus largely depends on what needs to be visualized or analyzed as much as who will be viewing it.*

Figure 2.21

The dialog box for stories in Vico's Constructor. (*Image courtesy of Vico.*)

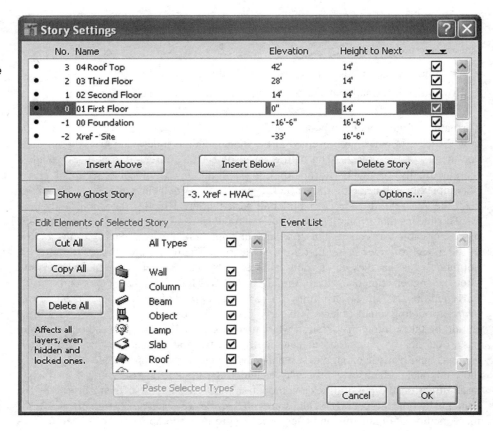

A recurring question is whether to model any of the temporary unseen work of the project. This work can include the trenches for underground utilities (and the soil piles next to the trenches), the formwork for concrete, or scaffolding for construction, construction trailers, lay-down areas for structural steel, waste collection facilities, etc. Modeling these types of objects is often useful for the visualization of site utilization, safety issues, installation clearances and sequences, etc. The level of detail of an object is not exactly the same as the level of complexity of an object. The detail mostly refers to the accuracy of the model object in relation to the actual real construction component; the more detailed a component is, the more realistic it will appear. The level of complexity generally refers to the nature of the information contained or linked to the object. A floor system could be represented by a simple slab that contains very complex attached information; information regarding formwork, its division into various areas for concrete placement, or steel reinforcing specifications could all be linked to the slab object. If we created the floor from several components that all together created the floor object, it would be very detailed even though it might not have complex information attached to it. Fabrication models are the best examples of models that clearly contain objects that may be both very detailed and complex. When a very high level of detail and complexity is necessary in a specific area, it may be possible to model only a smaller portion of the entire project to that level of detail. (See Fig. 2.15 for an example.)

The different types of models that can be specified can be grouped as follows:

1. *Conceptual or schematic models.* This model type has a low level of detail and information content, and a high degree of abstraction; it is conceptual in nature.

In the early stages of a project, the purpose of the model will primarily be design-oriented. Alternative design proposals may be compared and discussed among the project team members. The model will become the basis for the consultants to generate proposals in their own areas of responsibility, and a way for the designers to develop the project and communicate the design intent to other project team members. The coordination of the various parts of the project can be addressed from the very beginning of project development.

Preliminary approvals can be obtained, and early feasibility, marketing, and constructability studies can all be done with a schematic model. Such low-level detail models can also be very effective for responses to RFPs (requests for proposal) and initial project presentations. A schematic model can also be used to generate a construction sequence to demonstrate the time line of the development of the construction phase of a project. Visually relatively rich images may be generated from a model at this level of development.

The images in Fig. 2.22 are extracted from a 1.5-minute-long movie; they serve as an example of a very basic schematic model that was created to make this construction sequence study, that shows progressively more of the construction in place. Such a sequence analysis can begin with the site excavation and end with the completed project—the date will show in a corner of the screen; the construction schedule has now become visual. Site utilization and equipment placement can all be part of the dynamic analysis of the construction activities. It is remarkable how much information and understanding can be gleaned from such a simple model.

2. *Design models.* These have midlevel detail and information content.

The design model is used to develop the more detail-oriented elements of the project. At this point the team will have agreed on the basic project design. Many details will be developed at this stage of the project, and they have to comply with the required parameters such as budget, construction schedule, and available resources. A design model will have representations of all major components such as walls with doors and windows, accurate plan dimensions, basic structural elements (columns, beams, bracing, etc.), accurate floor-to-floor heights, rudimentary mechanical systems, vertical circulation designs, roof design, shading devices, etc. During this phase the primary purposes of the model are design analysis (and preliminary coordination), communication (and presentation) among the project team members, and submittals for outside approvals.

Design models are generally produced by the architect and may include components from consultants such as the structural and mechanical engineers. See Figs. 2.23

Figure 2.22
Toronto high-rise condominium project. (*Image courtesy of Lease Crutcher Lewis, Seattle, Washington.*) See also color insert.

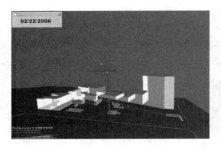
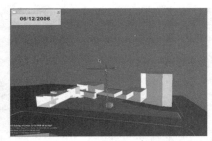
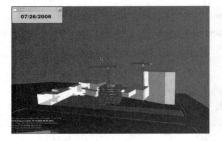
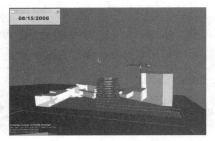
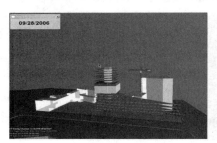
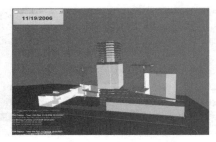

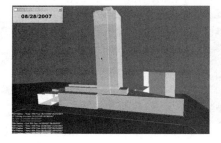
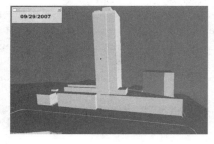

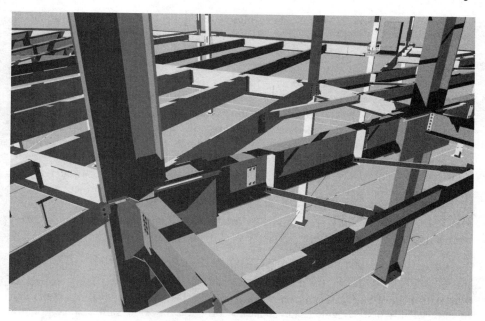

Figure 2.23
Structural design model. Sutter Surgical Hospital North Valley. (*Image courtesy of RQ Construction.*)

and 2.24. A model with this level of detail typically contains information that is traditionally found in the *design development* (DD) documents of a project. Such models can easily be used for presentations to design review committees, potential project investors, etc. A word of caution: To the layperson a model of this level of detail will appear to contain all the information required for construction. Unless it is properly presented, this may lead to false expectations on the part of a viewer who does not share the understanding of the project team who generated the model.

This type of model may also be expandable to a new level of detail that would enable it to evolve into the next category of sophistication. This will have to be planned, however, so that the modeling strategy will take this into account and not make it unnecessarily complicated.

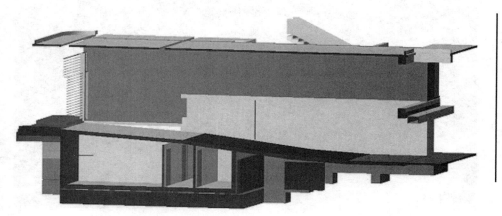

Figure 2.24
Architectural design model. The software can cut out any portion of the model to facilitate viewing the interior structure and details from any angle. (*Image courtesy of Vico.*)

3. *Construction model.* This model has a middle to high level of detail and information.

The construction model is a much more detailed version of the simulation which may include enough details to study interferences between different model components, such as structural and mechanical systems. A model of this level of development can be used for constructability studies, detailed cost analysis, construction schedule sequence generation, energy analysis, etc. At this stage it becomes worthwhile to consider the utility of the simulation in the management process. Will the model act as the single depository for all project-related information? Will the administrative project information be connected to the BIM? How could this be done effectively? The answers to these questions require a more advanced understanding and deliberate planning throughout the BIM process. It will depend on many factors, such as the nature of the project, the available experience, etc., whether developing some of these BIM processes will be wise or not. These areas certainly are not widely practiced at this time and will most likely evolve a lot during the next few years.

At this time in the development of BIM processes, it is unlikely that a construction model will be provided by the architect. In most cases it will be the general contractor who will make the necessary effort to assemble a BIM with this level of detail. This level of BIM will specifically address the construction processes, after the completion of the design by the architect. Due to the nature of the contract of the architect it will be the architect who will prepare the construction documents for building permits etc. These drawings may be produced from a design development level model and thus not require any additional model development on the architectural side. The necessary construction details are typically developed in the 2D drawing environment. The general contractor will thus either develop the DD model or generate a new model based on the construction documents from the architect. See Figs. 2.25 and 2.26.

Figure 2.25

Construction model of Sutter Surgical Hospital North Valley. Overall coordinated systems. (*Image courtesy of RQ Construction.*)

Figure 2.26
Construction model of Sutter Surgical Hospital North Valley. Coordinated mechanical systems with some fabrication level detail. (*Image courtesy of RQ Construction.*) See also color insert.

4. *Shop drawing model.* This model has a high level of detail with necessary information for fabrication.

Many manufacturers now use models in lieu of shop drawings to fabricate their components. Fabrication models (see Fig. 2.27) may be very useful to integrate with the other systems models for clash detection (interference studies). The timing of the production of such models becomes an issue. It is clearly an advantage to work with a modeling tool that permits the development of a schematic design model into a fabrication model, without having to begin over again with a different tool because the level of detail changes. The use of compatible software tools (interoperability) will be an issue between the persons who design and those who fabricate, so that already existing models can be used to further develop the project information. The fabrication models may often be created within the context of another already existing model, such as the architectural and/or structural model (see Fig. 2.28). It will thus represent a component with a different level of detail development than the context models (which will often be the result of an earlier phase of the project). In concept this is quite acceptable as long as the project team is aware of this and its implications, e.g., the lack of detail in some parts of the model, such as the modeling of the pipe hangers, but not the related inserts in the slab above. This would be the result of the mechanical model containing the pipe hangers, but the structural model missing the concrete inserts.

5. *Detailing model.* This model has a high level of detail of a specific portion of the project.

Detailing models are generally for visual analysis only and will typically not contain much other information; they often exist apart from the BIM of the project. The results

Figure 2.27
Fabrication model being generated from design model in Tekla Structures. Same column-beam intersection before and after the creation of the connection. (*Image courtesy of Tekla.*)

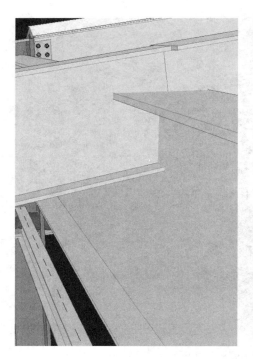
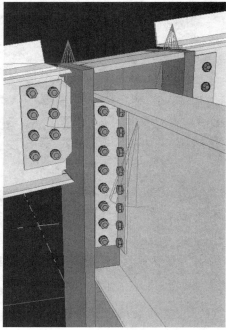

of the analysis and development of the detailing model, however, can be used to further refine the BIM, and thus can be beneficial for the whole project.

It may be useful to make a model of a specific area that requires greater development or further analysis to resolve some specific issues. In this case, rather than modeling the entire project to that level of detail, only the area in question needs to be modeled to

Figure 2.28
Ductwork and cable tray fabrication model being coordinated with architectural model. (*Image courtesy of RQ Construction.*)

that higher level of refinement. For example, this could be a specific corridor in a hospital where all the utilities need to be arranged and distributed in a small space, or the installation of a specific piece of equipment, or the construction of a difficult detail such as a curtain wall connection. See Fig. 2.14 for an example.

Detailing models are actually study models where the nature of modeling can be beneficial to resolving detailing problems. See Fig. 2.29. Since they will generally remain outside the BIM, it is often not important what tools are used to construct them. Such models also will not necessarily be shared with all who benefit from the BIM, but be a specific tool that produces an understanding that can guide the further development of the most useful level of abstraction of the BIM components of the project.

6. *As-built model.* This level of detail may depend on an already existing BIM.

Developing an as-built model should be addressed from the beginning of project planning so that it does not become a hardship at the end of construction. A *properly updated* BIM will in fact be the as-built model by the time the project is finished. The protocol developed for the updating of the models and project information during the preconstruction phase needs to be adapted and continued into the construction phase so that the model can remain a current and accurate reflection of the state of the project.

An already existing facility may need to be modeled to manage or plan alterations to that facility. In this situation the model may be constructed from the existing drawings or from new survey information about the existing facility. Such survey information could be generated with traditional measuring methods, or it could be generated by 3D laser scans. The resulting point clouds from the laser scanning can then be used to build a 3D model that matches the points of the *point cloud*. Laser scanning can potentially

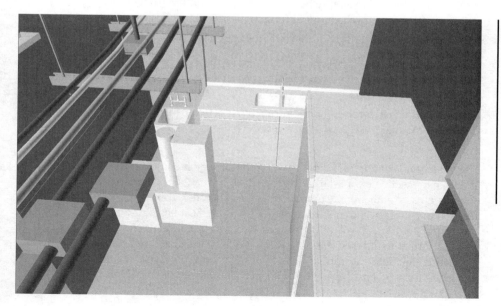

Figure 2.29
Detailing model to study light fixture layout for a typical room. Sutter Surgical Hospital North Valley. Modeled in Constructor by Vico. (*Image courtesy of RQ Construction.*)

also be used in new construction to document as-built conditions and compare them to the design model to check installation tolerances; this area is currently being developed and rapidly gaining in popularity.

7. *Operations and maintenance model*. This model type can represent various levels of detail.

A model used to manage the operations of a project can have numerous purposes, and the requirements for the model will need to be planned and implemented similarly to the other BIM processes discussed in this text. Models used in this phase will frequently have been inherited from the planning and construction phases of the project and may need to be adapted to their new purpose. The first considerations are often to update the latest BIM to accurately reflect the necessary as-built conditions of the project.

Facility managers can benefit from links among the model components and the O&M manuals (electronic versions). Modeling the contents of the building for inventory and tracking purposes can also be beneficial. Monitoring temperatures and energy consumption can be connected to the BIM. All these uses will require special adaptations for a BIM that was handed down from the design and construction project team.

The Nature of Information

This pertains to all information that is part of, or connected to, the components as well as the physical information inherent in the model itself (i.e., size, location, etc.). It is important that all information required to make an actual analysis be available from the BIM. The basic informational questions are as follows:

- What type of information will need to be attached to (embedded in) the model components? What level of detail will be required?
- Will the information simply be available (linked to) or also require a certain amount of processing (i.e., scheduling information, productivity rates, etc.)?
- What is the required format for the information?
- Will the information need to be exported (quantity takeoff, cost estimates, etc.)?
- Is the information imported (database link) or created in the model components (parametric objects)?
- What information will be required by the team to perform all its tasks in a timely manner?

Component information is primarily visual information and resides in the nature of the model part itself, i.e., a wall with material information, or quantitative information, such as area, volume, etc. Components in a 3D model also have specific locations in relation to an origin and to one another. This is the most basic information contained in the 3D model file. This is also the most likely information to translate correctly from one file format to another; e.g., if a Revit model is translated to be used in the Bentley or Vico compatible file format, it is likely that only this type of information will be available in the other software tool's format. This is why interoperability demands such attention in this field. There are numerous groups working on interoperability standards, and the most common platform at this time is the Industry Foundation Class—**IFC** format. If a model can be translated to the IFC format, it will generally carry much more of its attached information with it to its translated version.

In Fig. 2.30 note how few parameters can be set and how limited the information about the object is.

Parametric information is editable information contained in the parametric object. This is not an external source of information—it is embedded in the object, and therefore the model. Some of this information will be visual, while much of it can also be intellectual, such as part numbers, or material-related qualities, such as

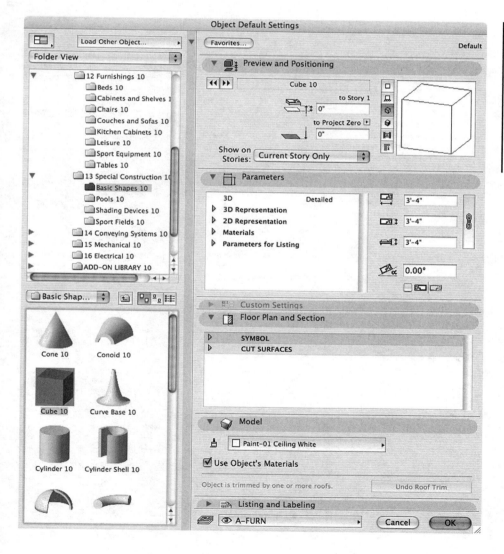

Figure 2.30

Dialog box for a simple object in Constructor by Vico. Note how few parameters can be set and how limited the information about the object is.

density (providing weight based on the geometry of the object), *R* value, etc. See Fig. 2.31.

Linked information refers to information that is actually not part of the model, but is connected to the model through visible or invisible links. Visible links can be "flags" that will open a window or file when clicked to display that file, invisible links could be, e.g., connections to a database with cost information. When two files are linked, changes in one will result in adaptations in the other linked file, and vice versa. An example of this is the link between a Vico model and its Estimator database that results in a cost estimate; changing either the model (quantities) or the database (unit cost) will result in an update of the cost estimate (see Fig. 2.32).

Figure 2.31

The dialog box for a parametric truss object in Constructor by Vico. Note how many parameters can be set and how detailed the information about the object is.

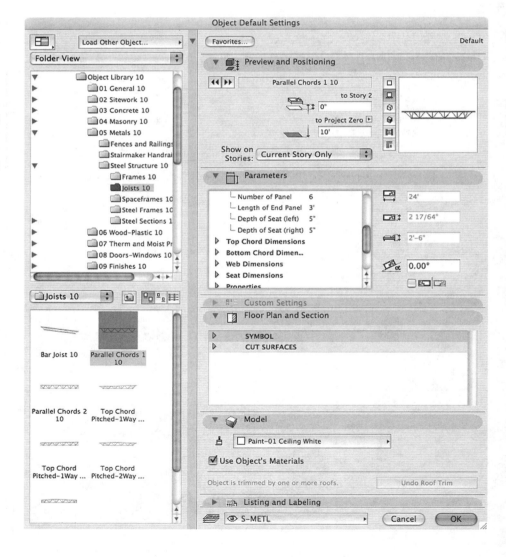

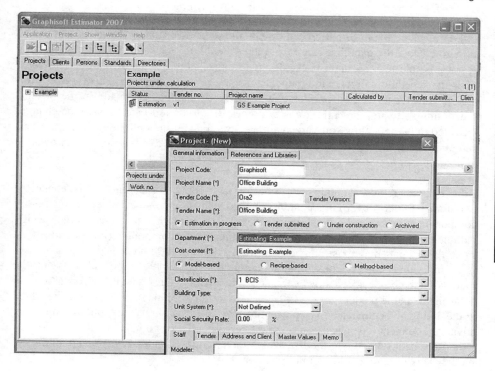

Figure 2.32
The dialog box for the link between Estimator and Constructor by Vico. The quantitative model information is fed to Estimator where it is calculated for total cost based on the unit cost assigned from the database in Estimator. (*Image courtesy of Vico.*)

External information refers to information that is generated separate from the BIM, such as a construction schedule, manufacturers' specifications of products, etc. External information may be linked to the model or remain autonomous. It is possible to provide a reference to a catalog without creating a link to an electronic file. Since not all information will be available in a compatible format, it may necessary to keep it accessible in printed form, as an external reference.

In all cases with information management it is critical that all users be able to discern whether they are accessing the latest (and only) version of the information. This is a huge challenge in the construction field where many individuals will generally be updating project information independently and concurrently. This clearly also applies to conventional construction project management. There is almost no area of project management whose improvement could provide such important benefits for the project.

The Nature of the Link between Model and Information
The information used in BIM will be of varying types, and the nature of the information will in many cases imply the nature of the link between the information and the 3D model. The specifics of the link will describe how information is processed. The transfer of information between the model and the estimating software designed by Vico for the Constructor suite is through a third file that both the model and the estimate files need to be linked to. Either file can then be updated and can transfer its information to the other through this third file; in this example information can flow in either direction.

There are other examples, like the import of a project schedule file into the modeling software, where the information can flow in only one direction. In such a case it is possible to change the data that came from the scheduling software into the model, but it is not possible to send them back to update the schedule in the scheduling software. Thus the schedule will have to be updated separately and manually. This type of information transfer also often implies that when some changes are made in the original scheduling software, the entire transfer process has to be repeated to have the changes reflected in the modeling software again, i.e., the transfer may not be incremental. This can be rather daunting on large project models, and *it is a good reason to run trials of all anticipated processes in the planning stages of the BIM.*

Library parts represent another type of information link; a model file will be connected to a library folder (or file) that contains all the usable components. When such a library component is introduced into the model, it will be programmed to contain some specific parameters that reflect the characteristics of that specific component (information). The same library part may exist numerous times in the model, and each of these instances is an individual component containing its unique information; the link between the model and the library does, however, need to be maintained so that this information can be available in the model file (see Fig. 2.33). In most cases this information can be edited in the dialog box connected to (representing) that specific library part, but in some more advanced connections it is also possible to create a list of components (i.e., a door or window schedule) and edit the list, which then in turn edits the components in the 3D model. This is an example of a bidirectional link.

If the model file is not connected to the library containing this specific library part, it will not show up in the model. All components made with the object tools, such as walls, roofs, and slabs, do not require attachment to a library.

Figure 2.33

All three beams are the same library object, with different parameter settings in the same model. The model was made in Constructor by Vico. (*Image courtesy of Vico.*)

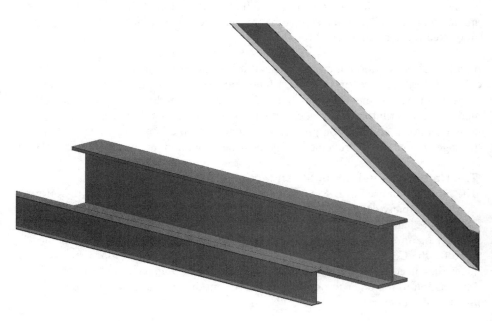

The widespread use of AutoCAD has also made **X-refs** a familiar concept. The link between the host file and the X-ref is similar to the library part, but the X-ref has no intelligence (no parametric qualities) and can only appear as it is. The advantage of the X-ref is that it can appear as often as needed in as many files as needed and only exist once itself. Thus if the X-ref is changed, its appearance in all host files will update itself as soon as the link between the X-ref and the host file is updated. The library part concept has all these qualities, and can also be programmed to appear uniquely in each of the host files utilizing that library part, and thus is referred to as an *intelligent* object.

Planning BIM Implementation

The implementation plan will follow directly from the desired goals for the BIM and the model specifications. This plan describes the deliverables, the process required to produce the desired result from the BIM, and the resources necessary to accomplish these goals.

To successfully plan this phase, it is important to know the requirements for information and the associated formats. Each goal should have a clear outline describing the tools and efforts required to realize it.

Step 1 is the description of the deliverables, step 2 outlines the required processes to accomplish the deliverables, and step 3 consists of the selection of the persons on the team who are best able to facilitate the first two steps. Things rarely turn out as anticipated, however, and having a detailed plan will help to better respond to the circumstances of the process as they present themselves. *The BIM process is a planning and managing process for building construction projects, and it is important for this process itself to be planned and managed carefully.*

Understanding the BIM Deliverables

What exactly is this process supposed to accomplish? How can it best be described? What are the required BIM project deliverables exactly, and when are they required? What are the major milestones in the project's development?

The answers to these questions will come from the work resulting from the previous sections about the purpose and the specifications of the BIM. When the goals and the level of detail for the information have been determined, it becomes possible to define the deliverables related to these goals. For example, once it has been decided to coordinate the MEP design and installation through the BIM, the required level of detail of the models will be determined by the project's characteristics (e.g., will the pipe hangers and insulation be modeled? etc.), and it will become possible to determine the exact deliverables for the necessary processes.

It is also helpful to identify both the customer and the supplier in relation to each of the deliverables. This definition will help to focus on the desired quality of the product and its timely completion. In many cases the deliverable for one phase will be the starting point for the next phase in a process. Breaking down the steps and outlining the relationships among all the parts and players help the project team to manage this development and the flow of information. The implementation will be easier to understand and plan if the deliverables are simple and straightforward; it is therefore helpful to break a complex process down into several smaller and simpler ones.

It is also useful to create a schedule for the deliverables of the BIM process; this will facilitate the procurement of the correct resources at the right time. Commitments will have to be obtained from all project team members to honor the schedule and deliver on time. A tool such as Commitment Manager can be helpful in implementing this discipline. The transparency of the BIM process can be useful in the enforcement of a certain degree of responsibility regarding the honoring of commitments by all team members. The serious effect of noncompliance on the whole project will also be a stimulus for cooperation of the whole team. Case 1, Chap. 5 describes this process in greater detail. See Fig. 2.34.

The physical format of the deliverables needs to be defined; e.g., how the output will be presented or used (i.e., slideshow, movie, spreadsheet, pdf, printed document—color or black and white, etc.) needs to be specified exactly.

Choosing the Methods

Developing a project BIM will consist of various processes, in which much information is generated and managed. The specific procedures can be seen as the methods used to develop and process the project information. These methods need to be identified and described so that the simulations can produce the desired results.

The purposes of the BIM and the resulting specifications will describe the methods required to accomplish the deliverables. Typical questions that need to be addressed are

Figure 2.34
Diagram showing the agreement protocol for a team. See more on this in Case 1 in Chap. 5. (*Image courtesy of AgileWorkforce.*)

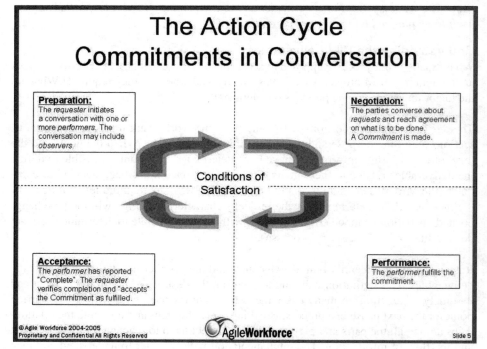

as follows: What type of information will need to be attached to (embedded in) the model components? How many different levels of detail will be required (for different components, or project phases)? Will the information simply be available (linked to) or also need to be processed (i.e., scheduling information, productivity rates, etc.)? Will the information need to be exported (correct file format)? Is the information imported (database link) or created in the model components? What information will be required by the team to perform all its tasks in a timely manner? These questions are very similar to the questions that begin the specification planning process, but in this round the potential tool to accomplish these tasks has to be kept in mind. This is a selection of both the process and the most likely tool to accomplish the process to the best advantage of the project. The team needs to be careful not to either choose or disqualify specific tools based on team members' skills (or lack thereof) at this stage; but instead should try to determine from a functional standpoint what will be the best tool for the work to be accomplished. There is always an opportunity to either find the necessary talent or compromise the tools, if need be.

The specific tools that can accomplish the necessary tasks will also determine the required skills from the project team. There is a large range in the ease of use and learning curves for the various software tools used in the BIM field. It is not always realistic to accomplish all the things the software companies claim their products are able to produce with the available skills of the persons on the project team. The saying "A bird in the hand is better than ten in the bush" is very appropriate in relation to software claims. The author cannot recommend experimenting with software on any project where the schedule matters (some exceptions may apply). This refers to both new and unfamiliar software, as well as version updates for software that is already in use by a project team.

Careful planning of the deliverables will formulate the required processes enabled by the BIM. The amount and type of information available at any given phase of the project can be a critical factor and can greatly influence the timing of the processes. Most of the early processes will relate to project planning, i.e., the design and development of the project and its systems. The implementation of these processes is organized into three stages:

The first stage is information gathering. This is the information that will be developed into the BIM and reflects the creation of the conceptual and schematic level information about most aspects of the project.

The second stage is the iterative analysis of the BIM that will lead to the further refinement of the information in the BIM. This analysis phase (and its associated processes) will generally begin just after design has commenced and sometimes continue until the project is completed. Examples of analytic processes are the consideration of alternative solutions to any part of the project or its systems and an analysis of the effect of these alternatives on the overall project (e.g., its cost).

The third stage of implementation methods is the management of the processes that will generate the required information. An example of such a process is the coordination of building systems through clash detection. When clashes between system components are identified, this triggers a process of its own to address the inconsistency. The project team members who are responsible for the clashing components need to collaborate about a resolution; then the 3D model needs to be amended, and another clash detection cycle needs to be run to verify that the solution accomplished the desired result and did not generate new problems elsewhere. Thus the actual clash detection process belongs to the iterative processes of stage 2, while the management of the clash detection process and the implementation of the solution to a clash are part of the management of processes of stage 3. It will help to remember both the process and the management of the process; and to keep the distinction between them in mind. It is not uncommon that a team will be focused on getting the process in place, and not be able to benefit from it because management of the process is lacking.

Defining the Project Team—Members and Skills

Who will be on the team to accomplish the necessary tasks? How will these individuals accomplish the work? Do these individuals have the necessary skills to get the work done efficiently? Training may be required to get individual skills up to the necessary standard, and it may be well advised to arrange a project team training session focusing on collaboration techniques. A communication protocol needs to be developed to support the goals of the team and keep the deliverables on schedule.

The skills of the individual project team members will largely determine the roles that will be played throughout the project's life. In relation to BIM, three types of roles can be defined that are centered on specific skill sets, and understanding these will help to build an effective project team.

See more about the roles of the BIM team members in Chap. 4.

BIM IMPLEMENTATION

The BIM is implemented in the reverse order of the planning of the implementation. The project team will be brought together first, based on the plan; then the processes will be implemented and adjusted accordingly, after which the deliverables can be produced. This has strong similarities to the method used by a structural engineer to calculate a structure by starting at the highest level and working down to the foundation, while clearly the constructor will begin by building the foundation and continue erecting the structure from the bottom up. In reality, good planning will include several back-and-forth journeys along such a path. Each trip up or down this planning sequence will generate information that will allow certain changes and adjustments to be made that help to refine the result. This also parallels the information feedback loop upon which much of BIM development is based.

It is helpful to begin the BIM application to projects on a manageable scale. Most project teams will find it challenging to have access to enough persons with enough skills to get very deeply into the BIM approach in the beginning. *It is, however, extremely useful and productive for a project to have these methods implemented at any level, and care should be given to developing a comfortable level of application for the given project and project team.*

Selecting the Project Team—Team Information Processing

Who is on the team, and what is their role? What are their skills, strengths, and weaknesses? See Fig. 2.35. Assess the available human resources in detail, and develop a list of missing skills on the team. Skills for the BIM process can come from either in-house team members or other members of the project team, i.e., the consultants or subcontractors; or, if necessary, they can be contracted out to consultants who are not otherwise part of the project team. The advantages and disadvantages of these options will need to be understood clearly before making any decisions in this area. The fact that "BIM is not about the model, but about the understanding that results from the modeling process" makes it a large advantage for the project to keep this process confined to the project team. Only if the project team members do all the work themselves will the understanding about the project gained from creating and handling the BIM remain within the team. In other words, if the modeling is outsourced, the understanding gained by the modeler will not be available to the project team to the same degree as the understanding of a team member modeler. The interactions among the team members are extremely beneficial to the advantageous development and understanding of the project.

All team-related processes need to be addressed at this time, including roles and responsibilities, contractual relationships, collaboration incentives, communication protocols, etc. The team will have to go through all sorts of team dynamics before the project will have taken its course; it is not possible to overestimate the importance of preparation.

Project Team Dynamics

The team structure has to be defined so that each member's role in relation to all the others on the team will be clear and productive. This can be represented in an organizational chart showing the relationships and responsibilities of the team members. This structure will also result in a communications protocol that establishes the flow of information for the various processes.

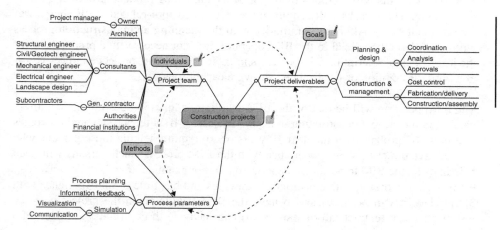

Figure 2.35

Diagram showing the relationships among the components of a construction project.

The actual methods and expectations for communications need to be described, discussed, and put in place at this time. It is important to define the methods by which the team members will exchange information among one another; this will depend on location and accessibility issues. The advantages of collocation cannot be overstated; in a process that is so dependent on successful collaboration the ease and reliability of communication is critical. Dr. Renate Fruchter's contributions to this area are discussed under "Project Management" in the section "BIM Planning" earlier in this chapter.

Ideas that will promote collaboration, i.e., regular meetings, smaller subteams for tasks, clear expectation of deliverables, team evaluations of deliverables, team decisions related to process, quality issues, etc., rewards (financial) for schedule gain, rewards for conflict resolution, etc., should all be addressed in the initial phase of the BIM process. Thorough preparation is very beneficial; the more predictable the team dynamics are, the more reliable the results will be.

Team Roles

The three primary BIM-related roles that emerge from this process are the BIM manager, the BIM operator, and the BIM facilitator. Each of these roles came from the different responsibilities and skills associated with the various tasks connected to the practice of building information modeling and model-aided construction management.

The BIM manager is the person on the project team who will manage most of the BIM-related processes. This role requires a good understanding of the concepts and applications and a familiarity with all tasks related to the planning and managing of a construction project. The role can also include leading the project team through the BIM process on a personal level, i.e., the selecting and training of specific team members to ensure that everyone is able to perform her or his tasks satisfactorily and that all goals are reached. These various expectations make this role similar to that of the traditional project manager with the addition of the BIM-related activities. This role carries most of the responsibility in relation to both project management and BIM management.

The second role is that of BIM operator. An operator will perform the BIM process-related tasks. This will include creating models, analyzing models, processing information, etc. These tasks will require more developed tool-related skills, but fewer management skills. Although familiarity with the planning and construction process will certainly be beneficial to the BIM operator, it is not necessarily a prerequisite for the job. This job description will be very similar to the current "project engineer" position with the addition of BIM-related software capabilities.

The third position will be that of the BIM facilitator. This job does not have a direct parallel in the current construction industry. The use of BIM technology and processes will initially (probably for the next 10 years or so) require helping those persons who do not have direct previous experience with the BIM process; such persons will need help in using the BIM to be able to benefit from it. For example, if an installer on a project is used to working with construction drawings and has little or no experience with 3D models, it will be necessary to have the BIM facilitator on the project help the installer look at (extract information from) and navigate through the 3D model on a computer in the job trailer. If the BIM operators (modelers) are relying on information feedback from the field to incorporate back into the BIM process, it will be the BIM facilitator who can understand, collect, and provide these data in the correct format to be useful to the project team. This role would also include facilitating a project meeting (such as progress or coordination meetings) using the BIM as the basis for the discussions (and construction management tasks). The BIM facilitator can thus be a person who will function a little as the superintendent's assistant, someone who is at the construction site most of the time to help out with the model and other BIM-related issues, someone who understands how to navigate through the BIM world and help others explore this environment—a bit like a knowledgeable BIM tour guide.

Developing the BIM Processes—Project Information Processing

After the team has been assembled, it is time to assess the specific processes the team members will be implementing. This relates to the "Choosing the Methods" section in the Planning BIM Implementation part earlier in this Chapter. The team members will now be prepared and scheduled to begin working on the deliverables. It may be necessary to adjust some of the methods that have been planned to achieve the deliverables in response to the actual skills and resources available to the project team. The processes that need to be put in place now are either information-related or tool-related. Information-related processes are directly associated to handling or generating project information, and tool-related processes are independent of the specific project, but part of the software tools employed to manipulate the project data. Although often addressed by the same project team members, these two categories of processes are very different in their relationship to the overall BIM process. It will help to keep this difference in mind.

Information Management

The basic question underlying this section of the implementation is: Are all the team members committed to the simulation processes (the creation and use of the model to achieve the deliverables)?

This question can be broken down into these:

- Who will model what?
- To what level of detail?
- And attach what type of information to it? By when?
- And what type of output will be produced from this information?

These questions are the same ones that were asked earlier in the planning process, only now they include names of people and dates of completion. In other words, there is now enough information available to create a schedule with resources for the BIM process itself.

Humans have the tendency not to dwell on questions such as these for too long; most often the process is just begun and intuitively (and from experience) sort of followed through as the circumstances best permit. It is usually only when something does not turn out as anticipated that questions arise, and some reflection and analysis begins to take place. This, however, is exactly what has been identified as one of the main reasons why the construction process on the whole needs to be improved. *Plan now, so that it does not need to be corrected later.*

To generate a list of processes (steps) necessary to produce the deliverables for the BIM, the overall BIM processes can be broken down into groups as follows:

- *Planning the project.* How is the project developed in the design phase?
- *Communicating the project.* How is the project information developed throughout these processes? How is this information delivered both to project team members as well as to outside entities such as financing agencies, permitting agencies, etc.?
- *Coordinating the project.* How are all the components of the project coordinated, i.e., the MEP and FP systems among themselves, as well as with the architectural and structural systems, underground construction (foundations) with underground utilities, or other existing facilities, etc.
- *Updating the project.* How will the BIM stay up to date with all design and information changes and developments?
- *Information feedback loop.* How is the information that is generated in all these processes being fed back into the loop to improve the process as well as the project (information)?
- *Tracking the project.* How will the actual project progress be tracked with the BIM? This applies to both to the planning and the construction phases of the project. Will an as-built model need to be delivered?
- *Delivering the BIM.* Is there a handoff of the BIM scheduled to the owner after completion of the construction phase?

These phases can result in a long list of processes required to accomplish the associated tasks. Frequently, however, it will be possible to derive multiple benefits from one or more of these functions. For example, during the planning phase it will be useful to have a preliminary cost estimate; for this to be possible we will need to attach some cost recipes to the model elements. The recipes will use the quantitative information from the model elements to generate a cost for that element (based on their link to cost information from a linked database). The additional benefit will be that since we have a 3D model with the elements necessary to create a simple cost estimate, we can also quickly generate a construction sequence showing the rough schedule and order of erection for the project. This will permit early considerations of construction site utilization and underground installation sequences from a visual standpoint. *It is good to begin with what is possible right now.* Plan a little bit of BIM, but plan it very well, and proceed. The experience will grow quickly, and begin to include many dimensions that could not have been planned in the beginning. Each project will grow in this fashion. The "planning well" will help it not only to work better, but also to grow faster on a more solid basis.

Tool Management

The processes will determine which tools are required. It is of course essential that these various tools communicate and function well together. **Interoperability** is a large and important area in the development of software.

The first step in mobilization of the software tools is the decision as to which software packages will be used for the various processes. This depends partly on the skills of the project team members and/or the requirements of the downstream processes.

Training needs to be considered; since this particular time in history can be seen as the dawn of BIM implementation, it will be difficult to find many individuals with a lot of experience and skills in this field. The regular scheduling of various training sessions can thus be beneficial for the development of a capable and productive project team.

Interoperability is a nagging issue when various types of models are going through the different processes within the BIM. The lack of interoperability can be a limiting factor to the BIM and needs to be considered early in the planning. It is advisable to run a simulation of the BIM process (yes, a simulation of the simulation) to test all the actual compatibilities and results of the planned processes as well as to test the skills of the team members. This would consist of taking a small portion of the project (or a sample project) and testing all the anticipated potential problem areas beforehand. This could also apply to the organization of the model and its information; in the case of very complex projects it will help to test the anticipated organization early so adjustments can be made based on the findings of such an experiment. Modeling a portion of the actual project will be very revealing in many ways. Without proper preparation and planning, it is almost inevitable to not feel that a large part of the initial modeling effort was wasted because the true nature of a project will only reveal itself once the project is better understood, and this will not happen without the necessary efforts that are best made by planning and modeling experiments.

Space and hardware issues are generally not likely to present problems; but need to be considered to make sure they are in harmony with the team goals. Many workstations will have multiple screens, and the physical location of workstations in relation to the other team members can have a large effect on their ability to collaborate.

The i-room is an idea that came from Stanford's **CIFE** (Center for Integrated Facility Engineering). See Fig. 2.36. The concept developed out of research of collaboration techniques in parallel industries such as automotive or aeronautic engineering. The

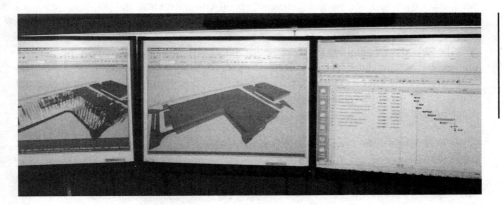

Figure 2.36
CIFE's lab space showing the i-room at Stanford. (*Photo courtesy of CIFE and DPR Construction.*)

automotive industry in Japan uses the *big room* concept, which is very similar to the i-room. The central idea is to put all the project team members who have to collaborate in one room together, and allow them full access to one another, so that they can work out their coordinated design solution together. The idea is excellent and has worked as well as could be expected in various attempts to implement it in the construction industry. It is clearly a challenge to bring together individuals from various companies and have them collocated for a longer time working out the design of a complex construction project. In practice it has been the general contractor who has been able to orchestrate such an endeavor successfully. See Case 1 in Chap. 5.

Networking is the best approach if the big room is not a possibility. Also at Stanford, Dr. Fruchter has established the Project Based Learning Lab (PBL) that addresses methods to collaborate on a project when the participants are not collocated. It is interesting to note that Stanford University has been researching and promoting methods to improve the level of collaboration in the construction industry for many years now. Both CIFE and PBL have developed various sophisticated techniques to help the construction industry.

Defining and Scheduling the BIM Deliverables— The Product

The critical questions for this phase are as follows:

- Based on the available resources and process skills, what exactly can be implemented, by whom, and how?
- What are the minimally required outcomes? What are the desirable outcomes?
- What are the required formats of the deliverables?
- Exactly when will who deliver exactly what?
- How will the deliverables be produced?
- What are the currently foreseeable problems?

It all begins with the desirable goals and the BIM specifications. Now that the processes have been listed, the specifications can be derived and a scope of work can be determined from the current understanding of the project. This specification needs to also include a measurable standard for the work to be delivered. Regular meetings will have been scheduled to track progress, follow up on commitments, and address questions from the project team members.

A BIM schedule can now be developed. This will indicate what will be accomplished by certain dates, how it relates to preceding and successive tasks, and who will perform the specific tasks. This schedule is closely coordinated with the actual construction schedule and describes the deliverables for the planning and management processes.

A method needs to be developed as part of the feedback loop that monitors the relevance of the model specifications and allows for adjustments to these requirements during the evolution of the BIM work. A system to track commitments from team members needs to be in place so that the project development can stay on schedule.

It is also useful to devote a few minutes in every (weekly) project team meeting to review the progress of all participants and have the team help with problems that any of the members may be dealing with in relation to delivery dates, available information, required decisions, etc. It is helpful to develop an open atmosphere in which all team members are encouraged to freely share their experiences and discoveries in relation to the BIM, its processes, and their effect on the project. Such sharing makes it more enjoyable and productive for all, and the help that can be available will often make the difference that will allow the successful resolution of problems that otherwise could impact the project schedule. Much of the tendency of humans to work independently is related to not wanting to expose a weakness; however, there is almost nothing more satisfying for a human than to help someone in need, and such an act will create a bond that will pay back in numerous ways. Fig. 2.37 shows three

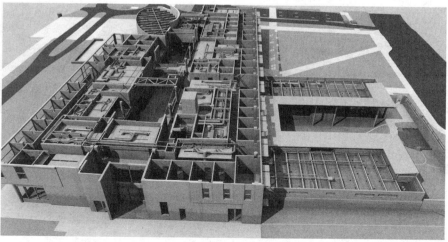

Figure 2.37
University of California, Santa Barbara, Student Resource Building. Modeled in Constructor and MicroStation TriForma, Rendered in NavisWorks. (*Images courtesy of RQ Construction.*)

Figure 2.37
(*Continued*)

views of a model of the Student Resource Building at the University of California at Santa Barbara, the first floor, the second floor, and the entire building. The viewing of these three scenes of the model can greatly aid in the understanding of the project and the relationship of all of its parts. Images of this type are an example of a deliverable for a presentation to the owner of the project at the design development phase of the project planning.

REFERENCES

1. Dr. Renate Fruchter, "Global Teamwork: Cross Disciplinary, Collaborative, Geographically Distributed e-Learning Environment," published in *Collaborative Design and Learning; Competence Building for Innovation,* eds. J. Bento et al., Quorum Books, Greenwood Publishing Group, Inc., 2004, pp. 265–298.
2. Ibid., front page.
3. Dr. Renate Fruchter, "The Fishbowl(tm): Degrees of Engagement in Global Teamwork," LNAI 4200, Springer Verlag, 2006, pp. 241–257.

3

Software Tools

INTRODUCTION

This chapter discusses the functionality of the software tools, and will aid in understanding the characteristics of some of the most common tools used for the BIM process. The author does not sponsor any specific software product, and the companies whose products are represented here are not the only ones producing software of this type. These descriptions are not included from a marketing standpoint, but as guidelines for the reader to compare different products available in the marketplace. It is important for the potential BIM manager to gain enough software familiarity to be able to select the most appropriate tools and deal with the vendors and technical support for these tools. It is also essential for all people involved in the application of the BIM processes to familiarize themselves with the software capabilities and to stay current in this field. Software changes continuously, and it is important to remain informed of the current state of the art of this technology. All software is based on a particular *architecture*, e.g., an approach to dealing with the organization of the information in the BIM; this software architecture changes less frequently than the particular functionality of the software. The descriptions provided by the software developers in their marketing materials will help the reader to become aware of some of the differences among these tools, and reading this book will give a good background for making a decision as to which tool is best suited for a particular purpose. It requires a good deal of research to update oneself with the state of the art of BIM software development, and due to its temporal nature, books will generally not be the place to look for the most current information about the functionality of a particular tool.

The software industry is a business, it is for profit, the software companies will develop what they think they can sell, and consequently they will also not develop anything they think they will not be able to sell. This puts the burden on the users (designers, fabricators, contractors, etc.) to educate the software industry about their needs. It also means that "what you see is what you get," and there is no guarantee about that which is promised by the software companies. Shop well, and keep searching for practical solutions that solve the problems at hand.

93

A huge area that is frequently overlooked is the training of software operators. This book addresses training in BIM processes; it does not address training in specific software tools, although this clearly is a requirement for anyone planning to use such tools. Most modeling tools will be intuitive enough to allow even the inexperienced user to build relatively simple projects in a fairly short time. The young generation just starting professional careers has been raised on video games and Internet exploration. This is both good and bad. The good part is that they are generally fearless about computers and will keep hitting various keys and clicking dialog boxes until some result is achieved; this, however, also includes the less desirable side of this approach—it often lacks discipline. There is only one way to master a modeling tool, and that is through discipline; without the necessary rigorous exercises the most one can achieve is advanced amateur status. Now it is fair to say that unless one is interested in becoming professional, there is nothing wrong with being an amateur. As a BIM manager, however, it is important to know the difference. An amateur model may be remarkably different from a professional one; inaccuracies or unclear organization in a model can make them virtually unusable for any number of analytic processes. It is thus imperative that proper training in a specific software tools be part of the preparation to implement BIM on a project. This training will frequently have to be provided by the software developer or an outside consultant. A word of caution is needed here: Make sure that what is promised by sales representatives will actually be deliverable; not all companies have a very good follow-up support record. Not all software is equal when it comes to learning how to use it either; the training of staff will generally require far more of the company's resources than the actual software purchase itself. Just as software salespeople are likely to promise more than they can deliver, software operators often represent themselves as being more capable than they are; in fairness to them, they do not know what they do not know, but that does leave the burden on the BIM manager who hires the operators for the performance of specific tasks.

Interoperability is a concept that is mentioned several times throughout this text. A separate book could be written about this subject; it is important, it is complex, and it is continually changing. This discussion does not address the subject in detail, but the BIM practitioner needs to become informed about the interoperability of the specific tools used on any given project; not just looking at the specification sheets of the software, but actually making the processes work on several files is a necessity.

It is shocking to realize how dependent everyone is on the various products that have been developed for use. For most users it is simply not realistic to customize such software.* The only hope is that the software developers will address the needs of the field, or (as is most often the case) the field will be able to adjust its practices to the capabilities of the available tools. Both possibilities may lead to unintentional but positive surprises, as well as to frustrations and setbacks.

---

*Frank Gehry is an exception—Gehry Industries developed a special version of CATIA, a French aeronautical design software, to address the architectural design challenges of Frank Gehry's work. This tool is now commercially available for those who wish to design these types of architectural forms.

MODELING TOOLS

The kind of information that is desired from the BIM will determine the type of model that is required, which in turn will lead to the nature of the modeling tool that can accomplish this. It may even be advantageous to compose the project of several models to be able to take advantage of different modeling tools' strengths.

Models are by definition **simulations**; a model represents something—it simulates it—it is an **abstraction** of the "real object." This also means that the model is *not real*; it is an abstraction, and there will *always* be a difference between the model and reality. It is extremely important to continue to remember this when using a model to facilitate the decision-making process in a project; sound decisions can be made only when the level of abstraction and the reliability of a model are clearly understood. *The implications of construction tolerances are important relative to model accuracy; tolerances are how reality deals with abstraction.* Generally 3D models do not address tolerance; they are exact, just as 2D drawings state exact dimensions for components. In reality, however, where the real components have to fit, tolerance is required because reality never matches the degree of perfection of the abstraction in a model.

A mathematical model can be composed of a structure of mathematical formulas representing a certain process, which can be studied by manipulating the variables in the formulas or by adjusting the formulas in relation to one another. Generally a model is created to aid in the visualization and understanding of a process, or an object. Models are used to represent, analyze, communicate, etc. If "a picture is worth thousand words," then it could perhaps be said that "a 3D model is worth a thousand pictures."

Non-3D Element Modelers (Process Modeling)

These types of models have been in use for a long time and can be seen as visual aids in process planning. Examples are Gantt charts for a schedule; graphs, bar or pie charts, etc., for spreadsheet information, drawings, and diagrams, and endless other model representations of information. The model represents the information in such a way that it allows the viewer to visualize its impact or relevance.

This does not refer to the modeling of non-3D elements in a BIM, such as project inspections, submittal approvals, etc. There are various methods to represent these sorts of events by hyperlinking placeholder 3D elements in the BIM to information of a non-3D nature.

Surface Modelers

Surface models consist only of surfaces (that have no thickness) to give a 3D look to their "hollow" forms (see Fig. 3.1). These models are generally only used for visualization, and typically they contain only visual information. Software programs such as SketchUp, Maia, etc., make surface models.

Most of the software tools used to make 3D images and animations are surface modelers; the results may be anywhere from very sketchy to photorealistic quality, and can be very useful for communication. See Fig. 3.2. Models produced in this manner may be able to help in BIM; i.e., it is possible to create a surface model of a HVAC ducting system and use it in a clash analysis in NavisWorks. A surface model will not be usable, however, for the fabrication of ductwork; a solids modeling tool will generally be used for that purpose. It may thus be more efficient to model the ducts with a tool that is designed to aid in the fabrication process in the first place. This also encourages collaboration with the mechanical subcontractor, so that he or she can produce the fabrication model that can then be used for a coordination/clash analysis. A word of caution about the timing of model production: A detailed production model can only be created once the necessary information for this level of detail is available. Therefore a certain type of model may not be available until a specific stage of the project's development; i.e., if a model is needed for clash detection between MEP and structural systems before the fabricators have produced the models, it will be necessary to perhaps have the designers produce the models. Only some, and not all modeling tools facilitate the development of a design model into a fabrication (or production) model.

A viewer such as NavisWorks will turn a solid model into a surface model; i.e., the solids will be represented by all their surfaces only. This "translation" allows the software to manipulate the information faster, thus making navigating through the model in NavisWorks faster and more practical for the user. The import of model data from a solids modeler will thus be limited to the 3D information that is critical to the functionality of NavisWorks; the nature of import and export functions between software tools is often limited, and relates to interoperability. It is the translator that determines exactly what information is brought across to the other platform, and how it is manifested in that new platform. Trial is the only reliable test of the utility of the translated format. This is why it is so critical to run a test simulation of all the processes anticipated during a BIM project; there can be no certainty

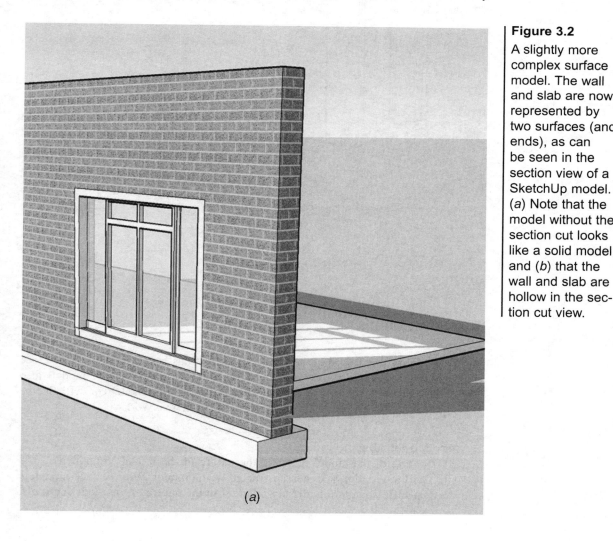

(a)

Figure 3.2

A slightly more complex surface model. The wall and slab are now represented by two surfaces (and ends), as can be seen in the section view of a SketchUp model. (a) Note that the model without the section cut looks like a solid model, and (b) that the wall and slab are hollow in the section cut view.

Figure 3.2
(*Continued*)

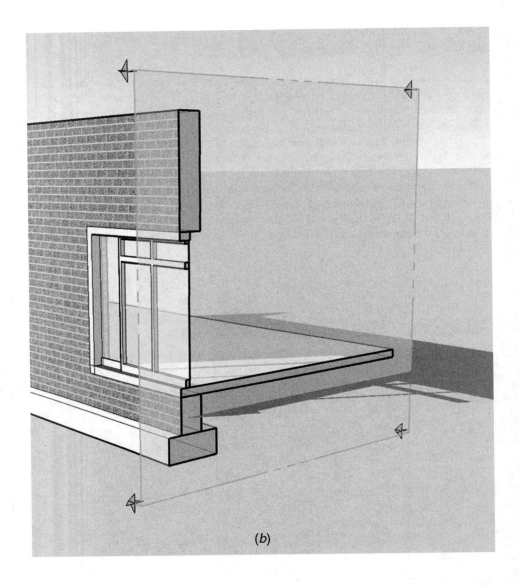

(*b*)

about the ability to perform certain analysis until it has been tried and proved (see Chap. 2). The fact that NavisWorks translates all models into surface models also means that models made by any other surface modeler, e.g., SketchUp, will also be usable for clash detection, sequence analysis, etc., in NavisWorks.

Surface Model Abstraction

The *abstraction* of the model refers to the nature of the model components; it is the way in which reality has been abstracted in the model. With surface modelers there is a specific abstraction already inherent in the nature of the modeling tools, namely, that all volumes are represented by their surfaces. The level of abstraction results directly from the requirement for detail in the model components. The more details are desired, the more realistic (less abstract) the model will have to be. This of course also directly effects the amount of modeling effort required to produce this level of detail.

Surface Model Organization

The *organization* of the model refers to the manner in which the model components are organized within the model. SketchUp, e.g., uses layers that can contain any components or parts of components. The layers can be shown or hidden, locked or unlocked, and greatly aid in the flexibility of editing the model. Due to its nature a surface of a 3D element in SketchUp consists of a plane with edges that are all individually selectable; it is actually possible for some of the edges and surfaces of a component (a form) to be in a different layer from the other edges and surfaces, something that can cause confusion with the novice modeler. Most surface modelers also permit the grouping of surfaces into objects (or components) that are not editable (other than scaling) until they are "exploded" into their constituent edges and surfaces again. When manipulated as a component or group, such elements can also be scaled in any or all dimensions to become functional in the project model. For example, a drawing of a floor plan or site plan can be imported as an object and then scaled to actual size to build the 3D model on its lines. See SketchUp exercises in Chap. 4. A door or window can be placed as a component into a model and scaled to reflect the desired size of that door or window.

Surface Modeling Tool Characteristics

Surface modelers create *only* edges, from which all planes and forms are constituted; all elements in such a model are represented by these edges. Of course the planes can have color and 2D texture that give them the look of a particular material. It is very similar to scene design for a play, or to constructing everything from paper, even the sticks that hold up the assembly. To build the more complex model parts, specific groups of edges and planes can be saved as components that may look similar to the "library parts" of a solid model. These model parts are not parametric, however, and still are simply collections of edges, with little ability to hold information other than their physical size and look. Groups of edges can generally only be scaled to become larger or smaller in relation to any of or all the X, Y, and Z axes, meaning that they can be stretched (or shrunk) in one, two, or three directions proportionally. When plan or section views of a surface model are viewed, they are collections of lines with empty space in between; they cannot show a distinction between the mass of a solid component and the space between the components. Thus if a drawing is needed, it will generally be necessary to do a bit of editing to turn it into an understandable document, with the necessary graphic information.

The 3D model, however, can look like any other and can be visually indistinguishable from a solid model. Thus it is often the tool of choice for the creation of flexible 3D models where the emphasis is on the visual information only, especially since the surface modelers are often faster and simpler to use.

Solid Modelers

Solid models are actual representations of real objects in 3D space, having the correct dimensions, location, and ability to contain other information about the object characteristics; e.g., a wall can consist of various thicknesses of specific materials that can then be used to calculate material quantities from the model. Solid objects represent the real objects both inside and out; in other words the walls have an actual thickness and "look solid" in a section view. See Figs. 3.3 and 3.4. A model is an abstraction, however, and there is a limit to the detail that can (and should) be represented in a model. Solid model components have volume, even the thinnest elements will have a measurable thickness (unlike the surfaces in a surface model).

Solid Model Abstraction

The abstraction of the model will largely depend on the stage of project development and the level of detail required from the model for the analysis. A very schematic (massing) model may look at an entire story as one thick solid slab, while only modeling the basic structural elements will already provide much more information in a model that is still at a schematic level of development. The level of model abstraction thus reflects the project, its stage of development, and its needs; it is less dependent on the software tool chosen to create the model. The questions related to determining the level of model abstraction are as follows:

- What needs to be represented in the project model?
- How will the components of the project be represented in the model?
- How can the required information be attached to these components? See "The Nature of Information" under "Specifying the Model" in Chap. 2.

These three questions will enable the project team to determine the level of abstraction and detail that needs to be addressed in the model. As was noted in Chap. 2, however, a lot of planning will be required before the answers to these three questions can be clear in the minds of the project team members.

Most modeling tools will specialize in a particular level of detail. Solid models, since they can be designed to be useful for fabrication instructions for component manufacturing, are often of the most detailed nature. Whether the same software tool will also be fast and flexible enough to be used for the design phase of the same components will depend on the particular software characteristics. It is important to note here that the nature of the software tool is also heavily dependent on the discipline that it serves. The mechanical and structural fields are fortunate enough to have a fairly limited range of materials, forms, sizes, etc., that are used to generate their building systems. This comparatively narrow range of components makes it much more likely for software in these disciplines to be more advanced in its functionality. Tekla produces software tools that will let the engineer introduce loading configurations, lay out structural steel systems, analyze them for stress, deflection, etc., and then design and model the steel members and their detailed connections. The engineer continues to use the same file to either generate shop drawings for fabrication or send the model to fabrication, where the manufacturing equipment is set up to take its instructions from such a model. This is

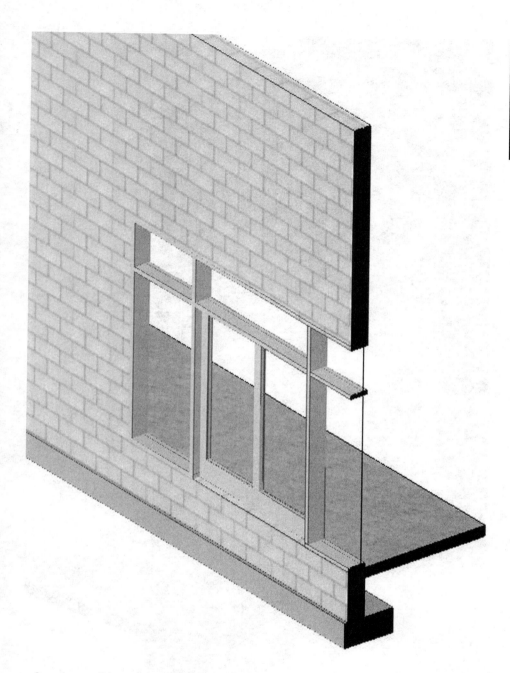

Figure 3.3
A section cut view through the wall showing solid elements as wall, slab, and window mullions, modeled in ArchiCAD.

referred to as Direct Digital Exchange (DDE) in the industry. The model may also be used during assembly to help establish the steel erection sequence. There exist mechanical HVAC ductwork and piping software tools that have similar functionality.

Tekla or other specialty modelers can also create a basic assembly of shapes, similar to what Revit Structure or Vico Constructor could produce. Such a simplified

Figure 3.4
(*a*) A section cut view through the wall constructed with individual concrete block library parts and some steel rebar, modeled in ArchiCAD. This model can show a partially constructed wall. (*b*) Note that the partially constructed wall is not a section cut and looks like it could also be a surface model.

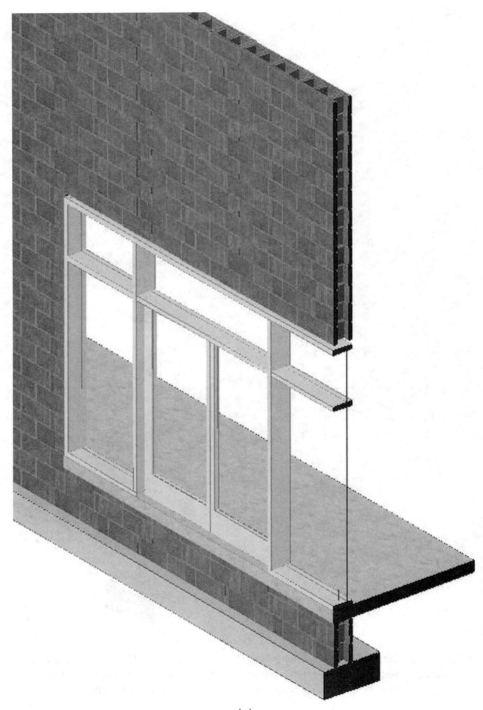

(*a*)

Figure 3.4
(*Continued*)

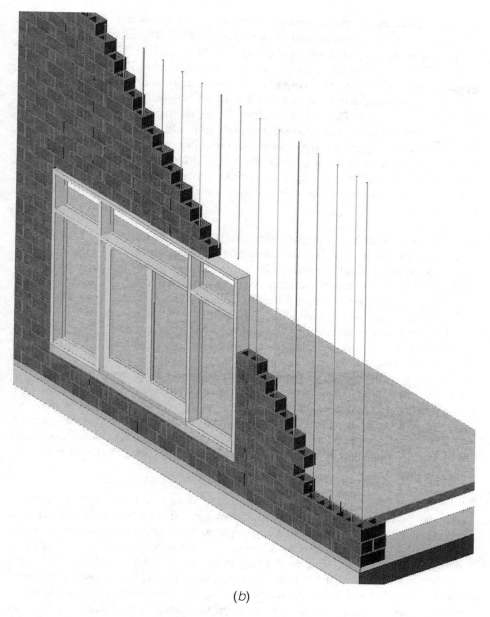

(*b*)

model would be usable, e.g., for developing floor-to-floor heights during design development, or to study the effects of alternative lateral bracing systems (at a schematic level) on the architectural development of a project. Once a structural system has been designed, a basic assembly of steel shapes can also be used to do coordination (clash analysis) with the various other building systems. Neither Revit nor Vico, however, (at this time) could develop its structural models to a greater level of detail that addresses fabrication requirements, or the design and analysis needs of the structural engineer. It also calls attention to the fact that if the structural engineer produces the initial design model in Tekla, it will then be useful in all other phases of the planning and construction process. The level of detail in the model can be developed based on the stage of the project and the available information. On the other hand, if such a model were produced in Revit or Constructor, it would not be able to be used for either structural analysis or fabrication purposes; and should the fabricator wish to use a 3D model, she or he will have to produce one of her or his own. This also holds true for the mechanical models of HVAC or piping systems. The idea of producing models from already completed designs by the consultants only makes sense when the consultants are unable to deliver such models and there is still value in conducting systems coordination exercises. It makes no sense at all for an engineer to make a model of a system that cannot be developed into a production model; it is simply the wrong software tool for such an application.

At this time it seems highly unlikely that a software tool that does not have the functionality to address both design and fabrication requirements should be recommended for use in a specialty field, particularly because there are very capable software tools on the market that do just that. It also does need to be noted that current standards of interoperability generally do not address the use of sophisticated production models for use in most other modeling software tools. The ability to analyze a "foreign" model is an extremely rare option, and the best that can be hoped for is the use of such a model in NavisWorks for viewing and clash detection against other models. The utility of an "abbreviated" tool such as Constructor or Revit MEP or structural is mainly for persons outside the specialty field, e.g., the architect or general contractor modeling the structural or mechanical systems strictly for his or her own purposes. While this may be the best alternative in the interim and not everyone on a project team may have modeling capabilities, it is clearly an inefficient way to address the overall project. In general it will be in the project team's best interest to have the specialty consultants and subcontractors model their areas of responsibility in their particular design to production ready software tools.

In the architectural area, it is the wide variety of materials, forms, objects, connections, and custom elements that makes modeling all this to a greater level of detail a large challenge. Curtain wall design appears to be the next area that may be evolving into a specialty area in relation to 3D modeling. However, a significant number of issues are part of the architecture of a project that are difficult to address in a model. This creates a different attitude toward the architectural model than toward the structural or mechanical models. In the mechanical and structural steel specialties there is a well-developed mechanism that takes a design into fabrication. There are almost no other areas in construction where this process has been developed to this extent due to the uniqueness of building projects and the variety in most other building parts. There is little opportunity to make an architectural model useful for fabrication purposes in general, and thus architectural models will generally show a much lower level of detail. There are some exceptions to this generalization; some general contractors are now trying to develop refinements for their self-performed work and analyze construction and assembly processes through the use of 3D models. This has parallels to the simulation of a manufacturing process to develop improved methods.

There are a number of sources for prefabricated 3D model components, many with a high level of detail. These are good labor savers in realistic models; some care has to be taken, however, to provide for artistic consistency in the model by not combining areas with high and low levels of abstraction and potentially creating confusion for the viewer. This phenomenon has similarities to 2D art and graphic design; an understanding of design principles and an aesthetic eye will help the delivery of a clear message with the 3D model.

Solid Model Organization

The *organization* of the model refers to the manner in which the model components (and connected information) are organized in the software file. Generally this organization will be related to the actual project, i.e., number of stories, number of wings, etc. The model organization is characteristic of the software, however; and it is the architecture of the software that will determine how a project model and its relevant information can be organized within the software file. Almost all software tools that create 2D and 3D objects and images allow the layering of the file contents. The layers are transparent sheets with names that contain various 2D and 3D content that can be shown or hidden, and locked or unlocked. Thus combinations of layers can provide selected views of the contents of the model that are relevant for any particular reason; e.g., showing only the structural layers will reveal views of the structural framing of a project, so when the architectural layers are also turned on, the model views will show both structure and architecture. The layers are also a means to select particular elements in groups. Generally layers can be edited, and content can be moved or removed from layers at any time. Use of the layer structure is one of the primary means of viewing and selecting/editing elements in a model. In general the layer structure will stay with the model contents when it is translated into another format for use in another software. It is thus advisable to choose an easy-to-learn naming system for the layers, so that people unfamiliar with the file can find their way around in it. A major difference between Revit and the other primary architectural modeling tools is the absence of layers in Revit. Elements are instead created as families and types and can also be selected as such. The project browser and the visibility graphics override determine what is shown or hidden, e.g., the electrical plan or the framing plan of the project.

Especially in the development phase of a project, the editing of both the components themselves and the attached information is continual. The components of the model therefore need to be well organized in layers (and/or stories, zones, etc.), so that at any given time they can be easily selected in the model. All components need to be organized so that multiple objects can be selected by type and edited in a single operation. At the same time the organization has to remain simple enough not to slow down the file manipulation, especially by others who will need to learn that organization before being able to manipulate the file freely.

When sequence studies are made, it is again necessary to be able to select groups of components to attach time-related information to them from the construction schedule. This operation can be tedious and needs to be properly prepared by an appropriate structure of the model parts.

This is similar to use of the model for cost analysis; specific cost information will have to be linked to each model component so that the quantitative information from the model part can be combined with the cost information from the database. A good model organization will simplify this task, and the model component structure has to be compatible with the cost database; e.g., the costs for material, labor, preparation work, etc., all have to be assigned to the specific appropriate model component in order to generate a realistic cost estimate.

Exercise projects are essential to develop a sense for a practical approach to model structure and object organization. This type of knowledge is best gained through hands-on experience. The planning discussions in Chap. 2 explain the need for preparing all the analytic activities for the BIM so that the models can be structured to best accommodate these tasks.

Solid Modeling Tool Characteristics

Most solid modeling tools have a lot in common. They all provide ways to manage building information. The nature of the specific information and the ways in which that information is connected to the model entities may differ a little depending on the software emphasis, e.g., whether it is an architecturally, structurally, or mechanically oriented design package. The user will create actual 3D components in the software and assemble them into a single model, of which multiple views are possible. The views do not exist independently—they are actual views of the single model entity; thus when a change is made in any of the views, it will actually be a change in the model, and therefore be reflected in *all* views of that model. Drawings become annotated views of the model, and the same holds true for changes made to the model; these are also directly manifested in all the drawings, thus ensuring an automatically updated project information database. Caution is required with the protocol regarding updating the various other forms of the project information, e.g., downloaded files, printed drawings, etc., which may or may not be the latest available version. When one is creating updates of files, it is best to choose a file name that will remain the same throughout a longer part of the (if not the entire) project. This has several advantages; first and foremost, when files are connected to one another, they find one another by name (and location), and thus it is very inconvenient when files are frequently renamed and all links have to be reestablished. Second, it is frequently unclear whether there exists a later version of a particular file that may be overlooked in that moment. It is the *archived* version of a file that needs to be identified as having a particular date or phase related to the project, but the working file should only be kept under its own—unchanging—name and should be the *only* working file for the project. This is a management challenge and a critical one to handle properly.

Most modeling tools will have a series of object tools to create the basic components that will comprise the bulk of the model for that particular functionality. The objects that cannot be directly created by these tools will need to be made up of several smaller components or imported as premade objects (library parts). Most software will come with such a parts library, and more and more manufacturers of construction materials are beginning to make "virtual catalog parts" available for the modeling profession. These library parts are often parametric and lend greater realism and accuracy to the

BIM; e.g., a piece of equipment will contain its connection and support points so that these details can be addressed accurately in the BIM. For example, door or window companies can create virtual models of their products that can then be inserted in the project model. This clearly will require interoperability since each modeler will have its own native file format, and to introduce an imported object will require a compatible format. There are also websites that sell model parts for specific software platforms; these premade library parts can make modeling easier and more realistic for the user. For a project with a specific need, it will be important to check on the availability of existing objects, as this could have a large effect on the required modeling effort. It is also important to verify the behavior of such objects and their ability to represent the actual needs of the BIM, as well as their ability to accept attached information for further analysis, such as cost estimates or sequence schedules.

Most solid modelers are also **parametric** modelers. This means that the model will contain parametric components that are characterized by programmable entities and may also have some intelligence in relation to one another. Both the elements created by the modeling tools such as walls, slabs, and roofs as well as the library parts, such as trusses, beams, and fixtures from a component library can be parametric objects. On the other hand, an object does not need to be parametric to be functional in a BIM. It is typically more convenient to model with parametric objects than to create unique objects for each element in a model. (However, even in a surface modeler, premade objects can be created to simplify multiple use of a particular model element.) For example, if a steel beam is a parametric component, it can be programmed to be whatever size it needs to be and can take on those characteristics in the 3D model; in addition, it may recognize the column to which its end is attaching and generate the appropriate connection (also programmed parametrically) in a semiautomatic fashion. Parametric components are powerful in their flexibility and ease of use; it is one of the primary means by which a BIM contains information and can function "intelligently." Another example of parametric qualities is the ability of a structural steel frame in a Tekla model to be stretched and have all the components (columns, beams, braces, and connections) automatically adjust themselves to the change.

The modeling tools also have means to use already completed work for multiple projects. Entire component assemblies can be turned into editable library parts and used in other locations or projects. A whole building could be a single component in a campus containing many buildings, thus becoming a 3D referenced object that exists independently in a separate file (where it can be edited). When one is creating complex project models, it is well worth it to plan the assembly of the project file carefully to optimize the production effort.

MODEL PRODUCTION

The actual creation of the model can be accomplished in a variety of ways. The best method is to have a design model produced by someone intimately involved with the design process. This will ensure that the understanding developed through the making of the model will benefit the project team the most, by keeping the project learning within the project team. A schematic model can usually best be produced by a single person; but the amount of effort necessary to produce a more detailed (advanced) model usually necessitates more persons. It is of course possible to have the model produced by a "model shop." In this case a set of documents describing the project will have to be provided so that someone unfamiliar with the project can build the simulation. Producing such a set of drawings will require enough time and effort that a model could have been produced by a project team and provided many additional advantages as well.

It is clear that a designer will derive much less benefit from having a model produced by an outside consultant. The outsourcing of modeling is primarily used by construction companies that lack the necessary resources to produce models in-house. It will quickly become clear that a lot of communication is required to be able to create an accurate simulation, and that this may be expedited by having the persons with the greatest project knowledge guiding those who are creating the models. Many questions (about the project) only arise at the moment someone tries to model it, because accurate visualization is required before modeling can take place. The modeling process is parallel to the actual construction (fabrication) process, in that the simulation is a representation of the actual project, and the whole reason to create a simulation is to find all those instances that had not been anticipated (or fully understood). A general observation is that if some aspect of a project is difficult to model, it will likely also be difficult to construct (but the reverse is not necessarily true—the fact that it is easy to model may not imply that it will be easy to build).

A BIM is likely to consist of a variety of models produced by different persons, possibly with different levels of detail, and with diverse software tools in unlike formats. Examples of models that may be produced to become part of the BIM include the following:

- Site model (context—land, buildings, landscape, etc.)
- Architectural model (walls, floors, roof, circulation, special objects, etc.)
- Structural model (structural systems)
- MEP models (mechanical, electrical, plumbing)
- FP model (fire protection)
- Specialty models (equipment, finishes, temporary construction—scaffolding, formwork, trenching, etc.)

Not only do these models represent a wide variety of types of information, but also it is possible to combine models with different levels of development; e.g., a schematic site model may provide the context for a production level MEP model together with a less detailed architectural model. Due to the variety of this list it is helpful to establish some ground rules for all these various models. First and foremost, a compatible file format has to be established. *Interoperability is critical.* This means that those models that need to be combined in a particular software have to be provided in a compatible format.

NavisWorks saves the day in this regard; it seems to be able to see almost any 3D file format and combine it readily with all the other formats it can read. This does depend, however, on whether what needs to be accomplished can in fact be done in NavisWorks—and NavisWorks does *not* do everything. It is in all cases well advised to run a test file through all the potential combinations and software tools, to make sure that the modeling is not in vain.

The second important ground rule is to establish an official origin for the project so that all models will register properly in 3D space. A practical way to accomplish this is to create a registration file that contains a cube with one corner as the established origin for the BIM. If available, it may be helpful to include already established grid lines and floor levels to help the other modelers begin their work. This registration file will then become the starting point for everyone else's modeling effort.

The third important ground rule is for all models to be as accurate as realistically possible; guessing is permitted only when there is no other alternative, and when something is guessed, it needs to be flagged so that everyone else will know it and not rely on its being accurate. Many unnecessary difficulties are introduced by careless inaccuracies.

MODEL ANALYSIS

The advantages of having the project team produce the whole BIM are immense, because it facilitates the resolution of many problems that need to be addressed before the model is considered ready for analysis. Viewing the model will be a predominant activity, since communication is one of the primary purposes for the model. Special model viewing software has been developed that allows the import of models from a large variety of other software products. These viewers permit the combination of many models into one viewable whole. Some of these viewers also allow other analysis to be made or other information to be connected to the model components (such as time-related information).

There exists another group of tools that perform quantitative analysis of a model; some analyze cost for a project estimate, others analyze construction time for scheduling, or energy consumption, or natural and artificial lighting levels, etc.

Most modeling software can be purchased "bundled" with compatible analysis software. There are also a number of independent software developers who have developed software tools that can import various 3D models and perform analysis on them. It is essential to verify that *all model sources* on a given project will provide models that can be imported into the analysis tools scheduled to be used for the project.

Qualitative Analysis

Qualitative analysis considers the nature of the issues, often irrespective of the quantities associated with it. The list of such processes is primarily visual in nature.

- *Communication and marketing illustrations and movies.* This is strictly visual content intended to give others an impression of the project. Almost all modelers will address this function; both surface and solid modelers will generally create good 3D images from a model. See Figs. 3.5 and 3.6a and b.

- *Constructability analysis.* Constructability refers to a visualization of the methods necessary to construct (assemble) a project; it is an inspection for practicality and is intended to spot potential difficulties. A certain level of detail will be required from the model to be able to visualize issues of interest. This process can be implemented with either solid or surface models. See Fig. 3.7.

- *Systems coordination and clash detection.* This is probably the most popular application of BIM models at this time. The clash analysis will find objects in the 3D model that take up the same space; thus they "clash." This can be a duplicate of the same object or one object touching or running through another one. This can be done with either solid or surface models. See Fig. 3.8.

- *Energy.* Energy analysis borders on the quantitative end and generally will require a solid model due to the information that needs to be available about the materials used for construction. The nature, size, and location of *zone boundaries* need to be calculated to generate heat gain and loss for each zone in the model. The model may be able to visually show hot or cold spots in the project through the simulation of certain circumstances and conditions.

Figure 3.5

A 3D floor plan for communication purposes, modeled and rendered in MicroStation TriForma. (*Image courtesy of Design Village.*)

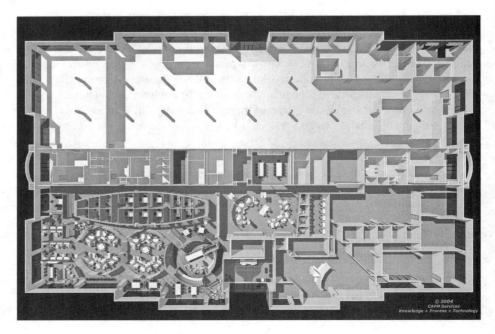

(a)

(b)

Figure 3.7

A detail of Fig. 2.6 showing constructability of underground utilities with respect to foundation location. (*Image courtesy of RQ Construction.*)

Figure 3.8

Coordination image of Ritz Carlton project in NavisWorks. Note the transparency of all architecture and structure for visibility of the MEP systems. (*Image courtesy of Q&D Construction and Swinerton Builders.*) See also color insert.

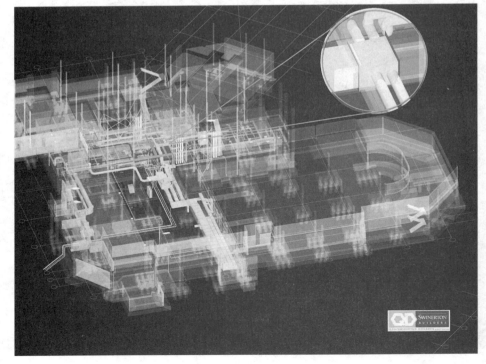

Sequential Analysis

Sequential analysis refers to studies that include time, both in duration and in sequence. These studies are very visual, although they also include a large amount of quantitative information, e.g., the amount of time required for specific tasks. The visual nature of the model provides a location-based element to the study; this will permit evaluation of issues such as work area definitions and crew interferences (and the rate of movement of a work area through the project).

- *Assembly and installation sequences.* Such sequences are visual interpretations of the model where components show up in time according to the construction schedule. This yields a movie showing the assembly of the project (or part thereof). Both solid and surface models can be used for this type of analysis.
- *Construction schedule and sequence.* This is primarily visual, although time is treated as a quantity. The construction sequence can be created with either solid or surface models. The link between the time information from the schedule and the model is typically one-way; changes in the model can generally not be sent back to update the schedule. Creating a schedule from the quantities in the model and linking it to productivity rates are particular to Vico Project Control at this time. This is a scheduling tool that has a bidirectional link with the model and is totally interactive; it requires a solid model produced by Constructor (Vico), or ArchiCAD (Graphisoft). Revit also advertises to have a bidirectional link to MS Project; the author has not yet verified this functionality.

Quantitative Analysis

Quantitative analysis involves measuring the amount of something in the project model and often combining it with other information. Most of the list is not visual in nature, but can often be represented in a spreadsheet or database format.

- *Quantity takeoff.* By virtue of the physical information inherent in the model components, the quantities of the various materials in the model can be extracted. This requires a solid model and interpretive information regarding the constituents of each model component.
- *Construction cost estimate.* The cost estimate is the product of the model quantities with the cost from a database. This also requires a solid model. Depending on the software, the nature of the link between the model and the database will vary.
- *Cash flow analysis.* Once a cost link has been established, the model can be used to track cash flow as construction progress is tracked in the model. This is a combination of the cost-estimating and the sequence-scheduling functions possible with a solid model.
- *Life cycle cost analysis.* This relatively new application of BIM is connected to cost control and energy consumption; and solid models are necessary. Both the operating cost (utility use, depreciation, etc.) of the project and the maintenance expenditures are tied to the model components to arrive at a life cycle forecast for the project.

There is clearly some overlap among these lists, and it is not intended to be exhaustive. This organization of the analysis functions helps to better consider them individually. Often the project team is interested in a particular analysis for the BIM; this list will identify some other related activities that may be relatively easy to accomplish because something similar is already being planned. It is a little like checking out what might be worthwhile to see in a city we are planning to visit for other reasons. Figs. 3.9 and 3.10 show the revealing nature of model images that may have been created for a variety of other purposes.

Figure 3.9

Presentation images of the Ritz Carlton project, modeled and rendered in Constructor. (*Images courtesy of Q&D Construction/ Swinerton Builders.*)

Figure 3.9
(*Continued*)

SPECIFIC SOFTWARE OPTIONS

Preparing for the Purchase

There are several major software developers that supply products with functionality in the BIM world; these represent the primary BIM tools for the construction industry. It is important to realize that there are many companies competing in this market and that all the various marketing claims will need to be substantiated carefully before purchasing decisions are made by the customer. Just as a buyer of an automobile would need to assess the need for a car to determine which model will suit that purpose, so will a software purchaser need to assess the requirements of the tasks carefully to choose among the various products addressing these needs. It is all too common that a specific product is purchased primarily on hearsay or assumed reputation, just so that the necessary research that would actually result in a more satisfactory purchase can be avoided. In an unfamiliar field it is

Figure 3.10

Presentation images of the The Carlyle project modeled in Constructor, rendered in NavisWorks. (*Images courtesy of Swinerton Builders.*)

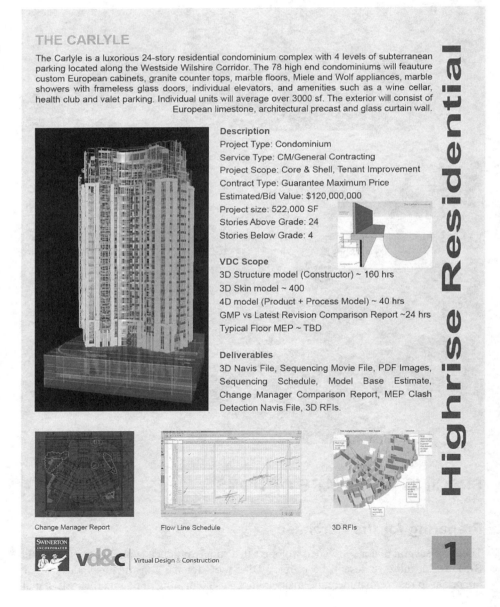

THE CARLYLE

The Carlyle is a luxorious 24-story residential condominium complex with 4 levels of subterranean parking located along the Westside Wilshire Corridor. The 78 high end condominiums will feauture custom European cabinets, granite counter tops, marble floors, Miele and Wolf appliances, marble showers with frameless glass doors, individual elevators, and amenities such as a wine cellar, health club and valet parking. Individual units will average over 3000 sf. The exterior will consist of European limestone, architectural precast and glass curtain wall.

Description
Project Type: Condominium
Service Type: CM/General Contracting
Project Scope: Core & Shell, Tenant Improvement
Contract Type: Guarantee Maximum Price
Estimated/Bid Value: $120,000,000
Project size: 522,000 SF
Stories Above Grade: 24
Stories Below Grade: 4

VDC Scope
3D Structure model (Constructor) ~ 160 hrs
3D Skin model ~ 400
4D model (Product + Process Model) ~ 40 hrs
GMP vs Latest Revision Comparison Report ~24 hrs
Typical Floor MEP ~ TBD

Deliverables
3D Navis File, Sequencing Movie File, PDF Images, Sequencing Schedule, Model Base Estimate, Change Manager Comparison Report, MEP Clash Detection Navis File, 3D RFIs.

Change Manager Report   Flow Line Schedule   3D RFIs

Highrise Residential

SWINERTON INCORPORATED

vd&c | Virtual Design & Construction

1

Figure 3.10
(*Continued*)

difficult to learn about a product and research its specifications; most potential buyers simply want the assurance that it will work, and they will try to just begin using it. This approach could easily lead to unanticipated problems, particularly in the area of BIM tools. With its relatively short history and complexity, building information modeling has created many unrealistic promises and expectations, on the parts of both the users and the developers of the software tools. Expecting to save money by upgrading an existing software license rather than investigating other potential tools could easily become one of the most expensive mistakes of embracing BIM technology. *The importance of a basic understanding of the concepts and applications of the BIM processes, to make intelligent choices among the available products, cannot be overstated.*

Once an understanding for BIM has been developed, answers to the following questions will help in choosing a particular product:

- What is the purpose of the software? Will it be used to make models (what will need to be modeled)? Will it be used to manage and view models? Will it be used to analyze models? What about the model is critical to its use, i.e., bill of quantities, visual 3D forms, central database, etc. (look at the list of benefits of BIM)?
- Who will be using the software? How will the software be learned? How long does it take to master the software? How often does the developer update the software? How much changes in each update? How long has the particular product been on the market, and how much has it changed over the last 10 years (not the company, but the software!)?
- What file formats are easily derived from the software? What is its native format? How can other file formats be imported (exported) from the software?
- Are there case study examples from other users who have done something close to what is required from the software? What exactly did it take to accomplish this? What were the major difficulties these users encountered? When there is a problem using the software, exactly how can it be resolved with the help of the software company (or other consultants)?

At this time there is no relationship in the author's mind between reliability and market share of the various software companies. Each product presented here is functional and needs to be evaluated on its own merits. Software vendors will frequently make unsubstantiated claims about their own or the competitors' products. The best advice is to question everything—ask for examples. If a vendor cannot specifically demonstrate something, it will warrant more research. (Many vendors are not particularly proficient in the use of the software they sell.) Most software companies will promise support and training; it behooves the buyer to check some references before making final decisions. The fact that everyone is using brand X means very little in the current BIM climate; interoperability is becoming a reality, and a product such as NavisWorks takes a lot of concern out of "being able to see someone else's model properly." It is useful to look at the history of the software company. A lot more can be learned about reliability of a product by looking at the track record than by listening to the sales pitches. Look at examples of the work produced by a tool, and make sure it is clear how that result was achieved exactly! Ask for demonstrations! Ask for a test drive! Do not buy from fear, buy from understanding! Committing to a particular software is like starting a relationship; it is difficult to just walk away from it, because it requires an investment that is far greater than the purchase price of the software boxes.

Software Descriptions

The following descriptions are just a sampling of the characteristics of some of the software companies and tools. It is by no means exhaustive either in relation to the companies producing software that may be used for building information modeling or in relation to the products available from any of the companies discussed in this section. It is also necessarily the case that even as this is being written, new functionality is continually being developed, and these descriptions of specific software characteristics will soon be out of date.

It is interesting to observe that in the marketing materials prepared by the software companies, it is generally the benefits of the BIM process that are being sold as if they were the advantages of the particular software. It is in fact difficult to distinguish among some of the features of these tools, and it is more important to understand the concepts of the processes, so that the user can recognize what the claims of the vendors actually apply to. Many of these claims in the description of a particular software tool can in fact be applied to almost any of the other software tools as well. This is like shopping for any item, e.g., a car; many of the differences among products may be very subtle. *It is thus the author's strong recommendation to test drive before committing to purchase. Put the software to a rigorous test, see if it actually does everything that is expected from it.*

NavisWorks

NavisWorks is the best place to begin the initial explorations into building information modeling. This is a viewer of models and has many useful applications in almost all phases of the use of the BIM. For anyone who has not been exposed to 3D models, it is a great place to begin to learn to view, navigate, and understand virtual environments. NavisWorks functions much as a video game, and since it is not a modeler, it also limits the severity and number of things that can go wrong in a BIM analysis.

The primary function of NavisWorks is to provide 3D model interoperability for the building design and construction field. Many different software tools are being used by many different disciplines that all produce 3D models in different file formats. Most of these tools do not import or export one another's native file formats, thus NavisWorks has provided a model viewer that can read almost any 3D file format. Not everyone will ever be using the same software for everything; thus the need for interoperability is fundamental to the successful implementation of the BIM process. A project team using BIM is faced with four major challenges that NavisWorks addresses: it can read different file types from various sources, it can import and handle huge files, it will combine different file types into the same file together successfully, and it facilitates graphical communications across the entire project team. At this time there is no other software that does this as well as NavisWorks, but there are rumors that several other companies are working on similar functionality.

One reason that NavisWorks can handle huge files and navigate through the virtual environments so effortlessly is that all models are translated into surface models. This necessarily removes some of the information (and most of the intelligence) from the original model, but that is generally not a particular problem. What is left is all the surface and spatial information, and that is enough to maintain all the visual data and perform sequence and clash analysis. The NavisWorks suite contains Roamer, which is the basic "engine" for NavisWorks and allows model combining and viewing. A free viewer called *Freedom* is also available; this can look at already prepared composite (or single) models in the correct file format. Freedom is for users who do not wish to analyze or manage projects, but simply wish to have visual access to the models. Special functionality can be added to Roamer with Clash Detective for coordination clash analysis, Publisher for providing files to be viewed with Freedom (the free viewer), Presenter for preparing high-end renderings of model views, and Time Liner for the creation of construction sequence analysis.

Clash Detective is the most popular of the functionalities of NavisWorks and the one that provides a quick return on investment. It is capable of finding and identifying all instances where model parts clash (take the same space in the model). This is invaluable for the coordination among building systems. The clashes not only are found and listed, but also can be managed through the same software until they are dismissed or resolved. Time Liner is very useful in providing a simulation of the construction (or installation) sequence of a project. By either importing a construction schedule from an outside software or building a new schedule in Time Liner, the 3D model components can be linked to a scheduled task, and thus can be seen appearing (or disappearing) in timed sequence. This is an excellent way to communicate construction progress visually. Autodesk purchased NavisWorks in 2007, and the entire construction community is watching what exactly will happen to NavisWorks now.

Many of the images in this book have been rendered in NavisWorks, and the two attractive images in Figs. 3.11 and 3.12 also attest to its capabilities in this area. There are of course software packages on the market that specialize in creating high-end

Figure 3.11

A sample of a detailed model "above the ceiling" in a medical facility, rendered in NavisWorks. (*Image courtesy of NavisWorks.*)

Figure 3.12
A sample of a model that has been rendered in NavisWorks JetStream Presenter. (*Image courtesy of NavisWorks.*) See also color insert.

rendered images from 3D models, but for its ease of use and high-quality output, many professionals whose purpose is related to the design and construction of the project (and not the rendering of it) seem to choose NavisWorks for the pretty images.

Google—SketchUp

The original SketchUp was developed by @Last Software and has swept the design industry by storm. It is almost irresistible, so simple, so powerful, so affordable. Now Google owns the software, and it appears to be a supportive marriage. SketchUp is a surface modeler; it is not trying to be a BIM tool, but it can be used as one anyway. Of course this means that its limitations have to be kept in (a "broader") mind. The limitations are primarily related to the type of information that can be contained in the model itself; that information is mostly related to size, location, and "look." It is not an object modeler, and thus it cannot be treated like one; the components only look like objects, but actually are just collections of surfaces (and can easily fall apart). The ways in which SketchUp *can* be a BIM tool lie in its phenomenal ability to quickly convey the essential information about a situation (mostly related to size, location, and look) into a 3D model. This model does not always need to be part of or be attached to a more complex BIM; it may simply be a communication tool for a specific issue. A SketchUp model can be imported into NavisWorks and seen together with any other model that may also be imported into the viewer. Once in NavisWorks, it is even possible to run a Clash Detection with the SketchUp model, or to use it in Time Liner; but again, its limitations have to be kept in mind, for it is not meant to be an information-rich modeler. The author encourages the reader to analyze the images in this book and study the uses for the various modeling tools to be able to develop a feel for the flexibility in this area. See Fig. 3.13.

Bentley

Bentley has produced software for design, fabrication, and construction for a long time. Presently the main product is called MicroStation TriForma, an extremely robust and stable 3D platform that addresses all the needs of the various disciplines required to develop and assemble construction projects. The company has a history of providing excellent support; and the well thought out software solutions leave the professional user little room for criticism. The only criticism that is sometimes heard is that the software is difficult to master, and that it requires a serious IT department to manage a

Figure 3.13

Bea Campus, San Jose, proposal modeled in SketchUp with Google Earth background. (*Images courtesy of Swinerton Builders.*)

Figure 3.13
(*Continued*)

network operating the Bentley's MicroStation software. For a professional, however, this is not a criticism, but a confirmation that the software is a robust, reliable high-end product. Many of the tools that are easier to learn and manage often are so at the expense of stability and functionality. Nevertheless, Bentley customers are generally large firms that build complex projects; thus for a smaller company it can appear too demanding to implement TriForma.

Bentley has thought through the BIM approach very carefully and recommends an evolutionary approach for its clients to fully transit to BIM (from the traditional 2D environment). Upgrades in the Bentley product line have never demanded large-scale changes or adaptations from the users; Bentley has developed its products and maintained stability and reliability throughout.

Bentley Building has chosen to address the fragmentation of the construction industry as the critical problem.[1] This fragmentation is experienced in the project teams that consist of disconnected people, in the construction processes that are fragmented into disconnected tasks, and in the fragmented tools evolved out of the disconnected construction disciplines. It is the cause of much wasted time, risked quality, and limited profitability and competitiveness. Bentley developed the "Build As One" motto, based on the use of a BIM as the hub for a collaborative approach to planning and construction. (See Benefits in Chap. 2.) Bentley also advises that starting over with a new, incompatible platform, as Autodesk suggests with Revit, is unnecessary to achieve the goals envisioned for the BIM approach to planning and construction.[2] The evolutionary path to software tool development serves the MicroStation TriForma users better, most have large investments in both training and software, and discontinuities in technology are undesirable. A second point on which Bentley disagrees with Autodesk is that of data management. Of the two possible approaches, with one being a **federated database** and the other being a **centralized database**, Bentley has chosen to develop the first option.

They found that developing a centralized database throughout all the phases of a project's life cycle is too risky to be reliable. Even though the centralized database is an attractive alternative for smaller projects, it quickly becomes unmanageable for larger, more complex ones where it ceases to be an option. When the various experiences of actual projects by different companies are taken into consideration, it becomes clear that the idea of a truly centralized database is fairly theoretical, it is a tempting idea, but always remains out of reach and cannot be implemented as would be expected; so far it remains intriguing but quite impractical.

Bentley focuses on supporting its products with a single comprehensive unchanging platform, on continually extending and improving its functionality, and on augmenting the software as necessary with collaborative products. It has evolved its CAD applications into BIM applications in a relatively seamless fashion. This will typically not be the experience of an Autodesk customer.

The database issue is a significant one and relates directly to planning. It is quite human to quickly get started and then solve the problems as they present themselves. The greater experience someone has in a particular area, the more planning will precede the actual start of the project and the more problems will be anticipated while there is still an opportunity to address them. The database problem is huge, and it behooves anyone contemplating a BIM approach to a project to carefully consider the potential difficulties of managing the project-related data throughout the life cycle of the project. *Experience in this particular area is worth a lot more than naïve enthusiasm.*

For examples see Figs. 2.14, 2.37, and 3.6 which are modeled in MicroStation TriForma.

Autodesk

Autodesk's main BIM product is Revit. This is probably the most widely used of the modeling tools; although it is also the youngest of the ones discussed in this book as well as the least mature. Autodesk's strength clearly is marketing; their market share with AutoCAD is enabling them to simply offer Revit as the next upgrade for their customers, hence its popularity. The fact that there is almost no continuity from previous attempts to address 3D modeling seems irrelevant—it shows a certain lack of consideration for the customer, which Autodesk can apparently afford. Many Autodesk customers are often simply unaware of any other software possibilities. Nevertheless, Revit is a serious BIM tool (it was already a modeler with good potential before Autodesk purchased it and when no one seemed to have heard of it), and the large user base will undoubtedly be very helpful in its further development. As mentioned in the Bentley description, Autodesk is billing Revit as a modeler with a centralized database; fortunately this is probably only wishful thinking at this stage. There is very little evidence that the data in a Revit model are any more centralized than those in a TriForma or Constructor model. When one is dealing with information in any BIM, it still needs to be managed wherever it resides, and simply having links to other locations does not centralize those data. Revit has very similar functionality to the other major solid modelers; in other words, the user can probably model just about anything in any of the software tools. There are various "bells and whistles" that may distinguish one modeler from another, but by and large the actual modeling experience of a seasoned user will not be that different from one software tool to the next. A greater concern is the ability to organize and manage the information that is collected in the BIM over the evolution of the project. Here also Revit is a serious contender, and even though it is particularly in the management of data that the modelers vary, all three are robust enough packages that it will take a lot of experience to understand which tool is the best for the specific projects and methods of a given design, management, or construction company.

Revit, e.g., does not use layers to organize its model components. It is unique in this feature, and the jury is still out on whether that is actually a feature or a shortcoming. On one hand, simpler is better, or is it? When a project becomes complex enough, it may just be an advantage to have additional means to sort its elements. It is useful to fully understand the nature of the tools used for these processes, so that solutions can be approached creatively and the characteristics of a specific tool do not become an obstacle.

Revit is able to link to MS Project and exchange scheduling information bidirectionally. See Fig. 3.14. It appears that the components in the model can be linked to multiple

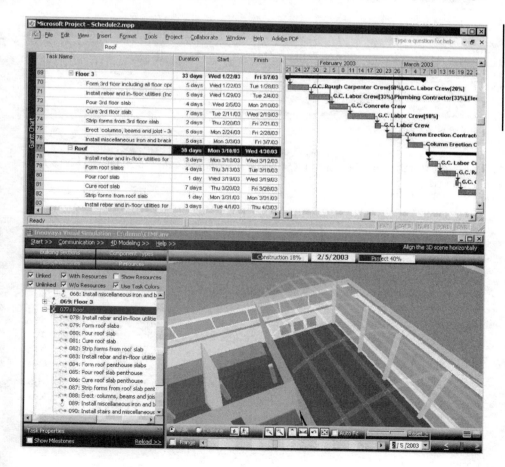

Figure 3.14

Linking between the Revit model and scheduling software. (*Images courtesy of Autodesk.*)

Figure 3.14
(*Continued*)

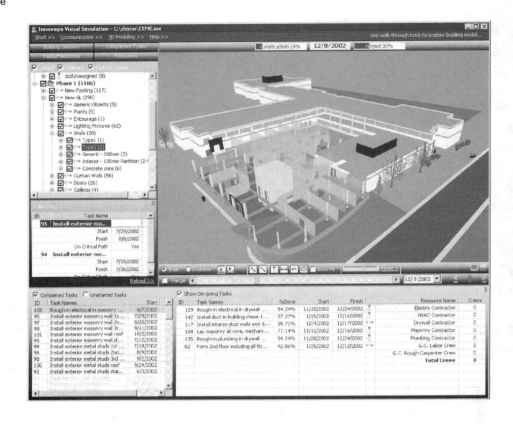

tasks in the schedule; e.g., a wall component may need to reflect the framing, the sheetrock installation, the door and window installation, and the finishing, all as tasks in a schedule.[3]

Revit also has the ability to export its model quantities to cost-estimating software. See Fig. 3.15. Due to the nature of the model, the quantities can be very accurate and thus reflect the status of the project design reliably. It appears that the connection is a one-way transfer of quantitative information and that all interpretations of this information are made in the cost-estimating software. Some questions are arising from users about the functionality of this link to estimating at this time.

Autodesk has also augmented its modeler with Revit Structures and Revit MEP. Both of these modules are designed to create specialty components to address the representation of the components for these disciplines. Whether the engineering design community will adopt these tools professionally remains to be seen. Revit Structures is not anything like Tekla, and there are any number of MEP modelers that will take these systems from the design through the fabrication phase. At this time the Revit modules for structural steel and MEP systems seem to be most attractive to project teams, where these systems models are not provided by the design consultant or the fabricator, and cannot be well coordinated without a 3D model (clearly a very justifiable use).

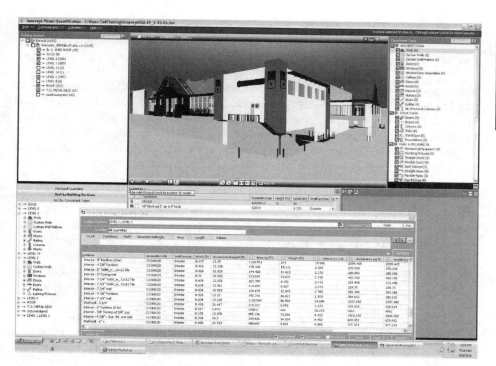

Figure 3.15
Linking between
the Revit model
and estimating
software. (*Images
courtesy of
Autodesk.*)

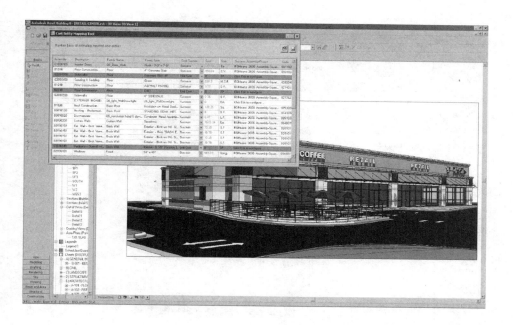

In summary, Revit is a young, but potentially powerful tool for the planning and management of construction projects. Only time will show whether Autodesk can develop Revit to keep pace with the demands of the design and construction industry.

The images in Fig. 3.16 show a Revit model addressing the GSA BIM requirement. As of 2007 the Government Services Administration (GSA) is requiring a BIM on all new projects. This requirement consists of an area analysis to facilitate space management in the planning phase and after construction of the project. This is an excellent way to introduce a complex concept in a simple fashion to the real estate industry. The GSA is the largest "real property" owner in the world, thus space management is a top priority for this organization.

Vico

Vico is a new company, but the engine behind its Constructor is ArchiCAD. In 2007 Graphisoft sold ArchiCAD to a German software developer and Constructor, its construction industry software suite, spun off to Vico Software, a newly formed company with the design and construction industry as its primary focus. The suite consists of the modeling engine ArchiCAD, which has been a professional solid modeler since the mid-1980s, and several modules that facilitate construction project management; Estimator, which is a cost database, a Line of Balance scheduling software called *Project Control,* and 5D Presenter which facilitates project presentations, all with a bidirectional link to each other and the model. As mentioned in the previous descriptions, the modeler is very similar to the other software modelers—test drive it! As a

Figure 3.16

A space (floor area) analysis in the Revit model (format based on the GSA mandate). (*Images courtesy of Autodesk.*)

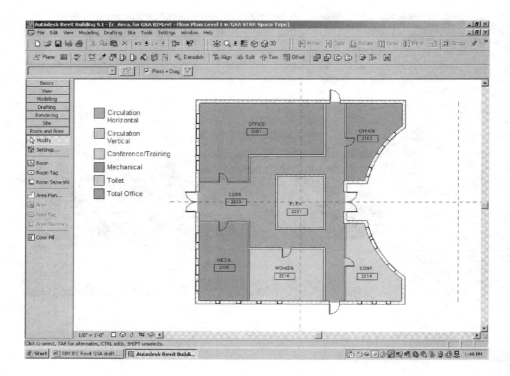

Figure P.1

The California Academy of Sciences. (*Image courtesy Webcor Builders, Chong Partners Architecture and Renzo Piano Building Workshop.*)

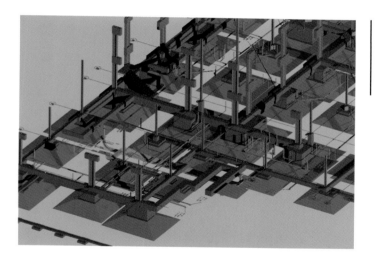

Figure 2.6

Composite models for underground utility coordination. (*Image courtesy RQ Construction.*)

Figure 2.14

Study model of building components. UC Santa Barbara Student Resource Center. (*Image courtesy RQ Construction.*)

Figure 2.17

MEP coordination for Sutter Surgical Hospital North Valley. (*Image courtesy RQ Construction.*)

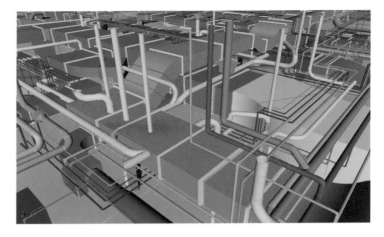

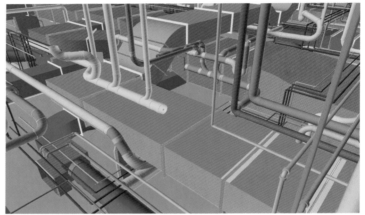

Figure 2.18

Sutter Surgical Hospital North Valley. (*Image courtesy RQ Construction.*)

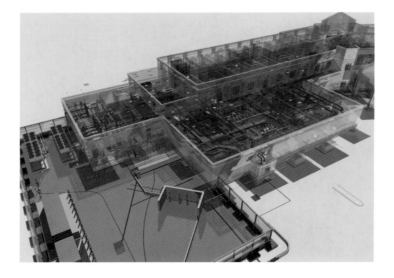

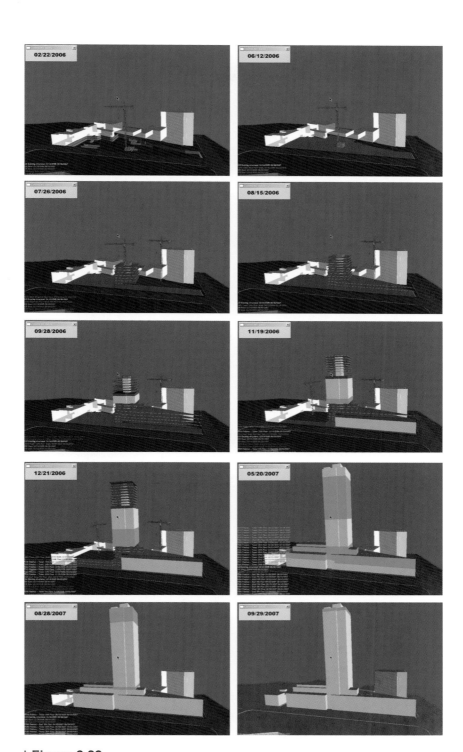

Figure 2.22

Toronto high rise condo project. (*Image courtesy Lease Crutcher Lewis, Seattle, Washington.*)

Figure 2.26

Construction model of Sutter Surgical Hospital North Valley. Coordinated mechanical systems with some fabrication level detail. (*Image courtesy RQ Construction.*)

Figure 3.6a

Interior renderings for communication purposes, modeled and rendered in MicroStation TriForma. (*Images courtesy Design Village.*)

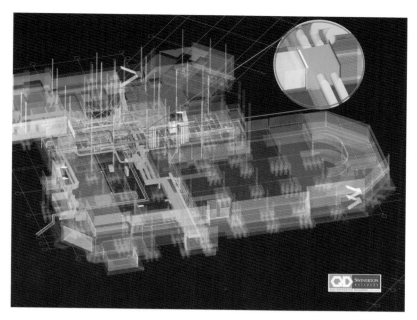

Figure 3.8

Coordination image of Ritz Carlton project in NavisWorks. Note the transparency of all architecture and structure for visibility of the MEP systems. (*Image courtesy Q&D Construction/Swinerton Builders.*)

Figure 3.12

A sample of a model that has been rendered in NavisWorks JetStream Presenter. (*Image courtesy NavisWorks.*)

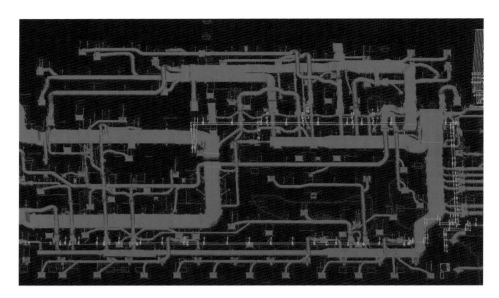

Figure 5.1.3

Snapshot of the mechanical system (HVAC duct, VAV boxes and Heating hot water pipe) of the first floor SE quadrant of the Camino MOB project. The medium and low pressure duct (shown in blue) and the heating hot water piping (shown in purple) allows other trades to determine the location of the mechanical systems in 3D and use it to route and coordinate their systems. (*Image courtesy DPR Construction, Inc., CA, USA.*)

Figure 5.1.5

Snapshot of the plumbing model of the first floor SE quadrant of the Camino MOB. The snapshot shows the waste and vents and the plumbing fixture locations (in green), the cold water supply (in blue) and hot water lines (in red). (*Image courtesy DPR Construction, Inc., CA, USA.*)

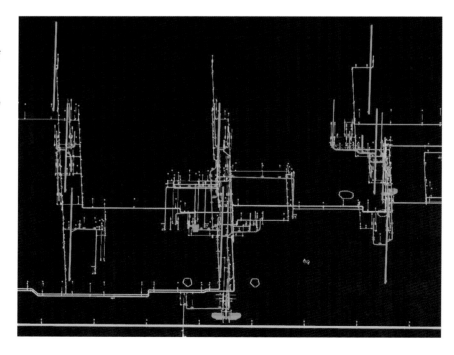

Figure 5.1.12

Clash between duct and sprinkler pipe (highlighted in red) on the Camino MOB. These clashes were identified by the Navisworks clash detection program. In a subsequent clash resolution session these clashes were resolved. (*Image courtesy, DPR Construction, Inc., CA, USA.*)

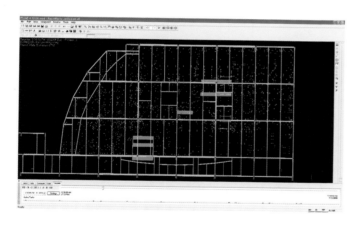

Figure 5.1.18

A snapshot of the 4D model from the Camino MOB project. The snapshot shows that the inserts (little dots in the screenshot) have been installed and construction of the full height wall framing (in green) is going on. (*Image courtesy DPR Construction, Inc., CA, USA.*)

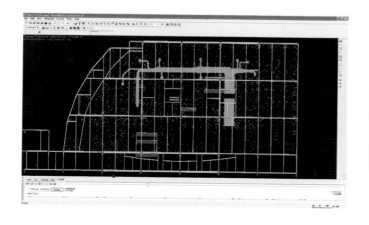

Figure 5.1.19

A snapshot of the 4D model from the Camino MOB project. The snapshot shows that the construction of the full height wall framing (in orange) is completed and the medium pressure duct (in green) is being installed. (*Image courtesy DPR Construction, Inc., CA, USA.*)

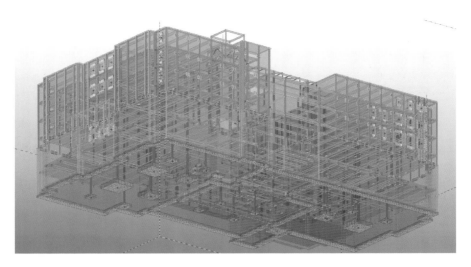

Figure 5.4.2

With Tekla we virtually build the building from the foundations up. (*Image courtesy Gregory P. Luth & Assoc., Inc.*)

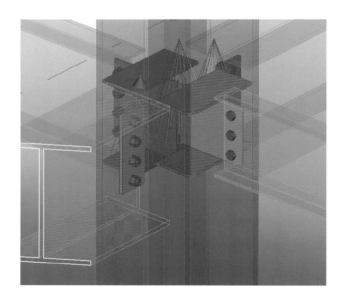

Figure 5.4.4b

We can model all of the reinforcing in Tekla such as the "U" bars around these windows. We can show recesses and inserts required to accommodate the stone trim in the façade. With Tekla, we can model all the steel connections—either conceptually or for final detailing. We can hand off the model to the detailers or complete it ourselves. (*Image courtesy Gregory P. Luth & Assoc., Inc.*)

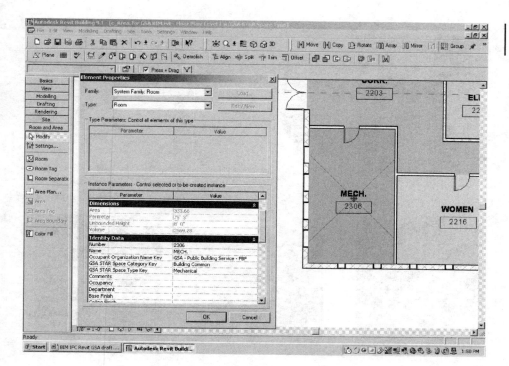

Figure 3.16
(*Continued*)

modeler ArchiCAD and Constructor are equal with the exception of some specific functionalities and object libraries that focus on either the architect's practice or the construction industry. The modeling is simple and straightforward to learn; the file structure is based on layers and stories that contain all the objects either created by the modeling tools or imported from object libraries. This is similar to most other modeling software. The Navigator is very effective in taking the user to any view of the model that has been saved (this applies to both 2D and 3D) and to any layer combination, etc. Since the software has had many years of development, it is very refined and has not lost the intuitiveness it was known for in the early 1990s, when it was one of the few professional 3D modelers in the marketplace (that still exists). It is easy to create custom objects with the modeling tools and save them as library parts. It is also not difficult (relatively) to create objects by writing code in GDL, which is not approachable in most other software tools. When one is making objects with modeling tools, they cannot easily become parametric objects; with GDL, however, there are almost no limits to the intelligence that can be written into the code of the objects.

The other components of the Constructor suite[4] are, however, the most interesting for their usefulness to construction project planning and management. Cost calculations can be created from the model by attaching a link from a recipe to a model part. A recipe is a description of the materials, labor, and resources that are required for a specific building component; it is part of the cost database. See Fig. 3.17. The object then provides the quantities that result in the cost calculation of that component. A recipe consists of one or more methods (project tasks like placing concrete, building formwork, etc.),

Figure 3.17

The structure of a recipe. (*Image courtesy of Vico.*)

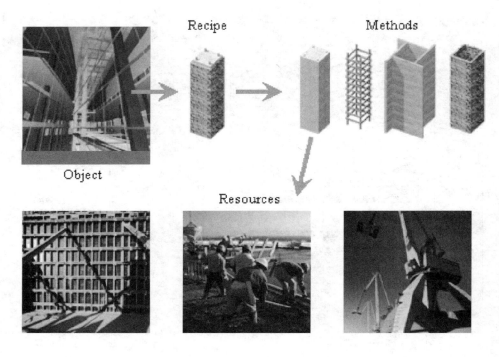

and a method consists of one or more resources (materials, labor, etc.). This gives recipes a flexibility that allows them to be used for almost any application, from representing a floor area with an overall square foot cost, to the analysis of a concrete element with all the details of formwork, reinforcing, finishing, etc. Such flexibility also permits the cost analysis of a project at any stage, thus facilitating the tracking of the cost changes as the design evolves. The refinement of both the recipes and the model parts over the course of the project's development provides a good cost management tool. Even though the management of the recipes can be tedious, it works well and once it is set up, it will remain functional for various projects where similar recipes can be used.

The scheduling tool in Constructor is called *Project-Control,* it is a Line of Balance Scheduler. A *Line of Balance* is a line that represents a task in a project, and its slope indicates the productivity rate of the task. The line thus shows both time and quantity of work as well as the location where the work takes place see Fig. 3.18. It is far more visual than a conventional Gantt chart, where the same information is not graphically represented, but buried in a dialog box. The Empire State Building was built in 13 months using this type of scheduling. Control connects the quantitative information from the model through the recipes in Estimator to the lines of balance in Control, both the quantity of materials and the time required to complete the task. Control then plots the lines and permits the manipulation of these lines to edit the time element of the tasks (not the material quantities, they can only be changed in the model); thus when a task starts and how long it takes can be adjusted until the whole project has been optimized

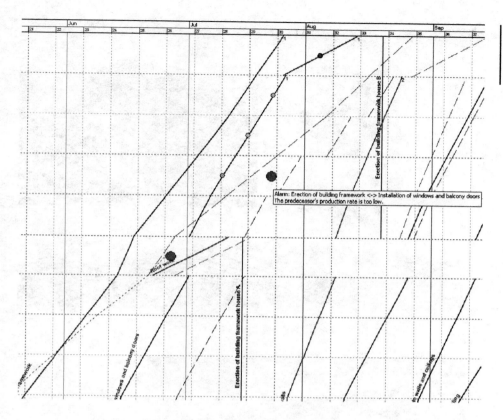

Figure 3.18
Line of Balance
Schedule. (*Image
courtesy of Vico.*)

in relation to productivity of crews and work locations in the project. Design updates are synchronized with the schedule by reimporting the model data from Estimator. The schedule can then be taken to the 5D viewer that will simulate it in a construction sequence.

Vico also describes its Design to Build and Build to Design ideas for the 3D model.[5] Design to Build represents building a model of the proposed project that reflects the actual construction techniques, including the actual tolerances of the objects in the model. This will facilitate proper coordination of the trades without incurring undue attention to unnecessary detail and accuracy. Build to Design then refers to the key model points being compared to the actual dimensions in the project by laser survey (or other means) to check the design tolerance compliance and ensure that prefabricated elements will fit.

The entire process of creating a 4D simulation can be described in steps.[6] The first step is represented in Fig. 3.19, the connection of the geometric model data to the recipe describing its methods and resources. The next step is the semiautomatic generation of a cost estimate and a schedule for the project based on the links between the information in the recipe and the model components, as shown in Fig. 3.20.

Figure 3.19

Build to Design.
(*Image courtesy
of Vico.*)

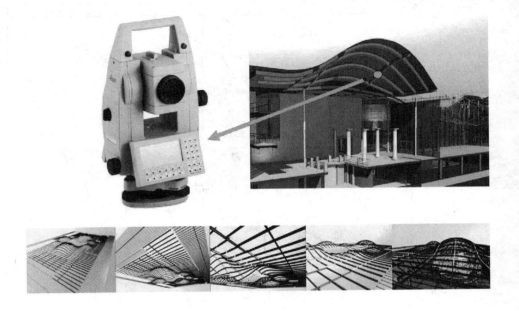

Figure 3.20

The 3D model
screen shows the
recipe connected
to the selected
objects; the
imported model
data in Estimator
(right) shows
recipes on top,
methods in the
middle, and
resources below.
(*Image courtesy
of Vico.*)

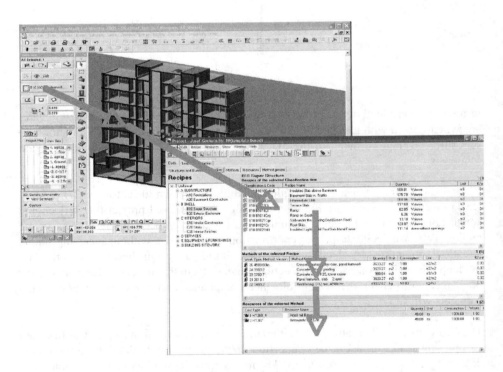

When design, cost, or time is changed, the other two are automatically updated. Few tools have this level of sophistication in their links.

Since the tasks of a construction schedule typically contain work that is to be done to multiple objects, i.e., a certain number of columns on a floor, etc., it is necessary to create zones to describe the locations in which the tasks are to be completed. This is step 3 in the process. See Fig. 3.21.

Once the zones have been described in the model by a line, the tasks and their respective recipes are automatically assigned to the proper zone. This now results in a *work breakdown structure* (WBS) that reflects the quantitative information of the project by zone or location, and this in turn is the basis for the *Line of Balance* schedule. Quantities from the methods and resources are the input for the calculations of task durations. The schedule results in activity durations, set by location (zone), assigned to the work breakdown structure. All 3D elements in the WBS have task connections, and the resulting 4D model can now be used for schedule simulation and analysis.

The different trades can be organized into task groups and identified by color in the 4D model, so that the activity can be visualized in the simulation. This level of visualization provides many possibilities to refine the construction process planning.

Tekla

Tekla is a Finnish software developer who addresses structural steel, steel reinforcing in concrete, and precast concrete modeling. The software is capable of taking the

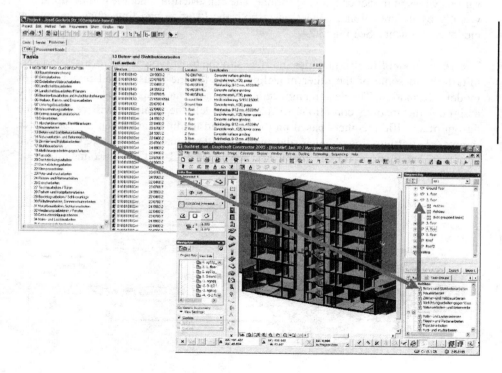

Figure 3.21

Tasks are mapped to objects, which belong to a construction zone, defined in the 3D model. (*Image courtesy of Vico.*)

project from the design phase, through detailing, into production and assembly. The engineer can create the model that begins the design and structural analysis process and pass it on for use in fabrication and installation. The software also has the ability to model reinforcing steel and precast concrete components for concrete construction. Tekla is a very focused tool, applied to a well-defined discipline; consequently it performs extremely well. Tekla models can of course be combined with models created in other software packages in viewers such as NavisWorks, so that the Tekla model can be used for construction coordination.

The modeling in Tekla is parametric; this means that the components of the model can be customized and edited at any time to suit the requirements of the project. This facilitates the model building or editing, and together with its graphical interface, Tekla is intuitive and not difficult to learn. There are three modules that can be added to Tekla Structures (the standard design configuration of Tekla), namely, steel detailing, precast detailing, and reinforced concrete detailing. Any and all drawings that are to be produced from the intelligent model will automatically represent the current version of the model and not require manual updating. Any of the building components can be modeled, from the steel connections and fasteners, to the railing, stairs, and trusses; if the available library components do not match the desired objects closely enough, then custom objects can be created from simpler elemental parts and saved as library parts also.

An advanced graphical input interface makes Tekla an excellent modeler and model manager, as well as making it very effective for navigation through the model and its various views in model or drawing format. The construction schedule can be simulated visually by the model and connected to both the location and time quantities of the model components. See Fig. 3.22.

The Tekla model file also includes interfaces to the most typical file formats and permits links to some of the other modeling tools for the transfer and integration of model information. The design engineer can begin the analysis of a steel structure by assigning the loading conditions to the 3D model; the analysis will result in the design of specific members based on the assigned loading; and when the loading or the model configuration changes, the analysis will automatically update the required structural calculations for the members. See Figs. 3.23 and 3.24. Connections are

Figure 3.22
Construction schedule to model connection in Tekla. (*Image courtesy of Tekla.*)

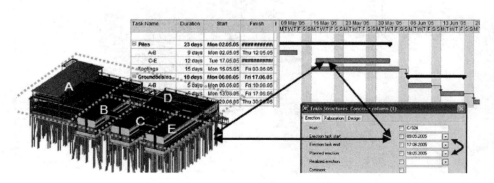

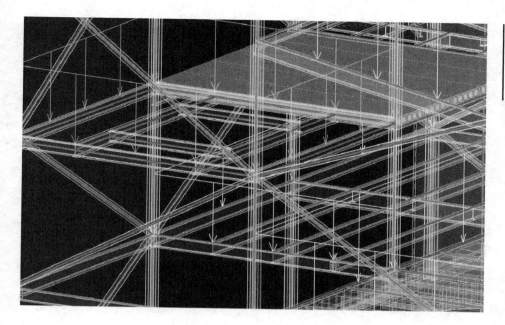

Figure 3.23
Loading assign-
ments in structural
model. (*Image
courtesy of Tekla.*)

(semi) automatically created by parametric design specifications and will update
themselves with layout (configuration) changes.

This same model can be developed into the fabrication model for the project, and then
continue its service during the erection process. The model use for fabrication is
referred to as Direct Digital Exchange. Either the design or the fabrication model will

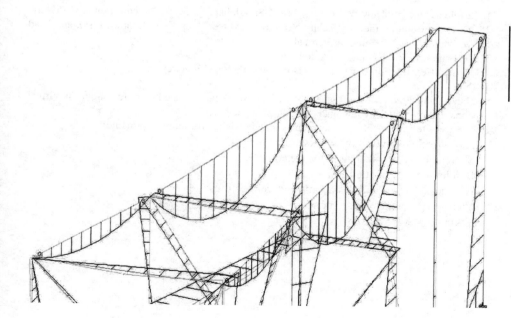

Figure 3.24
Structural analysis
in alternative
views. (*Image
courtesy of Tekla.*)

Figure 3.24
(*Continued*)

be able to function in the systems coordination process as well. Tekla's strength is software design and customer support. The software suite is soon to be expanded with various construction management modules.

REFERENCES

1. "Build as One" by Huw W. Roberts, AIA, CSI, Global Marketing Director, Bentley Building.
2. "Does the Building Industry Really Need to Start Over?", by Keith Bentley, CTO, and Brad Workman, AIA, VP, Building Vertical.
3. BIM and Project Planning, by Autodesk.
4. "Virtual Construction Benefits," by Dominic Gallello, CEO Graphisoft.
5. Ibid.
6. "Integrating Product Modeling with the Line of Balance Scheduling Technique in Virtual Construction," by Clay Freeman and Olli Seppanen of Vico.
7. The websites of the software companies may be visited for more information:
   NavisWorks—www.navisworks.com
   SketchUp—www.sketchup.google.com
   Bentley—www.bentley.com
   Autodesk—www.autodesk.com/revitarchitecturesuite
   Vico—www.vicosoftware.com
   Tekla—www.tekla.com

4 Learning BIM

INTRODUCTION

This chapter addresses how the BIM process can be learned (or taught) to both professionals already in the industry as well as students in university design or construction management curricula. The education of BIM concepts and techniques applies to a wide audience with a large variety of interests, who are involved in many types of construction projects. This chapter consists of three components:

- General learning characteristics
- Learning of the required skill sets
- Educating of construction professionals and university students

Observation of **human nature**: *For a person to make the effort to learn a subject well, it is either necessary to become passionate about that subject, or else make it an absolute necessity to learn it.*

The skills required to implement the BIM process are different from the already developed abilities we find among many construction industry professionals. Construction managers may typically plan only as much as seems to be absolutely necessary; all too often the construction schedule is a wall decoration in the job trailer. A deep commitment to looking ahead on a project is rare in the construction industry; this is probably due to the perception that the process itself can be fairly unstable. This could also become a self-fulfilling prophecy. The BIM approach includes a level of planning that has strong parallels to forecasting, or at least anticipating, the future of a project. A passion to try to see the future comes naturally to some, but not all; it generally requires a considerable effort to be able to predict with some level of confidence. BIM attracts people with the inclination and aptitude to observe and plan in enough detail to understand a project's current status so that its future can be better visualized (e.g., the champions in the construction firms already using the BIM process). It already has become the role of the university to introduce a person with these skills, in increasing numbers, into the construction industry to fill its needs.

Not everyone currently working in this industry will be entirely supportive of this approach. Many construction professionals are reluctant to embrace a new process and unwilling to make a large effort "to fix something that isn't broken." The facts, however, indicate that construction is the least efficient branch of industry; and it does need a major overhaul to become more competitive in view of the world's limited resources. The challenges of forming functional BIM teams are apparent. Most companies won't find the necessary experience in this field among their existing employees, and they'll need to train existing employees or find new recruits with the appropriate skills. This chapter will help to plan a strategy for the in-house training approach and will define the required skill set for new recruits.

LEARNING METHODS

The learning concepts discussed in this chapter relate to the BIM process from the three vantage points of (1) motivation, which is required to overcome (2) obstacles to the learning process and (3) recipes for success, which suggests five specific applications of learning principles.

Understanding these three subjects can make learning BIM a positive experience.

Learning is cyclical and iterative. It starts with the acquisition of knowledge, leading to the application of this new knowledge (practice), which results in the evaluation of the practice experience. This brings us full circle and introduces new learning (understanding) from the evaluation that leads to more practice, more evaluation, and so on. As understanding increases, the ability to acquire new knowledge will also increase. This development of greater understanding and the ability to apply it can be seen as the development of a skill. The development of a BIM is also cyclical and iterative; the creation of a BIM represents the learning about the project.

Learning takes place in three connected areas:

• Concepts
• Tool and process
• Applications

The learning cycle in Fig. 4.1 implies that learning in these three areas often takes place simultaneously and can thus be more difficult to observe.

Motivation to Learn

Having the right attitude is a key factor in achieving goals. Motivation results directly from attitude. Because it's important to be committed to the efforts necessary to reach goals, it's critical to set goals which are clearly achievable. Motivation to continue learning will come from the perceived progress toward these goals. For optimum results, it's necessary to have a learning plan with measurable milestones that indicate progress that will result in the motivation to continue. This learning strategy will consist of

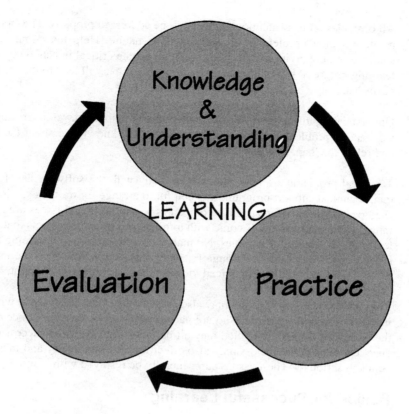

Figure 4.1
The learning cycle.

- Understanding the goal
- Planning the path to the goal
- Creating milestones along the path

Planning the learning strategy is parallel to the BIM process itself and based on the same principles. It's unlikely that this process will be "overplanned," and most difficulties are likely to arise from lack of planning.

All initiatives begin with motivation; and most efforts are also likely to end with the lack of motivation. As Confucius said, "When the goal cannot be reached, do not adjust your goal, adjust your steps."

Obstacles to Learning

Most obstacles in the learning process can be related to stemming from one (or more) of the following problems:

- Lack of understanding the process—conceptual issues
- Inability to use the required tools—technical issues
- Circumstances—environmental issues

All obstacles require attention and need to be addressed properly. The first step toward resolution of a problem is to understand its nature. Help may come from various sources, and creativity and problem solving become critical in achieving a satisfactory learning progress. It will ultimately be motivation that will lead to the resolution of the obstacles.

Understanding the nature of the problem will help to develop an approach to it. Conceptual problems are generally addressed with knowledge about the BIM process and relate to Chap. 2 of this text.

Technical problems are best addressed directly with the software developers through their technical support program. It is helpful to arrange for training sessions with qualified persons from the respective companies so that technical issues are kept to a minimum. Many software tools come with tutorials and practice projects that are helpful in learning the required techniques. No matter how thorough these training tools may be, however, it is advisable to arrange for hands-on sessions in which the use of the software is demonstrated and practiced to make the learning more efficient.

The circumstances of learning may also present obstacles; the space in which the learning takes place, the persons who are part of the process, the experience of the faculty, the budget of the program, etc., may all be factors affecting the success of the experience. Circumstantial factors may also effect motivation directly and therefore need to be taken seriously. These issues can generally be resolved with common sense.

Recipe for Successful Learning

Successful learning is enhanced by a number of steps that were developed in the BIM curriculum at California State University, Chico. These steps are based on the experiences gathered with the students' practice projects in the university laboratory, and the professional training workshops and seminars provided by Construction Simulation Lab. The most successful learners are passionate about the subject and their relationship to it. Success is directly dependent on the wish to attain it; generally, without a strong desire only half-hearted efforts are possible. The attitude about making extra effort needs to be very positive, especially in BIM; additional work can easily pay off in multiple ways, by saving time at a later stage in the use of the BIM.

Taking shortcuts in learning BIM is not recommended; don't even think about shortcuts until a number of successful projects have been completed. If you decide to depart from the well-traveled road, you had better either know the way or have a very good map. As Johann von Goethe said, "It is not enough to take steps which may some day lead to a goal; each step must be itself a goal."

Use Real Projects

The use of real projects makes educational exercises much more meaningful. Whether the model is being designed (as in architectural or engineering studios) or built from the design drawings, the reality factor of an exercise can have many positive effects. It is almost unthinkable to come up with a hypothetical project that would have the complexity and meaning of a real one (no matter how small). Most students respond very positively to practicing on real projects with real parameters in a real setting. Even though these are only exercises, the students enjoy it when simulations parallel the real world. The connection with an actual project also provides a reference point against which the team's accomplishments may be measured.

Using an actual project additionally may provide the possibility to learn firsthand from the actual persons playing the roles in real life. This has proved very informative in classroom situations, as it transforms the experience for the student into an internship-like relationship. Students enjoy meeting a person who is professionally playing the role they are studying for.

The use of the existing information of actual projects also makes the challenges of the simulation realistic. Solving problems that are too simple will not help much when it is time to handle reality; and most students enjoy being challenged. If the project is too large or complex, there are usually ways to simplify the exercise to make it manageable.

In exercises with hypothetical situations, the project and its circumstances are usually oversimplified. Even though the simple approach may have benefits in learning some of the basic concepts or techniques, it needs to be limited to very few, small exercises, since it does not adequately prepare the student for the actual BIM process.

Collaborate

Collaboration is a fundamental concept to the whole BIM process. It helps a learning team to become a *team*, overcome obstacles, and make progress. A common difficulty lies in not knowing what to do next. Without anyone there to rely on for help, it will be important to have a team that can deal with problems by collaborating to generate possible solutions. Learning collaboratively is excellent preparation for the psychological mind set necessary to work with the BIM process.

Team members have to develop collaboration skills, and learn to work with outside consultants. The teacher of the class may function as one of the consultants, but so may the software developer or the construction company representative for the class exercise project. The class will respond positively to working on a real project and have some of the professionals working on the actual project come to speak and consult with them about their work. In most cases, however, it will be the faculty (or team coach) who will play that role and advise them in their project-related questions. In the professional setting, a practicing team will need to get guidance from a team coach. Even though the teams appear very democratic, they need to be led by a capable person (coach or captain) who helps steer the team into the correct decisions for the sake of the project.

The BIM process involves many roles and disciplines. It's important for a student to have played the different roles of the various team members working on a construction project. The collaboration of the students on the team will also permit them to play a variety of these roles throughout the exercises and gain experience that will further enhance their ability to collaborate.

The persons who will ultimately be able to address and solve all issues related to this process need to be carefully selected and trained. Team building skills are not addressed here, but it is important for team members to have the ability to develop the skills discussed in this book, as well as the understanding of what it really means to be a member of a team.

Prepare

The importance of proper preparation cannot be overestimated. It is necessary to plan the entire process and create intermediate and final goals for all stages of the work. As with construction scheduling, the process needs to be visualized and evaluated throughout its development.

A simulation of a smaller portion of the project will help with the planning of the entire project simulation. This is a critical step especially since, without the necessary experience to make informed decisions, it will probably be necessary to reevaluate and adjust the approach significantly after this step.

Plan in detail—schedule with diligence. This is discussed in detail in the "BIM Planning" section of Chap. 2 of this book.

Be prepared for the unexpected. Learning BIM is no different than anything else in life; unforeseen difficulties (or perhaps windfalls) will likely arrive. When the unexpected happens, it needs to be analyzed. The work schedule needs to be consulted first, to assess foreseeable changes. This will make it clear whether the approach needs to be adjusted to accommodate the new situation.

Set Deadlines

Deadlines are a practical way to keep a process on track. It is critical to establish several intermediate deadlines and a final completion date. Most humans work better with deadlines, and need to learn not to take longer than necessary because of starting too late.

The intermediate deadlines will help to maintain the schedule and provide milestones at which progress can be evaluated and necessary adjustments can be made. These deadlines may also help to make the team's effort more consistent throughout the course of the project. Each deadline is an opportunity to apply the iterative "evaluation and adjustment" cycle.

Persevere

Last but certainly not least, do not give up!

At some time during the course of each class project, it is important to explain to the students how much they have accomplished and how much their understanding and ability to manipulate the BIM have improved in the previous few weeks or months. At a certain point, students will likely become aware of how much they do not understand. This is natural, just keep going—"this, too, shall pass."

It is important to follow all steps accurately and diligently. Make the extra effort to do it correctly because it is worth it! If things go wrong, start over. It will generally be easier that way.

SKILL SETS

The skills for creating and managing a building information model fall into the following three categories: software tools, management processes, and project team roles. The tools are typically technical, the processes are chiefly conceptual, and the roles are primarily psychological and social. However, there is a generous amount of overlap, and interaction, among all three of these areas. Each BIM exercise contains elements from all these areas, which reinforce one another to create an understanding of the entire skill set. These three skill categories will apply to the development of the component models that need to become part of the BIM, as well as to the ultimate management of the BIM as a complex entity. This represents the entire scale of project-related activities from the detailed to the general. It is helpful to work on both ends of this scale and to address the individual models, i.e., architectural, structural, MEP, etc., as well as the BIM in which the component models are brought together in a viewer or other analytic tool. Addressing all parts at the same time is working on the entire project, not just addressing isolated exercises that deal with simple elements out of context. Working on a project will provide the opportunity to learn how the individual elements relate to the whole, and interact with one another. The understanding of one concept will readily transfer to some of the others and therefore speed up the learning process.

Tool-Related

The operation of the various software tools is critical to the application of the BIM process. The nature of the tools is addressed in Chap. 3 of this book. Exercises related to learning the proper application of the tools will focus on the correct visualization of the objects (and concepts) that are to be modeled, the accuracy with which the objects are represented, and the organization of the model parts. There is further related discussion about model structure and model organization in Chap. 3.

Project Visualization

It is critical to develop the ability to visualize the components of the intended model, and to understand the relationships of the various components to one another, so that ultimately the entire project is visualized and represented as a 3D model. Architects and engineers are likely to work with modeling exercises that focus on creating a design concept and the necessary software skills to model and develop it. Construction managers, however, are most likely to learn the software by building a 3D model from the drawings of an already existing design.

The two processes have a lot in common, even though they are inherently very different. The design student in the first case may never work with a drawing during the entire process; all visualization may be represented either in the software model or in the student's head. The internal communication, necessary to develop the concept, takes place entirely between the modeler and the 3D model in the software. In the second case of the construction manager, the modeler works from a set of drawings and needs to be able to interpret these drawings, visualize the project, and model it in the 3D software (build the simulation). In the first case, the modeler works from the general to the specific; it will require several design iterations to be able to produce a certain level of detail from a conceptual model. In the second case, the detail has already been developed (as represented in the drawings); the challenge now is to effectively model to a specific level of detail. In the first case that level of detail will not be available until it has evolved from the project's development. These different types of modeling relate to the project phases; both will have their application in realistic BIM management.

In both cases the learning process is essentially that of evaluating the simulation and checking it against the modeler's understanding of it (the internal visualization) so that the model can be adjusted as required. In other words, the learning is centered on the ability to develop the model into an acceptable representation of what is visualized. All exercises need to focus on gaining control over the modeling software. *It is easy to fall into the trap of wanting to adjust the model based on the ability to control the software.* It is more important to learn the tools well enough to be able to model what is required, in order to avoid having to compromise the model. It is critical to learn to be professional in the use of the tools.

Most modeling software represents the basic construction components with basic modeling tools (i.e., slabs, walls, roofs, and various objects); however, there are always challenges that require the fabrication of special building parts, representing more complex objects, from basic modeling forms. Since the model is a schematic representation of an actual structure, it is necessary to choose the appropriate level of detail to represent the critical components of the project. Becoming more familiar with the software tools and having a better understanding of the purpose of the model will make these decisions more comfortable. With respect to this subject, there is no substitute for software skills, creativity, and experience.

Model Accuracy

Accuracy is of the utmost importance in the BIM. In schematic level models, although the actual (final) dimensions of objects are not usually known, it is still important to try to be as accurate as possible to facilitate the further development of the model. More detailed models need to be absolutely accurate, as any inaccuracy can become the source of great difficulty in further model development or analysis.

In the class exercises students have the unfailing responsibility to avoid fractional dimensions whenever possible, in other words, to be accurate and not just close. This is a critical habit, and it takes very little additional energy to do it right. It will save enormous amounts of time and energy during later stages of the model development. One of the current areas of research in the BIM field is **tolerance.** Tolerance is what makes theoretical components fit into a real world. Models are theoretical and thus need to be "perfect" from a design standpoint, tolerance is what is built in so that the real components will be able to fit in the assembly. This subject relates to the use of the model in place of traditional shop drawings for fabrication purposes, where accuracy is clearly necessary for successful production and installation.

It is also readily apparent that in the combination of several models into a viewer, it is critical that all models "fit" in relation to each other. This is referred to as *registration.* Registration needs to be planned beforehand and executed meticulously. Careful collaboration, so fundamental to this process, is required to have properly registered models in the viewer.

Simulation Structure

A BIM may contain vast amounts of information, and the organization of this information is critical to the successful analysis of the project. Learning how to organize information in the BIM is an important skill. The modeling software has its inherent architecture that organizes the model components and the informational links to those components. Thus the way the modeling software organizes the project information needs to be the basis for planning the effective use of the BIM. Chap. 3 on software tools discusses the nature of model organization.

When a model is exported to a viewer such as NavisWorks, it will retain its organizational structure. This will directly influence the ability to select the components in the viewer and in turn the viewer's ability to analyze the model. Running a construction sequence is directly derivative from the layer structure in the native modeling software and needs to be preplanned while constructing the original model in order to facilitate the selection of specific model components in NavisWorks. For example, visualize a structure with a large floor slab that will be constructed in three sections. It will be necessary to model this slab in the three sections in the original model, in order to be able to select the three sections individually in the viewer so they can individually appear in the construction sequence. If this is not addressed in the planning stages, it will either be more work in the viewer or require breaking large components into smaller sections in the modeler and reimporting the project to the viewer.

Generally it is almost always possible to correct anything at any time in the model development process. However, it is likely that it may require more work in some cases than in others and thus may result in a compromise from the original goals for the simulation. This type of compromise may be avoided by proper planning or with adequate experience with BIM development.

Process-Related

To facilitate project planning and management with BIM, the differences between the standard project delivery methods and BIM methods must be addressed. As explained in the introduction of this book, the BIM process is very different from our conventional design-bid-build process. So far the BIM process primarily finds its utility in the design-build and design-assist delivery methods. The process is based on collaboration and thus encourages the formation of the project team who will work from its initial conception until its final stages, which may even include the postconstruction functions of the project (i.e., operations and maintenance). Having the entire team cooperate from the beginning has clear planning advantages, but also introduces a certain degree of complexity that requires care. Collaboration also relies on trust among the team members. It is precisely this trust that allows a new form of communication (information processing) to emerge. Trust and collaboration will result in the largest advantages of the BIM approach—a group of individuals who will work together cooperatively to better understand the project and serve the project owner.

It is the process that enables the team, and the team that requires the process.

Communication

When working with a 3D virtual building, team members are no longer expected to imagine how the project looks; the project can now be seen in images from the virtual model. Communication is drastically improved because all team members "see" the same thing, allowing the team to address any issues represented in the model. Managing this communication becomes a challenge because of the increased amount of collaboration involved. Continual evaluation of the communication protocol is important so that adjustments can be made as required. During the BIM exercises, remember to establish communication channels and monitor the flow of information between the team members. Regular team meetings will establish whether the process is successful or not.

Information Management

Information can be space- and/or location-related, in which case it is visualized in the 3D model. Information can also take the form of reports, instructions, etc., in which case it can be a file-connected to a model part, or a file-hyperlinked to the BIM. Furthermore, there may also be time-related information that can be visualized through sequence simulations tied to a schedule or calendar. The concentration of so much project information in a BIM is a major development for the ability to manage project-related information. This concentration of information, plus the fact that there is an attempt to minimize duplication of information, makes editing and updating much more efficient than traditional project delivery approaches.

Information management is closely related to the tools used to process this information. BIM exercises should include components that require the organization and editing of information, i.e., the attaching of a cost database to physical 3D components, assembling a cost estimate report, changing unit costs, etc.

Coordination

The connection among all parts of the project information within the BIM makes it possible to focus on its coordination. Traditionally having information spread over various locations has made it very difficult to check for duplication and errors. Merely visualizing a project can be a big challenge and typically only addresses location-related information; tracking written and time-related information increases the level of complexity a great deal. Coordination applies to all information for a particular project; some filtering will need to be applied to address the major potential conflicts first, so that more detailed areas can be addressed once the major components work in harmony. Coordinating means to adjust different elements of the project in order to create a harmonious (coordinated) whole. This is the result of visualizing, understanding, communicating, and collaborating. Examples of the necessity for coordination are common in construction projects; especially among the subcontractor trades (HVAC, plumbing, electrical, etc.), where it is critical to coordinate design and installation activities. Since each of these trades is generally performed by a different group of individuals who all have to work and install their equipment into a very limited amount of space in the project, this area is the prime target for 3D coordination. Properly coordinated activities will result in more efficient use of time and materials in the project. Clash detection in 3D models is the most effective tool available for virtual coordination, and it should be an integral part of a BIM exercise. Another example of a coordination exercise is the analysis of a construction sequence of the installation of the underground utilities and the foundation work for a project. This sequence needs to include the excavations, soil storage, equipment locations, etc., of the entire process.

These exercises should also contain opportunities to address the hierarchy of coordination, i.e., to work from a large scale down to a finer scale. A sense for the proper filtering of information that is to be coordinated needs to be developed; this will help to keep the coordination effort realistic. A strong practical construction experience is very valuable for this sense of realism.

Role-Related

The introduction of BIM in the construction management process also requires special handling of the personnel. The following three new roles are proposed to formulate an effective BIM team: a *BIM manager*, a person who coordinates the team that is responsible for the production and analysis of the BIM; a *BIM operator*, the actual person doing the work of creating and analyzing the simulation; and a *BIM facilitator* who will help persons with the viewing and retrieving of information from the BIM. Collaboration is critical in the BIM process and needs to be exercised at the earliest possible stage. Almost all the BIM team roles will involve a lot of collaboration. An ego-centric or independent approach by any of the team members can easily undermine the efficiency and possibilities of the team as a whole. In a well-functioning team, all members will support one another and understand their mutual interdependence. A successful BIM team functions more as a harmonious family, a happy music ensemble, or a successful sports team, than as a corporate entity.

For the students of BIM to become better prepared for participation in an actual project, it is extremely useful to integrate the education with practical construction experience to the largest degree possible. The actual construction process has to be visualized properly to be able to build an effective model. This is an important reason to stress the collaboration between the students and persons with enough field experience to address constructability issues.

BIM Manager

The BIM manager will be a "people person" who is able to communicate on a personal level and quickly assess how to improve collaboration on all levels among the team members and outside contacts. She or he is the strategic planner of the project. It is the role of the BIM manager to determine how the BIM can best serve the particular project. The critical factors will be the client's requirements or wishes, the experience of the project team, and the availability of resources (personnel, software training, tools, etc.) The goals for the BIM process need to be analyzed and evaluated by the BIM manager so that a plan can be developed. This role requires thorough knowledge of the processes and tools necessary to create and analyze the BIM. Direct modeling experience is not required, but an understanding of the process and its limitations is important to optimize the planning of the project.

A BIM manager's plan will contain the following:

- Who will model and what tools will be used?
- What will be modeled and to what level of detail?
- What information will be required and who will provide it?
- Which analytic processes will be required and who will perform them?
- How the models will be structured and detailed to make the analysis possible?
- What the time frame will be for the various milestones of the BIM production?

BIM Operators

The BIM operators are the BIM team members who are involved in the production and analysis of the BIM. This will include all designers and consultants who build 3D models of their parts of the work, as well as all others who interact with the BIM from any informational standpoint, i.e., estimators, schedulers, fabricators, etc. These persons have to be very familiar with all aspects of the tools required for their work. No effort should be spared to adequately train in the use of such tools. Generally much more time and effort is wasted in inefficient use of a tool than would have been spent properly training for it. Training is the most likely area where shortcuts appear attractive, but consequently also where the largest inefficiencies can result.

BIM Facilitator

It is likely that the BIM will primarily be planned and created in the office, but that it will also be extensively used on the jobsite for management purposes. There is an advantage to separating these two functions so that the BIM can be more fully integrated into various construction site operations. It is powerful to have a BIM at job meetings where the discussions can be aided with the visualization and communication advantages of the 3D model and its possibilities. A BIM facilitator would be primarily jobsite-based and would facilitate the use of the BIM by those physically constructing the project. He or she would be instrumental in aiding the superintendent to establish communications with, and among, the subcontractors. This role will require understanding of the viewing software and the structure of the component models. The facilitator will help the retrieval of information from the BIM at the jobsite. He or she will navigate through the model and help the builders to understand their work better with the aid of the BIM visualization.

Thus all three roles will need to be addressed through the BIM exercises; and each student should get some experience in each role, to better understand the functioning of the whole project team on a BIM facilitated project.

THE LEARNERS

The term *learners* refers to the people requiring training to learn and implement BIM processes. There currently are a number of construction companies that are already utilizing and developing building information models and have begun implementing the BIM processes in various kinds of projects. The case study chapter of this book, Chap. 5, provides some examples. The construction industry at large is now becoming aware of the tremendous potential of this new development. To be successful with BIM it is critical to have qualified people working with the process. Several companies are expressing concern about the necessity of including BIM education into the construction management curriculum of university programs. There are several universities looking into the possibilities of developing such a curriculum; but as of Fall 2007, developed BIM programs are difficult to find. This is significant, since it takes a few years to bring such a curriculum to a productive level. At CSU Chico specific BIM classes have been taught since the Fall of 2004, and the first few qualified graduating students were ready to enter the industry in the summer of 2007. These classes had been in preparation for about two years before commencing.

During the last few years of teaching BIM, it has become apparent that the field has particular characteristics that make it more attractive to persons with a specific type of personality. A desire for organization and accuracy is important, and an affinity for working with computers is also essential. The desire to plan and control and a passion for scheduling and coordination are important for the BIM manager. Many professionals and students in construction management do not necessarily fit this profile. The industry will soon be desperate for persons with qualified BIM experience, and the minimal activity in education in this field at this time is alarming. Since the professional builder already has the necessary skill set to deal with the construction profession, it will not take a lot of training to develop proficiency in the BIM process. On the other hand, as has already been noted, not every individual currently in the construction field will necessarily be a good candidate for BIM training. It is a reasonable goal to encourage construction professionals generally, to become at least literate in the BIM world.

Project Owners

Benefits

Project owners can benefit from understanding the concepts of BIM and its business implications. The reduction of risk and waste and the ability to improve the construction schedule and reduce the time spent on rework, etc., are generally the most interesting benefits to a project owner and can lead to lower project costs and earlier occupancy. The BIM is also potentially able to enable life cycle cost analysis such as energy consumption, project maintenance, facilities management, etc. The owner can purchase the as-built in the form of a BIM, so that further use can be made of it during the occupancy of the project for operation and maintenance-related management. Project owners will likely benefit most from BIM in the following four ways:

Risk Reduction   Risk is a large (but often difficult to see) cost in most construction projects. When using the BIM process, much of the risk is removed from the construction planning and management of a project. This is largely due to the fact that the process requires greater planning, collaboration, and understanding of the project among all the project team members. See more in Chap. 2.

Waste Reduction   The reduction of waste in a project is closely connected to the decrease of risk. Waste comes in the form of lost time, wasted material, and lost opportunities. With better understanding of the project and the ability to coordinate the production of the components, more of the project can be premanufactured (rather than constructed on site) and thus installed with less waste and need for rework due to field conflicts. See more in Chap. 2.

Scheduling Advantages   A greater understanding of the related processes required for a construction project inevitably results in a better ability to schedule its activities. Test scenarios can be visualized in 4D sequences to help communicate the advantages and disadvantages of various scheduling options.

The line of balance'scheduling method of Vico's Project Control can be applied to maximize the productivity of the construction activities in the project and minimize the time and resources required for the same product.

Life Cycle Management   When a BIM is used for construction management, there are many reasons to maintain the BIM as an updated as-built version of the project. When construction is complete, this BIM will additionally benefit the owner since the BIM will be available for the postconstruction management of the project. Space and furniture allocation can be developed for the life of the project, as well as the maintenance and operations records and requirements for all the building systems. The BIM may also be used for energy consumption analysis, lighting studies, etc.

Contractual Issues   The most frequently asked question is, Who owns the model? The answer depends on who paid for it and how it is to be utilized. Both liability and cost become factors to consider in the contractual description of the BIM and its use. In principle, there does not need to be much difference between the responsibility for the traditional construction documents and for the BIM. The difficulty seems to arise from the fact that the BIM may be actively updated throughout the course of construction. The construction documents are rarely updated. They are principally amended with RFIs, change orders, etc., but the original documentation is unlikely to change significantly. This makes construction team members much less concerned about the safety of the information. With the BIM it is an issue, however, who and how updates to the "contract model" are being made, and how the information is secured. Technically this is not as complicated as it may sound, and it is important for the owners to educate themselves to participate in these discussions. See more on this in Chap. 1.

Risk   Project owners are concerned with their risks. The BIM eliminates much of the project risk. It is important to define and manage the risks of the different team members. Building contractors are often concerned that the additional cost of creating and managing the BIM will benefit them proportionally, and that the project owner is not only one to reap the rewards. *The best way to reduce project risk is to truly share both the risk and the benefits of this reduced risk among all the project team members.*

The project owners will thus most likely learn about BIM through these areas of primary interest to them. It is important to get a general understanding of the entire field and its possibilities and limitations, so that these particular areas of interest can be understood in their overall context.

BIM Specialists (Managers, Operators, and Facilitators)

Planning and Management

Currently the largest area of interest in BIM is in the development and management of the construction project. Various architects, engineers, and construction contractors are working with building information modeling to create and analyze their projects. The most common uses are systems coordination (e.g., clash detection and subcontractor communication and coordination) and systems fabrication (e.g., the mechanical subcontractor will design, lay out, and fabricate the ductwork with the aid of a 3D model). The project team will consist of all the persons who are responsible for the planning and production of the BIM, the owner, the designers, the managers, and administrators of the construction project. It is not necessary for all members to have the same understanding of the process, or the same skills in the application of the various processes related to BIM use and management. The variety of team members' skills will be a strength in the makeup of the team.

The management members of the team are those persons primarily concerned with the planning and administrative processes of the project. In some instances a BIM manager may also help with the production of models, or components, but management members will generally be utilizing the results of the modeling efforts of the hands-on team members. A thorough understanding of the concepts and processes is of primary importance for the BIM manager; the other management types will not need as thorough an understanding, however, and can rely on the BIM manager for expertise in making team decisions in this area.

The actual persons building the virtual models—BIM operators—will generally work for either the construction company or the consultants to the owner. These model makers will be like the drafters of the CAD age; instead of drawings they are now producing 3D models and attaching the necessary information to them. If drawings are required, for building permits, financing, etc., they can of course be created from the BIM. (The advantage is that the drawings will then inevitably reflect the latest state of development of the BIM.) Most of these modelers will be able to use the software tools, but the application of the BIM and management skills will remain with project management individuals. It will of course be natural for a BIM operator to migrate through the technical role into a management role. Persons in modeling roles will not necessarily be graduates from the university engineering or construction management programs, but likely also come from vocational training programs. At this time many construction companies that are in need of modeling for projects will have it outsourced. Outsourcing is addressed in Chap. 2 of this book under "BIM Concepts-The nature of the Building Information Model-Project Models-Model Sources."

Tools and Processes

The specific training for a hands-on operator is in the use of software tools and the processes that are facilitated by these tools. Training exercises can include the following areas of BIM activity.

- It may include the construction of virtual models in association with design team members or from already prepared plans for a project. The tools will be chosen based on the modelers' experience, software availability, and requirements of the task at hand.

- It will likely include performing the analysis of the BIM information that is required by the construction manager, in the day-to-day use of the BIM for the coordination and management of the project.
- It is also likely that the model will need to be updated regularly, to keep it a current as-built of the project. A protocol needs to be developed so that the work done by all the consultants is continually updated to the BIM. Potential effects of the differences between anticipated and actual progress on the project can then be analyzed.

Implementation

It may not be simple to find consultants who are able and willing to embrace the BIM process. Often one or more members of the project team will need to be trained to use the necessary tools to contribute to the process. The BIM process should be introduced into a construction company one project at a time. This will facilitate the training of people, and a "best practices" approach can be developed for the specific methods of the firm. The BIM process should be taken to a greater level of detail with each project, and it should be representative both of the firm and of the type of construction projects generally handled by the firm. This will allow a type of "project template" to emerge that specifically addresses the needs of the construction business.

Different levels of implementation may be desirable in response to the specific circumstances for each project. The example of the implementation of BIM set by the GSA (Government Services Administration) is a careful one; the GSA is starting with the use of BIM for space analysis. This will give a large amount of their users an opportunity to slowly familiarize themselves with the nature of the tools and processes without becoming overwhelmed by a large amount of detail early in the learning process. This approach is intelligent and sensitive to the nature of the audience.

The reality of BIM implementation needs to continually be taken into account in all training. Both the learning and the implementation of BIM processes will benefit from a strategic and well-planned approach.

University Students

The students attending university need to learn most of life's skills, in addition to the specific subject matter related to their course of study. These general skills will be developed along with the special skills addressing the BIM process throughout the length of the curriculum. It is important for all exercises to address a variety of many of the necessary skills. The skills that need to be learned are the ability to learn, read, write, apply math skills, verbally communicate, analyze problems, report on research, organize complex tasks, understand basic construction knowledge, understand basic construction management processes, etc. The proposed university curriculum is four semester classes long and incorporates the use of the software tools and the associated processes as well as a lot of construction project-related subject material. It is meant to fit into an existing developed construction management curriculum so that many of these general skills will be covered in the other classes. It is also recommended that the BIM classes be taken during the last two years of the CM curriculum. Care should be taken to coordinate the course content of the other CM classes to provide the BIM students with the necessary background in construction-related knowledge at the right time in their BIM curriculum.

The BIM Curriculum

The "new" BIM classes will address the creation and use of a building information model. These classes will presuppose a certain amount of basic construction knowledge so that the students can take existing plans and build a virtual project from them.

The BIM-related content of the university curriculum is essentially the same as the content required for construction professionals. The university classes, however, also contain general knowledge required to give the student an adequate background to understand the function of the BIM in the construction process.

The introductory class addresses the basic concepts and fundamental skills for construction management students; this class takes place within the first two years of the university education. The remaining four semesters develop an understanding of construction materials, processes, techniques, and representations in the context of the BIM and its processes within the planning and management of construction projects; these classes are scheduled for the last two years before graduation. All the exercises focus on the construction of simulation models based on documentation of existing projects. It begins with the careful analysis of drawings and specifications and requires the visualization of the project and its representation in the simulation. As the exercises progress through the four classes, the difficulty and level of detail of the subject increase. The first two classes address primarily individual skills such as modeling and analyzing models. The last two classes focus on team work and complexity that can only be addressed through collaboration. The last semester is devoted to real construction projects in progress, in collaboration with the company working on the project; this class is like an internship, and it gives the students a good basis for entering the industry with a professional level of skill.

A brief outline of a BIM curriculum can include the following:

Introduction Class—Construction Graphics

This is the introduction class for all CM majors, and it includes basic skills for visualizing, representing, and communicating construction concepts. Through lectures and exercises the students will learn basic skills that help them to understand graphical representations of construction projects.

- Visualization
- Representation
- Communication
- 2D, 3D, 4D, etc.
- SketchUp
- NavisWorks
- ArchiCAD

Introduction Exercises The exercises during this semester focus on teaching visualization and communication skills. After some smaller one-week problems, the students may download a set of drawings from the National Register of Historic Buildings, as their first major exercise, and build a model of Independence Hall in Philadelphia using SketchUp. See Fig. 4.2. This teaches the representational qualities of the drawings and connects them to a 3D compilation of these views into a model. The next exercise is a simple solid model of a small commercial building in ArchiCAD. This exercise introduces actual building components and their relationship to one another. At the end of

Figure 4.2

The Independence Hall project in SketchUp showing the imported drawings placed in the 3D model.

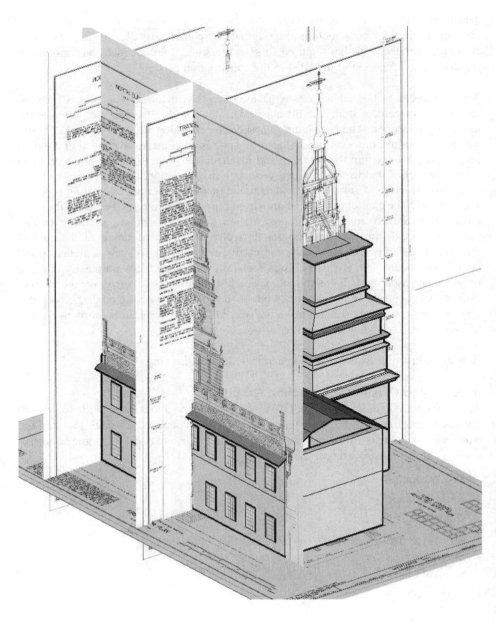

Figure 4.2
(*Continued*)

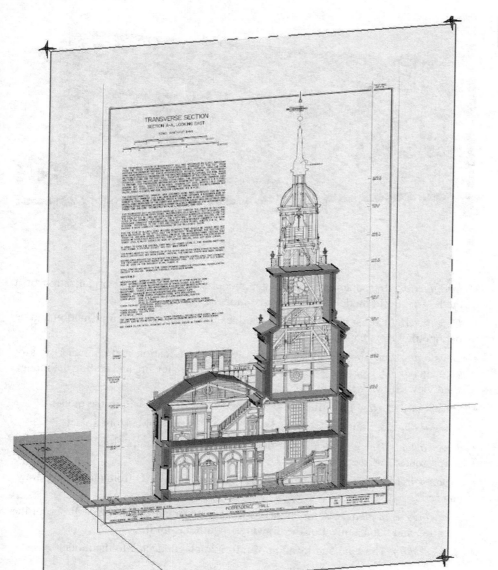

the model construction, the students will extract several simple drawings from the model and add dimensions and notes. See Fig. 4.3.

First-Semester BIM (after basic CM classes have been completed)

ArchiCAD is used to teach fundamental modeling concepts and techniques. Individual exercises have both construction and modeling skill challenges. Students will prepare by learning the general skills required to organize a 3D simulation model.

Figure 4.3

The video store shown in a cutaway perspective view.

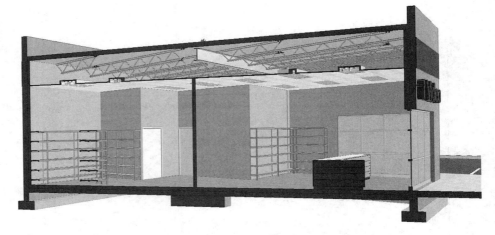

- *Introduction.* Introduction to computer models. The nature and organization of a model file. Solid models versus surface models.
- *Objects, GDL.* What is an object? What does it mean to contain information and be parametric? How can this be useful?
- *Developing and viewing forms—slabs, walls, etc.* Location and characteristics of elements in 3D. Geometry of modeling and location. Viewing and editing the model. Plan view, 3D views, section/elevation window.
- *Layers and stories.* The structure of the model. Navigating within the model.
- *Special objects.* Stair modeling and placement. Creation of custom objects.
- *Level of detail in a model.* What does level of detail mean? How can objects be "represented" as required?
- *Models from drawings.* A model will be created in ArchiCAD from an existing drawing set.
- *Drawings from models.* A model needs to have an organization that will permit the creation and management of the drawings required from it.
- *Project data.* The kind and location of information connected to the model.
- Introduction to complex models.
- *Presentations.*

First-Semester BIM Exercises

Exercise 2 is the first exercise where visualization is important. See Fig. 4.4. The model has to be constructed from two plan and two section drawings of the object. This exercise introduces complex organizations with layers and stories as well as multiplying and copying elements.

In Exercise 3 the student is provided with several drawings that represent the building and the schedules for the doors and windows. See Fig. 4.5. It is the first exercise where

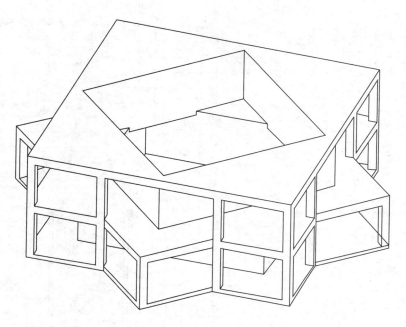

Figure 4.4
Model for
Exercise 2.

more realistic construction document information is presented to build a 3D model. Besides the emphasis on visualizing the project from the documents, it introduces parametric objects and custom library parts. The trim under the roof gables and the complex tower roof are the main modeling challenges in this exercise.

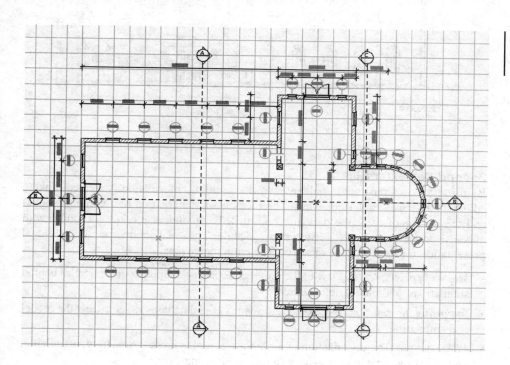

Figure 4.5
Drawings for
Exercise 3.

Figure 4.5
(*Continued*)

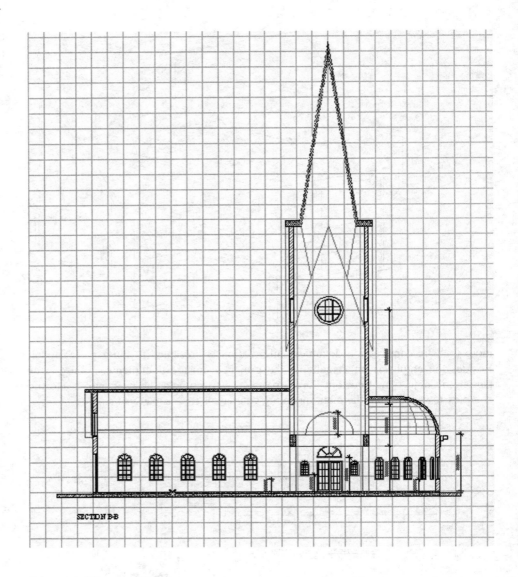

SECTION B-B

Second-Semester BIM

By using Vico's Constructor and NavisWorks, building information is created, linked, edited, and viewed in various ways. The focus is on the creation of a complex model and the management of the data attached to it. Each student produces a model with attached cost estimate and construction schedule. The final product is an individual presentation for each student's project. The class topics are:

- *Modeling principles.* Review of the previous semester. Emphasis on principles behind simulations, and model organization.

- *Importing information.* Use existing drawings (and databases) to construct the model and simulation.

- *File structure.* The organization of a file for a complex model. Attaching, organizing, and releasing outside information (imported drawings, etc.).

Figure 4.5
(*Continued*)

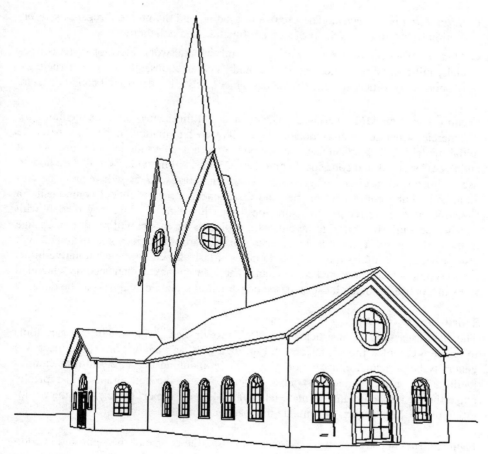

- *Model planning strategies.* What needs to be modeled? How much detail does the model need? What should be addressed, and how?
- *Building information.* What information should be attached and in which form? How is this information accessible and editable? Focus on the management of various information sources.
- *Estimator.* Recipe and database development linked to the model.
- *Project control.* Construction Schedule development based on the 3D model.
- *Object embedded information.* Parametric objects.
- *Hyperlinked information.* Connections between the model and outside information sources.
- *Model viewing and analysis.* Using NavisWorks to analyze the complex model.
- *NavisWorks clash detection.*
- *NavisWorks sequencing.*
- *NavisWorks rendering.*
- *Reporting.* Recording and communicating the results of viewing and analysis.

- *Information management.* The use of information and the protocol regarding information flow. How does the project team function and collaborate?
- *Modeling specialty items,* i.e., railings and other metal work, elevator systems, specialty utilities, large medical equipment and its connections, site drainage structures, temporary construction facilities and equipment, special underground conditions, etc.

Second-Semester BIM Exercises   The exercises of this semester treat a medium-size commercial structure which is modeled in detail by each individual in the class. After the initial modeling, each student will also produce more detailed models of the structural and HVAC systems and combine them in NavisWorks. All individuals will learn how to use Estimator, Control and NavisWorks. The Estimator exercises will require the creation of building component recipes and the connection of the model components in Constructor to these recipes in Estimator. This will result in a quantity takeoff with attached cost information. Editing either the recipe or the model will result in a change of the project costs. The productivity rates that are part of the recipes in Estimator will also provide time information for the duration of tasks based on the quantitative information coming from the model components. These durations can then become scheduled tasks in Control, so that a location based construction schedule analysis can be done.

Third-Semester BIM

The class uses Vico's Constructor, Autodesk's Revit, and various other software tools to create a complex model, attach relevant data to it, and analyze it. The project will generally be an actual construction project in its planning phase, e.g. a new campus facility. The architect, general contractor and some of the consultants will typically make the design and planning materials available and support the class in the exploration of a BIM approach to simulate the management of the project.

Each student chooses two areas to focus on during the course of the semester, in addition to the use of NavisWorks to manage the model. All work is done by groups and requires collaboration within and among groups and coordination of their work. The entire class will develop communication protocol and management structure for the exercises. The final goal for the class is a group presentation of the models, the coordination of the components, possible cost studies and construction schedule analysis. The students will select from the following potential teams:

- *Constructor modeling team.* Creating an architectural model.
- *Revit modeling team.* Creating an architectural model.
- *Tekla modeling team.* Creating a structural model. The construction of a virtual structural system that addresses all possible levels of detail.
- *HVAC modeling team.* Creating a model of the HVAC system, probably in Constructor but perhaps in another software package. Simulating the HVAC and possibly plumbing and electrical systems for a structure. Various levels of detail are possible.

This team will also model plumbing, electrical, etc., as required.

- *Site modeling team.* Creating a model of the setting of the project, including the underground work and temporary facilities for the construction process, landscaping, etc.

- *Estimating team.* Assigning cost information to the model components and creation of an actual project cost estimate, including soft costs.
- *Scheduling team.* Creating and importing schedules as well as developing time information for the model components and making construction sequence movies.
- *Detailed modeling team.* Using various software tools to create detailed models of specific building systems.

Fourth-Semester BIM

Modeling Steel Connections in Tekla   This last semester is used as an internship where the students create and analyze a model of an actual construction project in coordination with the actual construction company and project's consultants. This work consists of the application of the skills learned in the previous semesters.

The nature of the work will entirely depend on the requirements of the chosen project. The work environment and project team structure will mimic that of an actual construction business. Separate collaborating teams will be assembled for the creation of

- An architectural model
- A structural model
- A site model
- An HVAC model
- Models of other utilities etc.
- A cost estimate
- A construction schedule and sequenced animation

One student from each team will be responsible for coordinating the team's efforts and collaborating with the various other teams and outside sources. Several persons from the class will also be responsible for the larger management issues that relate to all the team's efforts, such as BIM planning and updating.

Third- and fourth-semester exercise examples include modeling structural steel columns, beams and bracing in Tekla.

The first step is the analysis of the structural drawings in order to visualize the arrangement of the structural elements. First the plan is consulted for the location and size of the columns and beams; then the column schedule will indicate the type and length of the columns. See Fig. 4.6.

This project provides students with very useful plan reading and visualization practice as well as a structural modeling exercise.

The level of detail attainable in the Tekla model allows it to be used in place of shop drawings for the fabrication of structural steel. Tekla software is used from the design and analysis phase of the steel through its fabrication phase. With a

Figure 4.6

(*a*) Plan view showing beam locations and sizes; (*b*) a detail view of the structural plan showing the column identification; (*c*) the column schedule; and (*d*) a 3D model showing columns and beams (on top of piles, caps, and grade beams).

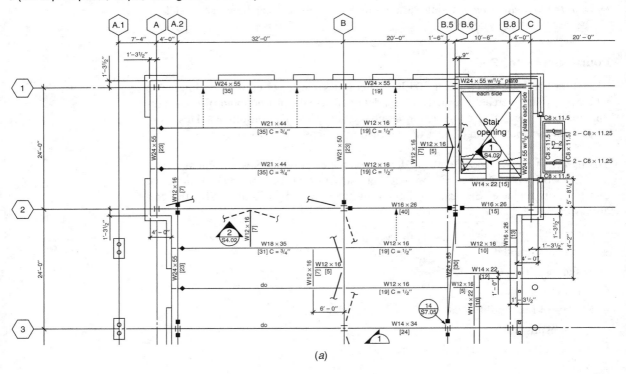

(*a*)

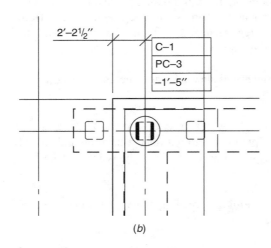

(*b*)

Figure 4.6
(*Continued*)

C–1	C–2	C–3	C–4	C–5	C–6	C–7	C–8	C–9
Typical perimeter column U.N.O.	Typical interior column U.N.O.			B & B.6/2 G.4 & H/3 B.5 & B.8/5	B.5/6	B/1 & 8 H/2	B.9/6 B.5 & B.9/7 H.4 & J.1/B.3	
							HSS5 × 5 × $^3/_8$	
W10 × 33	W12 × 50			W12 × 50	W12 × 50	W10 × 33		
						HSS6 × 6 × $^3/_8$		
W12 × 53	W12 × 87	W12 × 53		W12 × 87	W12 × 87	W12 × 53		W12 × 53
			HSS4 × 4 × $^3/_8$					
1 S4.01	1 S4.01	3 S4.01	3 S4.01	1 S4.01	1 S4.01	1 S4.01		1 S4.01

(*c*)

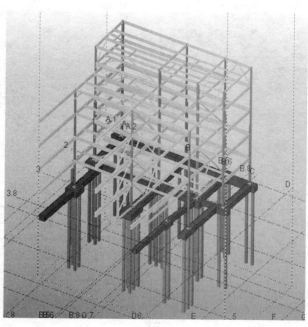

(*d*)

construction sequence analysis in NavisWorks it can also be useful in the assembly phase.

The following images (see Figs. 4.6 a and 4.7) show the steps taken by students to analyze the drawings in order to create the steel connections in the Tekla model.

Figure 4.7

(*a*) connection plan view; (*b*) connection elevation view; (*c*) elevation detail of the connection; and (*d*) a 3D connection detail in Tekla.

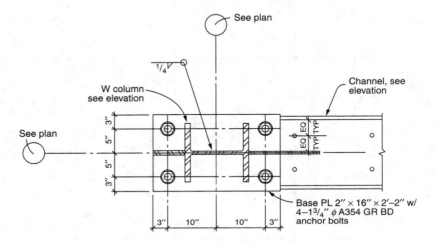

BASE PLATE

Plan detail	Scale: 1″ = 1′-0′	**9**
	KPFF K000O	S4.08

(*a*)

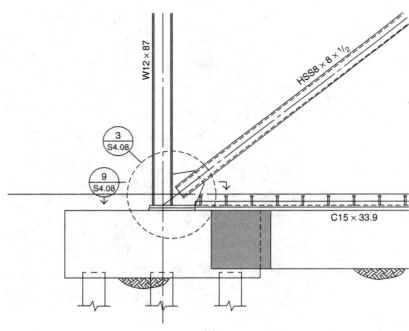

(*b*)

Figure 4.7
(*Continued*)

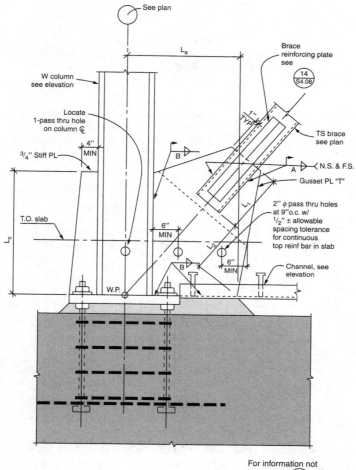

See plan

Brace
reinforcing plate
see
14
S4.08

W column
see elevation

Locate
1-pass thru hole
on column ℄

TS brace
see plan

4"
MIN

B

3/4" Stiff PL

1"
TYP

A ⟩ N.S. & F.S.

Gusset PL "T"

T.O. slab

L_c

L_a

6"
MIN

2" φ pass thru holes
at 9"o.c. w/
1/2" ± allowable
spacing tolerance
for continuous
top reinf bar in slab

B

6"
MIN

Channel, see
elevation

W.P.

For information not
noted, see 14 SIM
S4.08

BRACED FRAME CONN

Detail	Scale 1" = 1'-0"	**3**
	KPFF K000O	S4.08

(*c*)

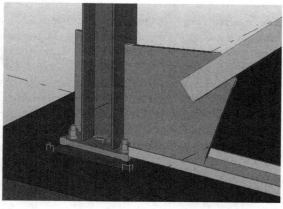

(*d*)

Figure 4.8

Plan model view
with 2D Autocad
background plan.

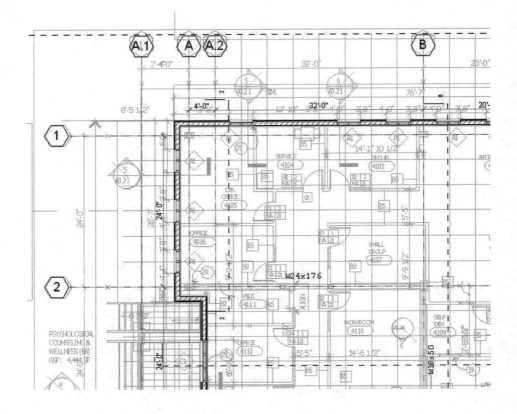

Figure 4.8 shows a plan view with the background 2D Autocad plan drawing being built upon in Constructor with 3D elements. This is an early stage of the model with only the exterior walls placed. Note also the duplication of the grid line system; this is a practical way to ensure that the X and Y coordinates of the model and the plan are registered properly. Part of the challenge in this exercise is the management of all the imported drawings and their layers in the model file. The drawings function as the base for the construction of the model. This speeds up the modeling considerably and functions as a good coordination check throughout the modeling process.

The images in Fig. 4.9 show the background 2D Autocad structural plan drawing being built upon in Constructor in 3D plan view and the section view of the same elements. This is an early stage of the structural model with some of the 3D structural steel elements.

NavisWorks is a flexible tool that permits the viewing of models in various ways, Fig. 4.10 shows two of the components of the complex model being analyzed for clashes, while Fig. 4.11 is a rendering created in NavisWorks for presentation purposes.

Incorporating BIM in Existing Classes

The use of BIM in education can serve to help in design, fabrication, or management-related training. These three areas will all require a different approach to the integration

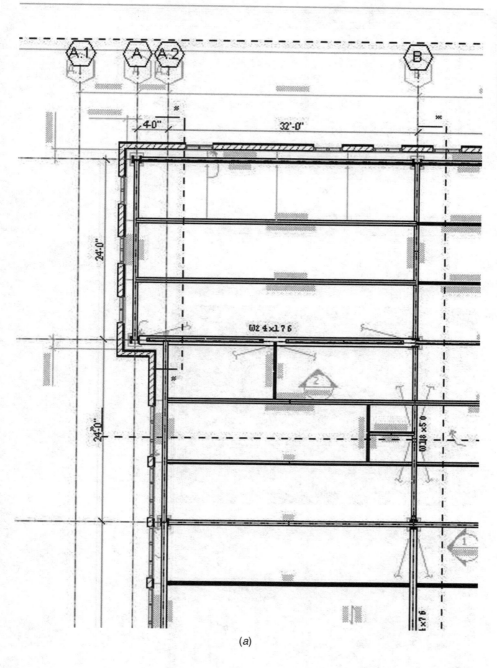

(a)

Figure 4.9
Constructor in (a) plan view with Autocad structural plan as background and (b) the section view of the same elements.

of BIM technology, and its application depends on the discipline in which it serves as a tool. In construction management it will not be used as a design tool, but may be used for management and fabrication. In architecture it will primarily be a design tool, and in some engineering disciplines it may serve in all three capacities.

Figure 4.9
(*Continued*)

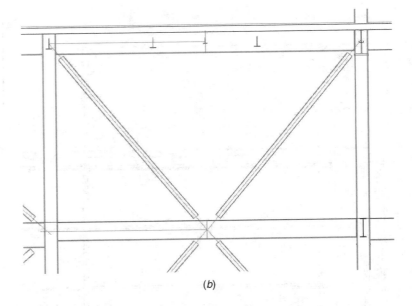

(*b*)

Figure 4.10

The combined
structural and
HVAC model
as seen in
NavisWorks.

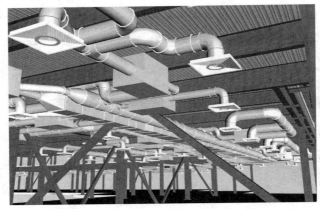

Figure 4.11

A rendered image
from NavisWorks.

Construction Management

When BIM is incorporated in existing construction management classes, it will perform very differently in beginning classes (first two years of the program), where the students have no prior construction knowledge, than in advanced classes (last two years of the program). The first two years of a curriculum in construction management are devoted to the familiarization of the students with the basic concepts and skills related to the construction industry. Learning the use of BIM can aid the students in learning to visualize components of structures and their relationships to one another. Building a project model also develops (and tests) the ability to visualize a project from construction documents.

Classical drafting is disappearing from the modern curricula. Drafting has traditionally been the best way for students to develop the ability to read plans and learn to visualize the relationships between 2D and 3D representations. The drafting exercises have not been replaced with anything equally robust to teach these critical skills. With the advent of BIM it is again possible to use the 2D construction documents of a project to build a 3D model, so that plan reading and visualization skills are developed in an even more efficient manner than through the old drafting exercises.

The introduction of BIM into classes which address estimating, scheduling, productivity analysis, etc., is even more challenging because it supposes a rather substantial understanding of the BIM and various analysis tools. To utilize the BIM in peripheral subjects, the students must already have completed the fundamental BIM training. This will allow the class to focus on the subject at hand and treat it in relation to BIM, rather than focus on the BIM process required for the specific subject. This also explains why it is important for BIM students to have enough understanding of all related construction management subjects to be able to understand and apply BIM concepts. Most exercises will consist of the interaction between both construction and BIM concepts and processes.

A SmartBoard is a good tool to engage several students at the same time in a BIM discussion. The interactive nature of this tool makes it ideal for educational purposes. See Fig. 4.12 where the SmartBoard at CSU Chico serves as a medium for a model analysis.

Figure 4.12

The SmartBoard in use by students and faculty in the lab.

Architecture and Engineering

Traditionally the architectural curriculum has been more ready to adopt the advantages of 3D modeling software to teach design skills. This makes it a natural fit for the transition into BIM. On the other hand, BIM is generally more focused on the development of models of structural systems, MEP systems, etc., the details of which are generally not the subject of architectural training. The architect's model is one of the components of the BIM, but it does not constitute the whole BIM.

The civil engineering disciplines are similar to architecture in the sense that they generally also represent one of the consultants of a construction project. This means that they too will produce one of the components of a BIM. Civil engineers will generally produce the structural framing model, or perhaps the earthwork model for the site of a larger project.

Other Disciplines

Mechanical, electrical, and plumbing disciplines also contribute components to the BIM. These models, like others, can begin as design models and be developed into coordination and fabrication models. The guidelines and suggestions of this book will apply in general, but the tool-related specifics can be very different depending on the particular software package.

The above mentioned characteristics for the design disciplines point to the relevance of collaboration between students in different disciplines. This will present a formidable challenge in most academic institutions. Some of the programs at Stanford University are the closest to addressing this multidisciplinary collaboration.

Faculty Preparation

It is clearly important to provide qualified faculty to teach BIM. During the first two semesters of the BIM curriculum, the content is technical and will require faculty capable to guide students through the conceptual as well as technical learning processes. This stage will require a lot of individual attention for the students. Actual experience with the software and good control over the student exercises are essential for faculty in this phase of the curriculum. The students will learn in various subject areas from these initial exercises, and a variety of questions may arise from their work. The student will generally need to learn to read drawings, understand the construction process, and try to come up with a way to represent construction objects by using modeling tools. The abstract nature of the simpler 3D models will need to be explained in detail to the student who has to be able to visualize the actual construction conditions and relate them to the modeling activity. Many questions will need to be answered appropriately in order not to discourage or confuse the students. This necessitates a certain degree of experience and confidence on the part of the faculty.

The third and fourth semesters will be much more varied for both the students and the faculty; and the role of the faculty is more like that of the BIM manager, while the role of the students is more like that of the BIM operator. This takes a little pressure off the faculty in relation to learning all the various software packages used in the process. It is nevertheless essential for faculty to be able to understand the concepts and technicalities of most of the software, but it is not necessary to be an expert with all the tools.

The students will learn fast and be able to get the necessary technical support directly from the companies that provide these tools. It is worthwhile to arrange for software representatives to schedule training sessions for the students in the use of those tools. The students should already have worked with the software somewhat, so that they will have prepared a list of specific questions for the session. The answers to these questions will often be the most useful part of the training, and they can often lead to quantum jumps in the level of understanding of the use of the software.

In general the faculty has the responsibility to stay in contact with the professional practitioners of BIM. The more varied and frequent the contacts, the more understanding and technical expertise will be available to the students. The preparation for the professional applications of BIM needs to be as closely aligned with the needs of the industry as possible. Most construction companies who are using BIM are very generous in providing help for educational purposes; and they are also eager to have the students properly prepared for their entry into the industry upon graduation. This gives faculty a unique position between the industry and the students in the classroom, a position that can be developed into a useful one for both the school and the industry.

5 Case Studies

The following case studies provide examples of the application of many of the concepts discussed in this book. A number of individuals have contributed specific projects in which BIM techniques have been applied. Each contribution is unique and interesting in its own right. There will be something here for everyone interested in the subject. It will also be clear that, throughout the contributions of the various persons who have helped to create this book, the messages are generally very similar; this should help to confirm that BIM is a vast change in process that will improve many aspects of the construction industry, by introducing a new level of collaboration rarely witnessed before in this field.

CASE 1: DPR CONSTRUCTION

Author's Comment

Dean and Atul have been working very intentionally to introduce BIM techniques and tools to DPR construction projects. Each experience has been planned and analyzed so that it would become a lesson for the next project. These developmental experiments have led to the following case study. It is possibly the most comprehensive analysis available of its kind and will be invaluable for anyone interested in implementing these techniques into her or his own work environment. This high level of development and implementation of BIM is commendable and rarely found in the construction industry, it shows the deep commitment of DPR to the improvement of building construction.

A Practitioner's Guide to Virtual Design and Construction (3D/4D) Tools on Commercial Projects: Case Study of a Large Healthcare Project

by Atul Khanzode* and Dean Reed†

Applying virtual building tools on fast-track commercial construction projects remains a challenge in the industry. The current traditional processes rely on two-dimensional

*Virtual Building Coordinator, DPR Construction, Inc., Redwood City, CA, USA
†Lean Construction Coordinator, DPR Construction, Inc., Redwood City, CA, USA

(2D) drawings and light tables and can result in costly errors and project delays. With the advent of virtual design and construction (VDC) tools, it is now possible to vastly improve the project delivery process. This case study highlights DPR Construction, Inc.'s real-world application of VDC tools and offers specific guidelines for industry practitioners on how to apply VDC tools, specifically three-dimensional and four-dimensional (3D and 4D) CAD for purposes that include sequencing and coordination of mechanical, electrical, plumbing and fire protection systems (MEP/FP systems). Key areas covered are as follows:

- How to set up a process to benefit from using VDC tools
- How to set up the organization to take advantage of what VDC tools have to offer
- How to be a learning organization that benefits from VDC tools

To drive true change and enhance the delivery process requires dedication, learning, and a willingness to experiment. It also demands shifting paradigms. What DPR has experienced is that the benefits are there for those who are willing to learn and become reflective practitioners. The lessons shared in this chapter are meant to inspire others to try VDC tools on commercial construction projects and help take the industry to new levels of performance.

Introduction

As DPR does with its construction projects, this study begins with the end in mind—reporting the results. Upon completing a 250,000-ft^2 medical office building (MOB) and adjacent parking garage for Camino Medical Group, an affiliate of Sutter Health, DPR realized the following benefits through the use of VDC tools (3D/4D CAD) for the coordination of MEP/FP systems:

- Virtually zero field conflicts among various systems
- Less than 0.2 percent rework
- Productivity improvement of more than 30 percent for the mechanical contractor
- Less than 2 hours per month spent on field coordination issues by the superintendent for the general contractor
- Only two field issues related to Requests for Information (RFIs)
- Zero change orders related to field conflict issues

These results are unimaginable for any modern construction project with the complexities involved in the project delivery and the systems.

What about this project makes it unique?

It is natural to gravitate toward the use of VDC tools. Although a factor, it was far from the sole determinant of the dramatic results achieved by this project team. The "yin" is the technology, and the "yang" is the process. Understanding how people work together, how to structure the process, and how to adjust along the way is an equally significant, if not more significant, determinant of project success. In short, a team of reflective practitioners, with the right tools, has the capability to achieve equally tremendous results. The following example of coordinating MEP systems using VDC tools helps illustrate the point.

Coordination of MEP/FP Systems Using VDC Tools

On modern day high-technology projects, MEP/FP systems account for about 40 to 60 percent of the total construction cost. The complexity of these systems has increased over the years. At the same time, the cost of materials has increased, and the availability of skilled labor to install these systems is steadily declining. Owners also are demanding that projects be delivered quicker and at lower cost. Project teams are constantly seeking newer and better methods to address these challenges.

One of the biggest areas of improvement is the design and coordination of MEP/FP systems. On many construction projects, the coordination is still done using 2D drawings and light tables in what is called a *sequential composite overlay process* (SCOP).[5] This method of coordination has proved to be inadequate and has led to many conflicts among systems, lack of confidence among subcontractors to prefabricate, rework in the field, and low productivity installing these systems in the field.

Project teams are exploring the use of virtual design and construction (VDC)[2] tools such as 3D/4D and collaborative project delivery approaches such as lean construction[1] to reduce the inherent waste in the traditional process and bring greater efficiency and productivity to the projects.

The authors have recently implemented VDC to manage the coordination of MEP/FP systems on two major health care projects in northern California. The results prove that there are tremendous benefits to applying VDC to coordinate the MEP/FP systems. On one of the projects, using the VDC tools combined with the Lean Project Delivery System (LPDS), for the coordination of the MEP/FP, the project team realized the six significant benefits listed in the "Introduction" above.

What does it take to achieve these results?

Based on DPR's experience of implementing VDC tools, combined with LPDS, on the Camino Medical Group medical office building, it requires the creation of a collaborative work environment, where multidisciplinary teams of designers and contractors can apply the VDC tools for the MEP/FP coordination process. The questions that project teams need to address include these:

1. How can one create a business case or ROI for applying VDC to the MEP/FP coordination process?

2. How can one set up a project organization to best utilize the VDC tools?

3. What roles should each of the project team members play in the coordination process?

4. How can one address issues such as sharing of models and drawings and other technical setup issues?

5. How should the coordination process be structured and managed?

6. How should the installation process be structured and managed?

The guidelines provided help address these questions and are therefore organized into the following sections:

1. The business case for applying VDC tools for MEP coordination

2. Role of the general contractor (GC) and specialty contractors in the coordination process

3. Use of the 3D MEP/FP models for prefabrication efforts

4. Levels of detail in the architectural, structural, and the MEP/FP models and potential benefits

5. The coordination process
   a. Set up the technical logistics.
   b. Kick off the coordination process.
   c. Establish the sequence of coordination.
   d. Manage handoffs between designers and detailers.
   e. Work in the "big room."
   f. Use 3D clash detection tools to identify and resolve conflicts.
   g. Manage the process using the Last Planner System.
   h. Make the final signoff.

6. The installation process
   a. Create the 4D models for MEP coordination.
   b. Update the 4D models for coordination.

The Case for Applying VDC Tools for the MEP Coordination Process

Owner Return on Investment   Minimizing cost escalation on capital projects is a tremendous pressure that owners currently face. In a market that has been escalating with material and labor price increases over the last few years, it has been even more challenging to predict costs over the duration of the projects.

The question many owners are bound to ask is, What value does the use of VDC tools provide?

The proper use of VDC tools has tremendous potential to reduce uncertainty, improve productivity and quality, and reduce the overall cost; but first the team should take responsibility for clearly identifying the return on investment (ROI) for the owner. VDC (3D/4D) modeling for MEP/FP systems coordination is an investment like any other. Currently, 3D modeling and coordination take more time than drafting in 2D space and overlaying the drawings on a light table. The 3D model-based process requires more planning and greater precision as the team is working with parametrically correct objects rather than lines and arcs. Another factor is that creation of the 3D models is best done by real builders: people who have put work in place and have learned 3D modeling. Such highly skilled builders are in short supply and command high wages. Case studies have shown that early subcontractor involvement in design allows the construction knowledge to be included in the design process.[4] With VDC tools, this knowledge can be captured in a virtual 3D model.

With all that being said, experience has proved that using VDC tools in a collaborative coordination effort up front allows a team to gain greater value during construction. The Camino MOB project reported an ROI of 2 to 3 times the original investment in VDC within 6 to 9 months. Savings accrued through greater prefabrication, elimination of conflicts among the various systems, reduction in change orders, and an increase in productivity of installation without crews struggling with other trades for the same space to install their components. The ROI is therefore accrued from the time design is completed to the time all rough-in activities for the MEP/FP systems are completed.

The owner, as the stakeholder with the money and final risk as well as the expectation of gaining the greatest value, must be willing to make the initial investment. As the investor, the owner should make sure that the construction contracts allow for the recapture of the cost of work savings to provide ROI. For example, the contracts for all the MEP/FP subcontractors were guaranteed maximum price (GMP) contracts on one of the projects. The team used VDC tools to eliminate the risk of missed coordination and was able to achieve higher productivity. Subcontractors also were able to return the savings to the owner's incentive sharing plan.

On projects using VDC in a collaborative effort, the owner should gain the benefit of anticipated higher productivity when the project GMP is set. On the health care project for Sutter Health, the approach of GMP with shared savings and an incentive plan worked; however, there are other approaches, such as partnering and self-assembled teams, that could also work just as effectively.

Role of the General Contractor and Specialty Contractors in the Coordination Process

The use of VDC tools requires the team to evaluate what role each member should play in the project delivery process. Each party brings a unique skill set to the table, and the use of VDC tools maximizes the benefits. The following are the roles that each party can play in the coordination process.

General Contractor   The GC enables the VDC process by acting as facilitator rather than author of the drawings. The GC enables and coordinates the handoff of information from the architects and engineers (A/Es) to the subcontractors as well as the modeling and coordination work itself.

The GC's role in initial modeling and coordination is much the same as that on the project as a whole: to develop a workable detailing schedule together with the A/Es and subcontractors to support the construction schedule. Once the schedule is established, the GC's project engineer assigned to MEP coordination works together with the detailers to achieve signoff milestones using the Last Planner System.[1]

Specialty Contractor   The specialty contractors are responsible for modeling their portion of work using 3D tools. On the Camino MOB project that used the VDC tools for MEP coordination, the HVAC contractor took a lead role in the coordination process.

The HVAC equipment, including VAV boxes, fire smoke dampers, duct shafts, and low- and medium-pressure ducts, takes up the most space in the above-ceiling space, and the detailers of other trades (plumbing, electrical, and fire sprinklers) would much rather know in advance how the HVAC equipment and duct shafts andmain ducts are routed since that has the greatest impact on how they will route their utilities. The HVAC contractor, therefore, should model at least the main medium-pressure and low-pressure duct lines and shafts so that other trades can coordinate and route their utilities around these duct lines.

The specialty contractors are also involved early in the process so they can provide input into the constructability and operations issues to the design team. Some contracting methods that allow for early involvement of specialty contractors include the design-assist and design-build contracting methods. In both methods, the specialty contractors are brought in early (somewhere between the conceptual and schematic design phases). In the design-build method, the specialty contractor is also the engineer of record for the MEP systems; in the design-assist method, this responsibility may rest with an independent or third-party engineering and design firm. Both models work well for the coordination process.

Use of 3D MEP/FP Models for Prefabrication Efforts

On the Camino MOB project, tremendous benefits of prefabrication have been attributed directly to the use of VDC in the MEP/FP coordination process. The HVAC contractor alone saved 33 percent of field labor hours by creating parametric and fully coordinated 3D models and then prefabricating the medium-pressure duct and low-pressure ducts.

Fully coordinated and clash-free, parametric 3D models of MEP/FP systems are a prerequisite for extensive prefabrication. The GC and subcontractors should set up an explicit target for prefabricating assemblies off-site at the beginning of the project. This provides a goal to track to and also motivates the entire team to use the VDC tools to create clash-free models of MEP/FP systems. The fabrication shops can then use these models for prefabrication, knowing with greater certainty that the assemblies they are putting together will fit in the field.

What to Model?

One of the questions that most teams have when starting the 3D modeling effort is, What should we model in 3D? This question should be answered by the whole team involved in the 3D coordination effort. The goals set out by the team for the coordination effort will play a big role in determining what to model. On most projects ME/FP coordination can be divided into two distinct efforts:

- Underground coordination of utilities such as plumbing and electrical
- Above-ceiling coordination of all the MEP/FP utilities

If the teams decide to do both underground and above-ceiling coordination using 3D tools, then elements such as foundations and framing are required for the coordination effort.

Another question is, What level of detail should be included in the model? There clearly is a tradeoff between the levels of detail in the model and the uses it can provide to the coordination effort. For example, inclusion of casework details in the architectural model is necessary for determining the exact locations of the plumbing rough-ins in the wall but is not needed for coordination and conflict detection with other systems such as HVAC. The project team should collectively decide the level of detail question.

The coordination of MEP/FP systems using VDC tools requires that project teams plan to create 3D models for the following:

- Architectural elements such as interior walls and ceilings
- Structural elements such as the main structural framing, slabs and foundations
- Mechanical systems such as ductwork
- Plumbing systems such as the gravity lines and hot and cold water piping
- Electrical systems such as the major conduits and cable trays
- Fire protection systems with the mains and branches
- Other specialty systems such as medical gases or others depending on the project

In the following sections, a summary for each of the various models is provided, followed by a table that documents what benefits are possible for the corresponding levels of detail in a particular model.

Architectural Model   The architectural model forms the basis of design and is used by the team members as a reference point for their own systems. Ideally, the architect should design in 3D space, rather than modeling 2D design drawings in 3D space. If the 3D model is created from the 2D design documents, it is critical that it be kept up to date (i.e., that it reflect changes in design).

Wall thickness and height, hard ceilings and soffits, suspended acoustical ceilings, and casework with correct fixture locations must be accurately modeled, because these are necessary for effective coordination of MEP/FP systems. On the MOB project for Camino Medical Group, the architect modeled the external wall panels, internal walls, doors, and the parking garage in 3D space (Fig. 5.1.1). Modeling these systems in 3D space is a must, as it allows the other team members to accurately locate their own systems. For example, the interior wall and ceiling model allows the HVAC subcontractor to locate the diffusers in the rooms and allows the electrical contractor to locate fixtures in the room accurately.

Structural Model   An accurate 3D model of the foundation system and vertical and horizontal structural steel framing is also a must for the MEP/FP contractors. If it is a steel-framed building, the model should also include connections such as gusset plates and brace frame connections.

The structural model should feature the miscellaneous metal supports and connection points to external building elements such as GFRC panels. All these details play a

Figure 5.1.1

An isometric view of the Camino Medical Office Building (MOB) project. The snapshot shows a three-story MOB and a two-story parking structure. This 3D formed the basis of the MEP/FP coordination for the Camino MOB project. (*Image courtesy of DPR Construction, Inc., California.*)

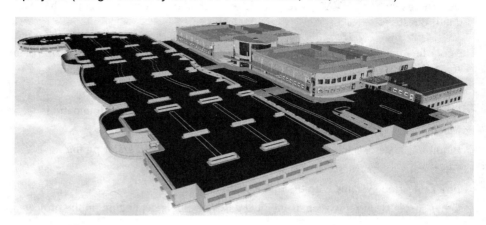

crucial role in the modeling of MEP/FP systems. For example, the underground plumbing lines and electrical conduits are located in reference to the foundations; the seismic bracing for the ductwork and other systems is located in reference to the structural elements such as slabs and steel beam and columns. Figure 5.1.2 shows a structural steel and foundation model of the Camino MOB that was created by the structural designer for the project.

As with the architectural 3D model, the structural model must accurately reflect design changes at all times, because detailing of the MEP/FP systems will be done in reference to the structural-steel framing.

If the design and coordination of MEP/FP systems begin before a steel fabricator is on board, then the steel model from the structural designer should be used as a starting point for the modeling of MEP/FP systems.

Ideally, the systems should also be checked against the fabrication level structural 3D model. The GC should request that the structural steel fabricator include a detailed 3D fabrication model in its price. The steel fabricator must also agree to make this model available to the detailing team just as soon as it has been reviewed and approved for fabrication. This fabrication model will show all connections and be much closer to what will be installed in the field than the structural engineer's model.

The steel fabrication model should be imported into clash detection software. This model should then be clash-tested against the MEP/FP systems that have already been clash-tested with the structural engineer's 3D model. If any clashes exist, they should

Figure 5.1.2

Screenshot of structural 3D model for the Camino MOB. The screenshot shows the beams, columns, brace frame connections, and foundation elements such as grade beams and spread footings for the Camino MOB. This model formed the basis of the underground and the above-ceiling MEP/FP coordination for the Camino MOB project. (*Image courtesy of DPR Construction, Inc., California.*)

be resolved, so MEP fabrication can commence with a high level of confidence that the MEP systems will fit in the actual structure being built.

Mechanical Model One of the main goals of the mechanical contractor is to be able to use the 3D model for the prefabrication of duct and piping assemblies and use it to plan activities such as installing inserts. Currently, major mechanical subcontractors already have the capability to produce 3D models of their systems but are hampered in their prefabrication efforts as they do not have the confidence that their systems will be clash-free in the field because other trades often produce their designs only in 2D space.

In a VDC-enabled 3D MEP/FP coordination process, all the subcontractors need to produce their designs as 3D models. This allows the mechanical contractor to have greater confidence that the assemblies will fit as he or she has coordinated them with other trades and their 3D models.

The mechanical model consists of

- HVAC duct
- Connections between ducts, hangers, and inserts
- Seismic supports
- Diffusers
- VAV boxes
- Fire smoke dampers (FSDs)
- Shafts, duct and pipe insulation
- Heating hot water piping

The duct and piping models are then used for prefabrication. The hangers, inserts, and seismic support model are used to install inserts and hangers. These 3D models also allow other trades to coordinate effectively with the mechanical systems. For example, Fig. 5.1.3 offers a snapshot from the mechanical model of the Camino MOB project and shows the medium-pressure duct, low-pressure duct, hangers and inserts, and heating hot water piping.

Figure 5.1.3

Snapshot of the mechanical system (HVAC duct, VAV boxes, and heating hot water pipe) of the first-floor SE quadrant of the Camino MOB project. The medium- and low-pressure ducts (in blue) and the heating hot water piping (in purple) allow other trades to determine the location of the mechanical systems in 3D and use it to route and coordinate their systems. (*Image courtesy of DPR Construction, Inc., California.*) See also color insert.

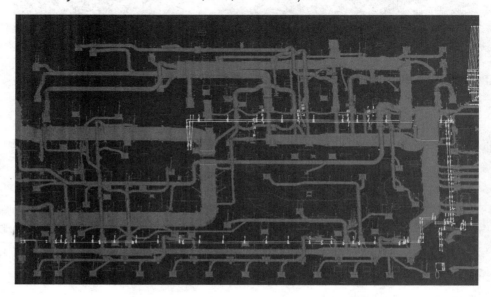

Electrical Model On most projects, the electrical systems typically do not occupy a lot of above-ceiling space and also have some routing flexibility due to the use of flexible cable and wiring. Although this can be an argument for not creating a 3D model of electrical systems, it should be understood that electrical subcontractors do use rigid conduits, cable trays, junction boxes, panels, etc., that do need to be coordinated with other systems. Therefore, the electrical contractor should model the branch and feeder conduits, all underground conduits, junction boxes, all lighting, all lighting supports for specialty lighting, all the cable trays and other supports, bundles of cables or wiring, and the outlets. This allows the team to coordinate with the electrical systems and the electrical contractor to prefabricate and prebend most of the conduits that need to be bent as well as precut cables and wires to the length required. Assemblies can also be created in the shop rather than the field. For example, Fig. 5.1.4 shows a screenshot of the electrical systems for the Camino MOB and shows the lighting fixtures, conduits, and cable trays modeled in 3D space.

Plumbing Model The two major plumbing systems on most construction projects are gravity-based systems to carry the wastewater and pressure-based systems to carry hot and cold water. In addition, specialty systems such as medical gases in hospitals are part of the plumbing system.

The challenge with gravity systems is that the systems should satisfy the slope requirements for the wastewater to flow from one end to another. This requires the plumbing contractor to have relatively uninterrupted sloped gravity lines, which is a significant challenge in the coordination effort.

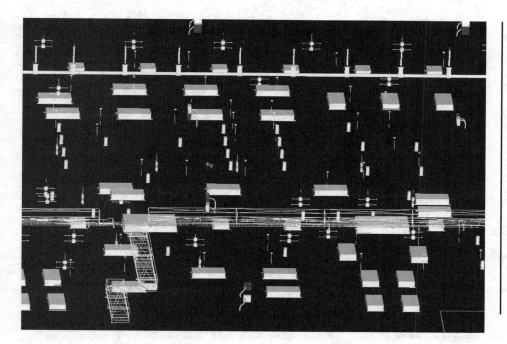

Figure 5.1.4

Snapshot of the electrical model for the first-floor SE quadrant of the Camino MOB project. The snapshot shows a 3D view of all the lighting fixtures, junction boxes, cable trays, and major conduit runs for this quadrant on the Camino MOB project. (*Image courtesy of DPR Construction, Inc., California.*)

As with the mechanical contractor, the plumbing contractor's objectives are to prefabricate the plumbing assemblies and determine the location of inserts and hangers by using the 3D model. Therefore, the plumbing contractor should model all his or her plumbing fixtures, graded cast iron pipelines, underground storm and sewer pipes, all major waste and vent lines, cold and hot water piping, seismic details, all boiler and other equipment, and specialty piping (such as medical gas piping) and specialty equipment. This detail allows the plumbing contractor to prefabricate materials in the shop environment. For example, Fig. 5.1.5 shows a screenshot of the 3D model with the plumbing gravity lines, fixtures, hot and cold water pipes for the first-ffloor SE quadrant of the Camino MOB project.

Sprinkler Model   The fire protection contractor should model the mains and branches, the drop pipes, and the exact location of drops in the ceiling. This allows the contractor to lay out the mains and branches, prefabricate and also install inserts before the deck is poured. For example, Fig. 5.1.6 shows a snapshot of the 3D sprinkler model for one of the quadrants of the Camino MOB with its mains, branches, and sprinkler drops.

Levels of Detail in Architectural, Structural, and MEP/FP Models and Potential Uses and Benefits

Two of the key questions when applying VDC methodologies to the 3D MEP/FP coordination process are, What level of detail should be included in the models? and What uses and benefits can a team obtain from the models? Table 5.1.1 summarizes answers to these questions.

Figure 5.1.5
Snapshot of the plumbing model of first-floor SE quadrant of Camino MOB. The snapshot shows the waste and vents and the plumbing fixture locations (in green), the cold water supply (in blue), and hot water lines (in red). (*Image courtesy of DPR Construction, Inc., California.*) See also color insert.

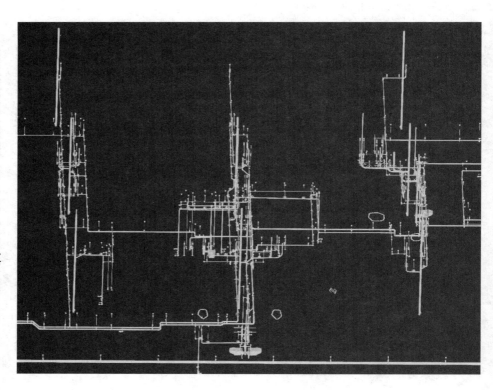

Figure 5.1.6
Snapshot of the 3D sprinkler model of first-floor SE quadrant of the Camino MOB. The screenshot shows the mains and branches and the sprinkler drops. (*Image courtesy of DPR Construction, Inc., California.*)

As indicated, there is a definite tradeoff between the levels of detail in the model and the benefits it provides in the coordination process. As a result, teams should identify what benefits they want out of the modeling and coordination process before deciding what level of details the models should include.

Managing the Coordination Process

Getting the Technical Logistics Right   Technical logistics plays an important part in the coordination process. It is likely that many models will be used on the project and each subcontractor will create her or his own model. Team members should agree on some basic rules at the outset of the project, so the sharing of electronic models is efficient and benefits the whole team. The issues that the project team should address include the following:

- Drawings are accompanied by standard word documents describing revisions therein.

- Drawings are posted to a project website, ftp site, or a document collaboration site determined by the team which includes the GC, subcontractors, owner, and A/E team.

- The collaboration site provides secure and remote access to all the model files.

- A clear file path structure is set up on the server to organize the model files and other relevant documents.

- Everyone works from and posts to the same server.

- The server is backed up every night.

- Borders and title blocks are not transmitted with the drawings.

- Insertion points for all drawings are based on the 0,0,0 insertion point established in the architectural drawings.

- Anything not intended to be seen in the drawing is erased prior to file transfer.

Table 5.1 .1
Level of detail in the 3D model and potential uses and benefits for each of the disciplines.

Model	Level of Detail	Uses and Benefits in MEP Coordination Process
Architectural model	Wall thickness and height	Required for routing main utilities, locating VAV boxes, identifying priority wall framing, wall penetrations, fire stopping
	Hard ceilings and soffits	Required for identifying HVAC diffuser locations, electrical fixture locations, routing of utilities
	Suspended acoustical ceilings	Required for identifying HVAC diffuser locations, electrical fixture locations, routing of utilities
	Casework with correct fixture locations	Useful for identifying the location of plumbing utilities rough-in in the walls
	Exterior wall/storefront	Useful for identifying the locations of rainwater leaders
	Shafts, wall chases	Required for identifying the correct locations of plumbing vents, HVAC shafts
Structural model	Foundations, grade beams	Required for coordination of underground utilities such as electrical, plumbing
	Beams and columns	Required for coordinating above-ceiling MEP/FP utilities
	Braces and gusset plates	Required for coordination of routing of MEP/FP piping
	Miscellaneous support steel such as exam light supports for medical facilities or Unistrut, etc.	Required for routing of MEP/FP utilities correctly
	External wall framing connections (such as connection between steel and GFRC panels)	Required to coordinate plumbing rainwater leaders
Mechanical model	Medium-pressure duct	Required for coordination and routing of other trades as well as prefabrication
	Low-pressure duct	Required for coordination and routing of other trades as well as prefabrication
	Shaft locations	Required for coordination and routing of other trades and for locating smoke dampers, etc.
	VAV boxes	Required for prefabrication purposes, coordination with HVAC heating hot water piping

Table 5.1.1
(*Continued*)

Model	Level of Detail	Uses and Benefits in MEP Coordination Process
	Fire smoke dampers	Useful for coordination, especially if walls are also provided in model
	Flex ducts	Useful for showing how low-pressure ducts connect to diffusers
	Diffuser locations	Useful for coordination of finish utilities with other fixtures in a room (electrical fixtures, etc.)
	Hangers and seismic bracing	Required for coordination and routing of other trades and for inserting deck correctly before installation begins
	HVAC piping to the VAV boxes	Main lines are required for coordinating with other trades, also required if they will be pre-fabricated; connections to VAV boxes can be left for field routing
	Rooftop equipment	Useful for coordinating with other trades (can be drawn as a 3D block)
Electrical model	Branch and feeder conduits	Required for coordination with other trades and for prefabrication
	All underground conduits	Required for underground MEP/FP coordination
	Junction boxes	Required for coordination with other trades
	All lighting fixtures	Required for coordination with other trades and finish utilities such as ceiling grid, sprinkler heads, HVAC diffusers, specialty lighting
	All lighting supports in case of specialty lighting	Required for routing and coordination with other trades
	All cable trays and other supports	Required for coordination with other trades
	Bundles of cables or wiring	Useful for coordination and prefabrication
	Outlets and switch locations in rooms	Useful for prefabrication but not required for coordination with other trades (typically modeled in 2D)

(*Continued*)

Table 5.1.1
(Continued)

Model	Level of Detail	Uses and Benefits in MEP Coordination Process
	Hangers	Required for coordination with other trades and for inserting deck
	Equipment panels	Useful for coordination with wall framing to determine backing, etc.
	Electrical rooms	Useful for coordination with wall framing and other trades
Plumbing model	Plumbing fixtures	Required for coordination with other MEP trades and casework
	Graded cast iron pipelines	Required for coordination with other trades and for prefabrication
	Underground storm and sewer pipes	Required for underground utilities coordination and for prefabrication
	All major waste and vent lines	Required for coordination with other trades and with architectural walls and shafts and for prefabrication
	Cold and hot water piping	Required for coordination with other trades and for prefabrication
	Hangers and Seismic bracing details	Required for coordination with other trades, inserting before installation, and prefabrication
	All boiler and other equipment	Useful for coordination (can be drawn as a 3D block)
	Specialty piping (such as medical gas piping) and specialty equipment	Required for coordination with other trades and for prefabrication
Sprinkler model	Sprinkler mains and branches	Required for coordination with other trades and for prefabrication
	Sprinkler head drops	Useful for coordination with finish utilities such as electrical lighting, diffusers, etc.
	Smaller sprinkler pipes	Required if hard pipe is used, useful if newer type of flex pipe is used

On projects using products compatible with the .dwg format or the Autodesk CAD file format, the following guidelines apply:

- Use only standard AutoCAD fonts in model space; do not use true type fonts or custom AutoCAD fonts.
- For all AutoCAD-based models each trade will use the EXTERNAL REFERENCE (X-ref) command to bring any drawing needed into the "background."
- X-ref's are not to be bound or inserted.
- All X-ref's are detached prior to transferring drawings to other trades.
- Nothing is drawn in paper space.
- No trades draw anything on layer zero (0) or Def points.
- Drawings are purged (AutoCAD purge command) and audited (AutoCAD audit command) prior to file transfer to get rid of any errors or garbage in the drawing file.
- Text is on different layers from the graphics so that the text can be turned off without turning off the graphic.
- Any thick lines to designate wall fire ratings are on separate layers.
- All layers are on and thawed.
- All entities are delivered with colors, line types, and line weights set by layer.

Kicking Off the Coordination Process—The First Steps   The first step in the coordination process is the kickoff meeting that involves all the team members (architects, engineers, GC, and subcontractors). The following guidelines should be discussed during the meeting:

- Get the technical logistics right.
- Perform the initial space allocation of the above-ceiling space.
- Determine the breakup of floor plans so they can be coordinated in smaller batches.

Figs. 5.1.7 and 5.1.8 show space and zone allocation tools with which to start organizing the coordination process.

Sequence of Coordination   Based on DPR's experience, the MEP/FP coordination process using 3D-4D tools is most efficient if it follows the sequence below:

1. Start with the 3D structural and architectural model.
2. Add miscellaneous steel details to the model.
3. Perform preliminary space allocation (as indicated in the previous section).
4. Identify hard constraints (locations of access panels, lights, etc.).
5. Draw the main medium-pressure ducts from the shaft out.
6. Draw the main graded plumbing lines and vents.
7. Draw the sprinkler mains and branches.
8. Draw the cold and hot water mains and branches.
9. Draw the lighting fixtures and plumbing fixtures.
10. Route the smaller ducts and flex ducts around the utilities drawn above.
11. Route the smaller cold and hot water piping, flex ducts, etc., last.

Figure 5.1.7

Screenshot of the initial space allocation of the above-space utilities for the Camino Medical Group project for DPR Construction. This space allocation allows subcontractors to identify the general location of their systems which they can use as a starting point and is also used as a general guideline for the modeling effort. (*Image courtesy of DPR Construction, Inc., California.*)

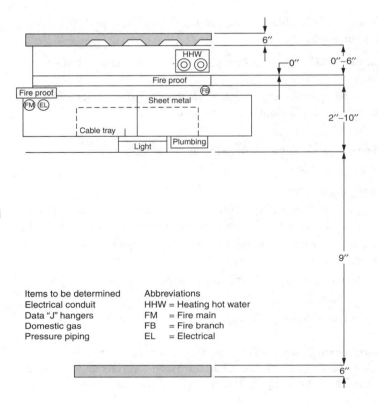

Items to be determined	Abbreviations
Electrical conduit	HHW = Heating hot water
Data "J" hangers	FM = Fire main
Domestic gas	FB = Fire branch
Pressure piping	EL = Electrical

Managing the Handoffs between Designers and Subcontractors' Detailers   In the U.S. construction industry, the traditional building process involves a host of specialty firms focused on a smaller portion of work. This is true for both the design and the construction phases of the project.

During the design phase, architects work with a host of design consultants, such as the structural engineer, acoustical consultant, and mechanical engineers, to complete the design of the facilities. During the construction process, the GC typically coordinates the work of many specialty subcontractors. There is no single master builder. In this environment, managing the handoff of information from designers (who are typically the engineers of record) to the subcontractors' detailers becomes extremely important. In a fast-track project, where design and construction overlap managing the handoffs between designers and subcontractors, it is doubly important. Significant time and money will be wasted if changes to the floor and reflected ceiling plans occur after MEP detailing begins.

The project team should collaboratively determine how the design will be broken down into small enough batch sizes that allow detailers to coordinate and complete an area so that fabrication can begin. This is an iterative process between the design and construction process. It is a balance between waiting until design is complete and turning over a small batch that is complete. However, many unanswered design questions

Figure 5.1.8

Screenshot of the floor plan divided into smaller areas (SE-A, SE-B). The project team including GCs, subcontractors, and A/Es helped in creating the breakdown of the overall floor plan into smaller areas for the Camino MOB project for DPR Construction. The smaller units or areas were then used to coordinate utilities included in the area. The areas also match the work breakdown structure created for the construction. (*Image courtesy of HPS Architects, Mountain View, California.*)

CAD File Naming Conventions

When naming drawings use the same name that the design team is using to name their drawing and follow it with a −XX. Replace the XX with your companies abbreviation. Use A/B to denote further break up of a quadrant for $1/4''$ scale drawings.

Example: M2.113A–SI

When transferring CAD files or posting on prolog for coordination please break down the files by quadrant to minimize the file size. This helps when importing all the files into navis.

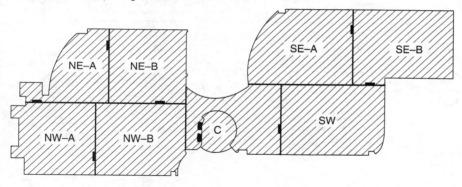

are dependent on completing the design for the remaining areas. Areas cannot be organized arbitrarily; the boundaries should be determined by system feeds and distribution. Rather than receiving handoffs for all MEP/FP systems in a specific area, handoffs could be phased by system. Major systems, which impact the whole design coordination process, should be finalized first. Waste and vent systems are examples, since they must be designed from the top down and impact all floors and connections below. For example, the Camino MOB project developed a process chart and document (shown in Figs. 5.1.9 and 5.1.10, respectively) to determine the handoff between the design and the construction teams.

This handoff is a result of honest negotiation with the A/Es. The GC should come to these talks with a clear understanding of the critical path. That said, it is just as important to listen and understand the real status of design. The subcontractors should be included along with the MEP consultants. Contractors should, e.g., be prepared to learn that the A/Es are struggling with design questions after the owner has accepted design at key milestones, such as 75 percent design development.

Figure 5.1.9

The handoff process developed by the Camino MOB design and construction teams collaboratively. It indicates that the design and detailing teams will work collaboratively at the beginning of schematic design stage (50 percent SD) and the detailing team for the subcontractors will start creating the 3D models at the detailed design stage and complete the modeling effort with a fully coordinated 3D design at the end of construction documents phase. (*Image courtesy of DPR Construction, Inc., California.*)

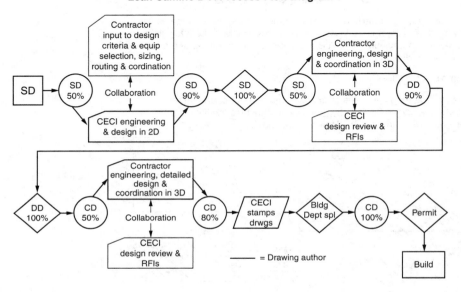

The entire project team should also be aware of the cost of starting the MEP detailing work too soon. It is always better to ask the detailing group to compress its schedule by working overtime than to start before design is fixed and then be forced to redraw and recoordinate to accommodate changes.

Working in a Big Room Coordination of design is an intense process. It involves designers and specialty contractors. The detailing work for each trade is dependent on information from the designers and other trade contractors. For example, the plumbing detailer is interested in finding out the location of waste and vent shafts from the design team and the location of the main duct runs from the mechanical subcontractor. At the same time, the mechanical subcontractor is interested in finding out information about the gravity lines from the plumbing subcontractor, so it can correctly locate its duct lines.

The coordination effort involves a fair amount of reciprocal dependencies that need to be resolved quickly. Latency in decision making can seriously impact a fast-track project schedule. These challenges are addressed by collocating the design and detailing teams.[6, 7]

Figure 5.1.10

The MEP coordination handoff document prepared by the Camino MOB design and construction team to manage the handoffs between the design and construction team. The figure shows the handoff schedule for the first-floor SE quadrant. The Camino MOB team used smaller areas to hand off the design information to the subcontractors' detailing team. (*Image courtesy of HPS Architects, Mountain View, California.*)

Camino Medical Group – Mountain View Campus   Rev. 6/1/05

MEP Overhead Coordination

First Floor South-East Quadrant

Schedule

A.	Information Procurement (CMG):	Target Completion Date – 5/27/05
B.	Design Period Duration (HPS/Design):	7 Days / Start: 5/27 – End: 6/6
C.	Shop Drawing Preparation (DPR/DA):	27 Days / Start: 6/7 – End: 7/13

Information Required / Responsible Party

1. User Acceptance of Floor Plans (CMG)	Complete 6/1
2. Radiology Overhead Equipment Weights and Attachment Layout/Dimensions (CMG/Siemens)	Due by 6/7

The goal is to create a collaborative work environment where the decision-making latency can be reduced. This is similar to the "Extreme Collaboration" (XC) approach[3] that is used by NASA scientists in designing space missions.

To foster a strong collaborative work environment, detailers must work side by side in one "big room" to model and coordinate their designs to meet the coordination schedule. Subcontractors, who are outsourcing modeling and coordination, are not exempt from this requirement. Outsource detailers are also required to work in the big room, not remotely.

Having detailers working side by side shortens the overall time for modeling and coordination and is more economical in the end for all concerned, because it eliminates the need for detailers to wait for postings to see what others are doing. The big room need not be at the jobsite; it can be in another location more convenient for the detailers. For example, Fig. 5.1.11 shows the big room that was set up by the Camino MOB project team. Detailers for the various specialty subcontractors sat in a single room; shared resources such as servers, Internet connection, printers, and plotters; and coordinated the design with the design team in this room.

Using 3D Clash Detection Tools to Identify and Resolve Conflicts   Commercial tools are currently available that allow project teams to combine models from multiple CAD systems into a single model and determine if two or more systems conflict with

Figure 5.1.11

The "big room" on the Camino MOB project with all the detailers from the specialty trades working together in a single room. The detailers used shared resources such as a shared server to post drawings and shared printers and plotters. All the coordination with the design team was done in this big room. All the construction documents were also generated from this one big room. (*Image courtesy of DPR Construction, Inc., California.*)

one another. One such tool is NavisWorks, which has a clash detection program that allows teams to automatically analyze the models for conflicts among systems. This tool was used on the Camino MOB project.

Conflict identification and resolution is an iterative process. First the models are combined into a single model, and then the clash detection program is run to identify clashes between systems. The clashes are then resolved in their native programs, and the iteration is performed until all clashes are resolved. See Figs. 5.1.12 and 5.1.13.

Creating the Modeling Coordination Schedule

The GC works with the MEP/FP subcontractors to establish the coordination schedule. This schedule is the work plan to ensure that clash-free drawings are in the hands of installation crews in time for penetrations and hangers to be installed prior to the placement of reinforcement and concrete on the elevated decks.

Figure 5.1.12
Clash between duct and sprinkler pipe (in red) on the Camino MOB. These clashes were identified by the NavisWorks clash detection program. In a subsequent clash resolution session these clashes were resolved. (*Image courtesy of DPR Construction, Inc., California.*) See also color insert.

The coordination schedule also sets dates for a final all-hands clash detection workshop for each area in time for prefabrication of assemblies to meet the master construction schedule. For example, Fig. 5.1.14 shows a simple Microsoft Excel table that represents the coordination schedule developed on the Camino MOB project. The coordination schedule was developed with the help of designers and subcontractors. The schedule was pulled from the milestone of the MEP insert start date. This means that the team worked backward from the MEP insert milestone date to determine the preceding activities and durations to meet this milestone date.

Steps to Develop the Pull Coordination Schedule

1. Agree on the master construction schedule milestone dates that will drive the coordination schedule. At the Camino MOB, these were the dates for placing concrete on the elevated decks and the start of overhead rough-ins for each trade.

2. Create a "pull schedule," working backward from construction milestones to determine insert and release to fabricate dates by area. Each trade needs to provide realistic lead times for fabrication and delivery of materials to the jobsite. The detailing team must review these delivery schedules and may need to request that some companies improve their shop lead times. Ultimately, the team must agree on a date for the Release-to-Fabrication Clash Detection Workshop (see Fig. 5.1.14), based on the earliest date for one of the contractors to place his or her fabrication order.

Figure 5.1.13

The clash between duct and sprinkler pipe identified in Fig. 5.1.12 has now been resolved by moving the sprinkler pipe out of the way. (*Image courtesy of DPR Construction, Inc., California.*)

Figure 5.1.14 shows a pull schedule that was developed by the Camino MOB team, which denotes both the insert milestone and the release to fabrication milestone.

3. The detailing team then needs to create a "work stream," which clearly identifies posting dates and coordination sessions with intermediate class detections, leading to both insert and release to fabrication sign-offs. Figure 5.1.15 shows an example work stream from the Camino MOB project.

4. Identify specific dates for sign-offs for the coordinated models. The sign-off should include the GC, the A/E team, and all the subcontractors. An electronic snapshot and a paper copy of all the modeled systems should be signed off by all the parties.

5. Finally, resource planning should take into account preparation of field layout and shop drawings after sign-off. Additional resources, working outside of the big room, may be required.

Applying the Last Planner System Every Day

The best system to manage this process is the Last Planner System (Ballard). The MEP detailing team should meet once a week to decide on the production plan for the next week. It is critical that each company commit to providing an informed *responsible individual* (RI), who is empowered to make promises to attend all the coordination planning meetings. This should either be a detailer or foreman working on the project.

Figure 5.1.14

The pull coordination schedule for the Camino MOB shows the target sign-off dates for each of the areas. The schedule was developed as a collaborative effort among the GC, the subcontractors, and the design team and was driven by the start date for MEP inserts. (*Image courtesy of DPR Construction, Inc., California.*)

Camino Medical Center
MEP/FP DA Team MEP/FP Design Coordination Schedule

Coordination quadrant	A/E drwgs for construction	Insert Navis file posted	Insert order	MEP insert start	MEP insert finish	Target release for fab sign-off	Fab order	Release for fab date	Date of DA team acceptance of SI medium pressure duct	Date of DA Team acceptance of of JWM DW&V
1st floor Southeast	11/22/05	10/18/05	1	10/27/2005	11/03/2005	12/07/05	1	12/06/05	12/16/05	01/02/06
1st floor Southwest	11/22/05	11/11/05	2	11/15/2005	11/22/2005	12/21/05	2	12/21/05	12/29/05	01/12/06
2nd floor Southeast	11/22/05	11/22/05	3	11/22/2005	12/01/2005	01/04/06	3	01/04/06	01/17/06	02/01/06
2nd floor Southwest	11/22/05	12/07/05	4	12/09/2005	12/16/2005	01/11/06	4	01/22/06	01/31/06	02/18/06
1st floor Northeast	11/22/05	12/28/05	7	12/30/2005	01/09/2006	01/18/06	5	02/05/06	02/14/06	03/02/06
2nd floor Northeast	11/22/05	01/16/06	9	01/19/2006	01/26/2006	01/25/06	6	02/19/06	02/28/06	03/18/06
2nd floor Northwest	11/22/05	01/19/06	10	01/24/2006	01/31/2006	02/01/06	7	03/05/06	03/14/06	04/02/06
3rd floor Southeast	11/22/05	12/07/05	5	12/13/2005	12/21/2005	02/08/06	8	03/19/06	03/28/06	04/16/06
3rd floor Southwest	11/22/05	12/14/05	6	12/19/2005	12/27/2005	02/10/06	9	04/02/06	04/11/06	04/30/06
3rd floor Northeast	11/22/05	02/03/06	11	02/07/2006	02/15/2006	02/15/06	10	04/16/06	04/26/06	05/14/06
3rd floor Northwest	11/22/05	02/15/06	12	02/15/2006	02/27/2006	02/17/06	11	05/02/06	05/11/06	05/30/06
1st floor Northwest	11/22/05	01/02/06	8	01/05/2006	01/12/2006	02/23/05	12	05/16/06	05/25/06	06/13/06
1st floor Center	11/22/05	01/11/06	13	02/24/2006	03/01/2006	12/21/05	13	06/10/06	06/19/06	07/08/06
2nd floor Center	11/22/05	01/27/06	14	02/27/2006	03/02/2006	01/11/06	14	06/17/06	06/23/06	07/15/06
3rd floor Center	11/22/05	02/21/06	15	02/28/2006	03/03/2006	02/17/06	15	07/01/06	06/30/06	07/29/06

Weekly Coordination Meeting Agenda

1. Check in with all attendees on whether they were able to keep their commitments for the previous week, from the last to the current meeting.

2. Looking ahead as far as possible, at least one week, the team should make requests and promises. This should be recorded on a simple *look ahead plan* (LAP), e.g., in Excel or MS Project.

3. Promises falling within the next week should be put into the production plan for the upcoming week. Individual detailers should be required to come to the weekly coordination meeting with their own weekly work plan. Every issue should be viewed

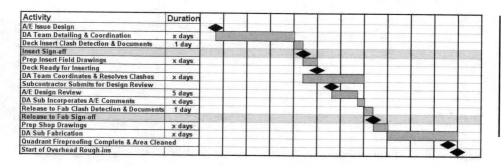

Activity	Duration
A/E Issue Design	
DA Team Detailing & Coordination	x days
Deck Insert Clash Detection & Documents	1 day
Insert Sign-off	
Prep Insert Field Drawings	x days
Deck Ready for Inserting	
DA Team Coordinates & Resolves Clashes	x days
Subcontractor Submits for Design Review	
A/E Design Review	5 days
DA Sub Incorporates A/E Comments	x days
Release to Fab Clash Detection & Documents	1 day
Release to Fab Sign-off	
Prep Shop Drawings	x days
DA Sub Fabrication	x days
Quadrant Fireproofing Complete & Area Cleaned	
Start of Overhead Rough-ins	

Figure 5.1.15

Design and coordination work stream for the Camino MOB project. (*Image courtesy of DPR Construction, Inc., California.*)

as a constraint that needs to be removed, and a RI should be asked to take action by a certain date. This make-ready work should be recorded on the LAP and fall into the production plan.

4. Commitments for the next week should be reviewed at the end of the planning session to make sure that RIs understand what they have agreed to do. Promises can only be made by RIs attending the meeting. The GC, representing the larger project team, must take responsibility for getting items from others not present in the meeting (i.e., foremen from the GC's own team doing self-performed work for whom she or he can speak). Figure 5.1.16 shows a LAP for the Camino MOB.

Daily Stand-up Meeting

Detailers working in the big room should meet face to face every day. Detailers not on-site can phone and log in using a Web meeting program.

The MEP detailing team will almost always be working to a very tight schedule, with no time to lose. The detailers should stop work for 15 minutes each day to check in with one another and the team lead on how they are doing. The question that should be asked and answered is, Will you be able to meet the promises you made to the team in the weekly coordination meeting?

"Constraints" should be discussed leading to commitments by team members to clear them. The GC representative should expect to come away with action items to work with people outside of the detailing team to provide answers and resolution on issues. For example, if the detailing team has a question about external wall panels, then the

Figure 5.1.16

The LAP developed by the detailers to manage the coordination process on the Camino MOB. (*Image courtesy of DPR Construction, Inc., California.*)

Starting	3/9/06		Reasons for Not Completing Work as Planned								
Ending	3/16/06										
PPC Analysis		1	Over-committed		Performer's other commitments prevented successful completion						
Activities Planned	0	2	Unanticipated Constraint		Something which had to be done beforw what was promised was not identified.						
Completed as Planned	0	3	Miscommunication		Performer didn't understand either the conditions of satisfaction or the due date						
Percent Planned Complete (PPC)	0%	4	Prerequisite Incomplete		Performer didn't receive perquisite information from another performer						
		5	Change in priorities		Performer decided or was directed not to perform the task because of a change in priorities.						

No.	Work to Be Completed	Locat ion	Company	Resp. Individ.	What Others Must Do	Due Date	Done? Yes	Done? No	Description of Issue Preventing Completion	Primary Reason No.
1	DPR to distribute schedule to new people	Bldg	DPR	DZ		3/16/06				
2	SI to provide need dates for umblicals firm locations	Bldg	SI	JS		3/17/06				
3	East Bay to provide delivery dates for refrig line and other above ceiling shop drwgs	1E	EBRS	JD		3/20/06				
4	CEI to post branch distribution 1st floor E & W 50%	1E&W	CEI	JM		3/21/06				
5	SI to post plumbing and piping 100% 1st floor E & W changes	1E&W	SI	KC		3/21/06				
6	SI to post HVAC 1st floor E & W 75%	1E&W	SI	JS		3/21/06				
7	WFP to post 90% FP 1st floor E & W	1E&W	WFP	DJ		3/21/06				
8	DPR to provide extra tables and white board for next week's meeting	Bldg	DPR	DZ		3/23/06				
9	DPR to review and report back on construction sequencing at 4hr wall area	Bldg	DPR	KM		3/23/06				
10	CEI to post cable tray & feeders 2nd floor E & W 25%	2E&W	CEI	JM		3/28/06				
11	SI to post plumbing and piping 50% 2nd floor E & W	2E&W	SI	KC		3/28/06				
12	SI to post HVAC 50% 2nd floor W	2W	SI	JS		3/28/06				
13	WFP to post FP 75% 2nd floor E & W	2E&W	WFP	DJ		3/28/06				
	Combined Plan Percent Complete for the Week						0	0	PPC for the Week	0%

GC representative should commit to getting the answer to the detailing team by coordinating with the designers and the wall panel subcontractor.

The last planner process and the daily stand-up meetings provide a great opportunity to learn as you go into the process. Each reason for not meeting a commitment is a breakdown and an opportunity to learn how to improve the process. This is part of being reflective practitioners. It will become clear that what was planned for at the beginning might or might not work, but if the team consciously chips away at it, success is inevitable. It does call for a collaborative environment, where all opinions matter and the entire team is actively engaged in a dialogue to improve performance rather than to assign blame for nonperformance.

When an environment like the big room is provided and a process such as the Last Planner System is used, it can be surprising how quickly the team comes together to solve real issues. This is the part of the plan—do—check—act cycle that is a must if this process is to succeed. After every meeting, teams need to ask, "What did we learn?" and "What can we do better?" That is the only way the process will improve. It will also become clear that although VDC tools are important, how they are used, what was expected to be gained through the use of these tools, the overall goals of the team, who develops the models using these tools, and how information to produce the right models with these tools was gathered, are just as important. A team should pay attention to these issues.

Using the MEP/FP 3D Models for Coordinating Installation
4D Simulation of Installation Once the MEP/FP 3D models for an area are fully coordinated, the installation of MEP work can be coordinated by attaching schedule dates to the objects in the coordinated 3D model to create a 4D simulation based on discussions with subcontractor foremen. See Figs. 5.1.17, 5.1.18, and 5.1.19.

After the final sign-off on the fabrication models and drawings, subcontractor foremen should first develop a schedule for their installations by area. This will most likely follow the fabrication and spool sheets they submitted to their respective shops. They arrive at the duration of the installation activities by identifying the quantities and applying an estimated productivity for their crews.

Once the duration is determined, the foremen will make the commitment to perform installation for specific dates on their weekly work plan (WWP). These dates can be obtained from the subcontractor's weekly work plan. These dates form the basis of 4D simulation. The foremen should then be brought together to identify and resolve scheduling conflicts by reviewing the sequence of activities in the 4D model. In these meetings, they will sometimes discover that the plan of work they have determined might cause time-space conflicts with other trades or lack of availability of lay-down areas. In these instances the foremen will need to agree to modifications to their original sequence, which will be the basis of the agreed 4D schedule.

The 4D schedule should be reviewed, and the status of each activity should be noted in the field foreman's weekly coordination meeting.

Figure 5.1.17

Foremen meeting on the Camino MOB project to discuss the construction sequence with the aid of 2D drawings and 3D-4D models. (*Image courtesy of DPR Construction, Inc., California.*)

Figure 5.1.18

A snapshot of 4D model from Camino MOB project. The snapshot shows that the inserts (little dots in the screenshot) have been installed and construction of the full-height wall framing (in green) is going on. (*Image courtesy of DPR Construction, Inc., California.*) See also color insert.

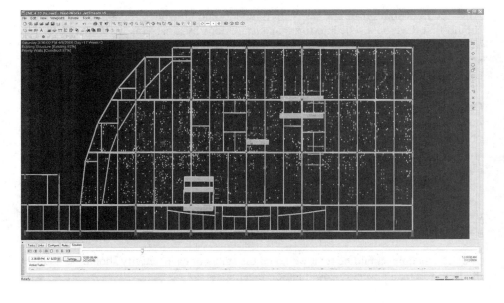

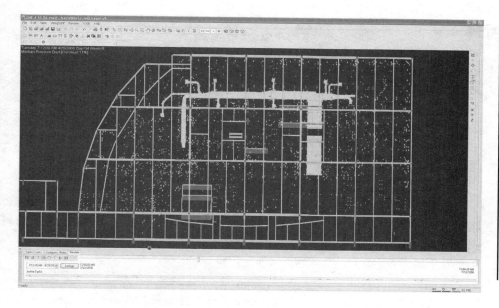

Figure 5.1.19
A snapshot of 4D model from Camino MOB project. The construction of full-height wall framing (in orange) is completed, and medium-pressure duct (in green) is being installed. (*Image courtesy of DPR Construction, Inc., California.*) See also color insert.

Benefits

The Camino MOB project team estimated that on a $94.5 million contract the client saved approximately $1.2 million, attributed to the modeling and coordination using VDC tools. Some of the specific benefits include the following:

1. *Increased field productivity.* The HVAC subcontractor was able to achieve a 20 to 33 percent increase in field productivity due to the prefabrication of systems that resulted from the use of VDC tools for MEP coordination. Figure 5.1.20 shows the actual field productivity of the duct and pipe installation work compared with the estimated productivity during the course of installation of both the duct and piping systems.

2. *Zero field conflicts among systems modeled and coordinated using VDC tools.* On the Camino MOB project, there were zero field conflicts among systems that were modeled and coordinated using VDC tools. Normally on comparable projects, the superintendents' estimate is that there would be about 100 to 200 conflicts that get resolved in the field if the SCOP method is used for coordination.

3. *Only 43 hours of rework out of 25,000 hours worked.* The team has only needed to complete 43 hours of rework out of 25,000 hours worked. Although there is not an official study as to how this compares to other projects, the project team believes that this is a phenomenal number compared to projects where the coordination is done in a 2D SCOP process.

4. *Only six RFIs related to field conflicts.* There were only six RFIs dealing with field conflicts. These RFIs were for conflicts between systems that were not modeled in 3D space. The project team members estimate that this is about 5 to 10 percent of what they typically see on comparable projects coordinated using the 2D SCOP process.

5. *Increased planning reliability on the project.* The Camino MOB project tracked the planning reliability using the percent plan complete (PPC) metric, which is the

Figure 5.1.20

Field productivity for sheet metal (duct) and piping compared to the actual field productivity. (*Image courtesy of Southland Industries, San Jose, California.*)

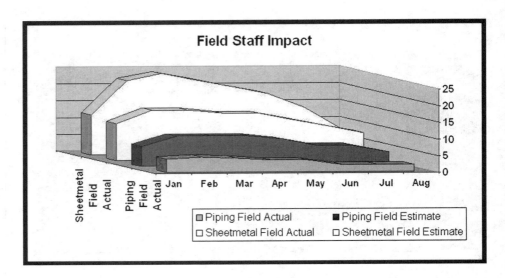

percentage ratio of tasks that were completed to the tasks that were planned. See Fig. 5.1.21. The project team's cumulative PPC is about 83 percent. The Lean Construction Institute estimates that the average PPC on well-managed projects is about 60 percent. This shows that the Camino MOB planning reliability percentage is much higher than that for comparable projects. Although there could be multiple

Figure 5.1.21

Cumulative percent plan complete (PPC) chart for the Camino MOB project through the end of 11/20/2006. (*Image courtesy of DPR Construction, Inc., California.*)

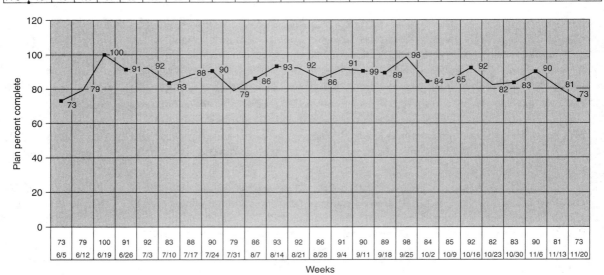

factors associated with this, the team believes that a higher level of confidence in installations and making reliable commitments due to confidence in VDC tools is one of the major factors in this increase in PPC.

Conclusions

This case study presented guidelines on how to use VDC tools for the challenging task of the coordination of MEP systems on a real construction project. Results from the experience indicate that project participants can gain tremendous benefits following the process outlined.

DPR continues to apply this process to other projects and will continue to refine these guidelines. The construction delivery process can be further enhanced by a systematic study and analysis of the handoffs that happen among a multistakeholder design team using VDC tools.

On the Camino MOB project, the project team felt that the use of models helped the design team members visualize and understand the construction sequence and ask questions that they traditionally would not ask until construction was underway. The A/E team members also felt that they had to play a greater role during the design coordination and provide information to the detailing team of the subcontractors in much smaller batches than they are used to. The project team also realized that numerous reciprocal dependencies exist among systems, and the use of VDC tools in a big room helped resolve some of these dependencies quickly rather than through the traditional method. This indicates that there is a greater need to study the application of VDC tools on other projects and a need for creating a new design coordination method that takes advantage of the VDC tools.

Although VDC tools have been around, these are truly remarkable times when project teams such as Camino MOB are seeing true benefits from the use of these tools in a collaborative environment. The Camino MOB experience points to the fact that we can improve as an industry by following the Deming cycle of continuous improvement, the plan-do-check-act cycle. With the VDC tools along with the right process, teams can gain this benefit from working together, developing a purpose, and adjusting along the way by creating a learning environment on the project. Our hope is that the book inspires others to emulate the experience of the DPR project team and to become reflective practitioners.

Acknowledgments

We would like to acknowledge Sutter Health, Camino Medical Group, DPR Construction, Inc., Hawley Peterson and Snyder Architects, Capital Engineering Consultants, KPFF Structural Engineers, The Engineering Enterprise, Southland Industries, Cupertino Electric, JW McLenahan Company, and North Star Fire Protection for contributing to this report. We would also like to thank Dr. Martin Fischer, Executive Director of CIFE, Stanford University, for his insights when the project team was developing the guidelines. Specifically, we would like to thank Yumi Clevenger of DPR Construction, Inc., for proofreading the chapter and helping make it better.

References

1. Ballard, Glenn, "Lean Project Delivery System," White Paper 8, Lean Construction Institute, Berkeley, California, 2000.

2. Fischer, Martin, and John Kunz, "The Scope and Role of Information Technology in Construction," Tech. Rep. 156, Center for Integrated Facilities Engineering (CIFE), Stanford University, California, 2004.

3. Garcia, Ana-Christina, et al., "Building a Project Ontology with Extreme Collaboration and Virtual Design and Construction," CIFE Working Paper 152, CIFE, Stanford University, November 2003.

4. Gil, Nino, et al., "Contribution of Specialty Contractor Knowledge to Early Design," *Proc. of the 8th Annual Congress of the International Group for Lean Construction*, July 17–19, 2000, Brighton, UK.

5. Korman, Thomas, Fischer, and C. B. Tatum, "Knowledge and Reasoning for MEP Coordination," *Journal of Construction Engineering and Management*, pp. 627–634, November–December 2003.

6. Levitt, Ray, and John Kunz, "Design Your Project Organizations as Engineers Design Bridges," CIFE Working Paper 73, CIFE, Stanford University, August 2002.

7. Thompson, J. D., "Organizations in Action: Social Science Bases of Administrative Theory," Transaction Publishers, January 2003.

CASE 2: RQ CONSTRUCTION

Author's Comment

RQ Construction has been looking for opportunities to implement BIM and found their chance in the Sutter Surgical Hospital project. This case study supports the fact that communications and commitment management are critical to the successful implementation of the BIM process.

BIM at Yuba City—Sutter Surgical Hospital North Valley

by Frank Peters, project superintendent RQ Construction

Sutter Surgical Hospital is a two-story ± 45,000-ft^2 steel framed structure on an empty lot in Yuba City, California.

This project is now under construction, the steel has been erected, and the rough-ins are just beginning. In planning and executing the modeling and coordination effort, the project team first *defined* the desired outcomes (required deliverables), then *designed* the systems to achieve the goals of the definition phase, and now is *building* that which was designed.

In the *definition phase,* the following points were noteworthy:

- RQ Construction solicited the help of SPS (Strategic Project Solutions) in creating a coordination planning strategy (see images of slide show explaining the process in Fig. 5.2.1a to g).
- Sutter (owner) didn't require any specific deliverable other than being sold on the "inherent advantages" of 3D modeling before physically building it.
- RQC thought there was probably some additional advantages to using 3D modeling but did not specify in detail. There was a desire to transfer what was learned from the modeling process back to the RQC design department.

Desired Outcomes

- Have gained a shared understanding of the value Sutter Health and RQ Construction are seeking through the use of 3D at the Yuba City project

- Have gained a shared understanding of the overall process in a design-bid-build scenario

- Have discussed and agreed on the solution for the use of 3D modeling at Yuba City to align customer value and RQ needs and wants

- Have discussed and agreed on next steps

(a)

Figure 5.2.1

Strategic Project Solutions plan. (*Image courtesy of RQ Construction.*)

Figure 5.2.1
(*Continued*)

Stakeholder Analysis

Stakeholders	What's the value for them?

Sutter FPD (Pixley)	• Demonstrate beyond what is currently being provided by others (e.g., lean)
	  – Predictability on schedule and cost
	  – Change control

Users' Group / Sutter North
 	
  –National Surgical
 	
  – Doctors' Group / Patients
	• Time to market
	• Efficient hospital so they can make money
	• Attract other doctors
	• Ability to do other procedures

RQ Construction	• Get additional health care work (inc. Sutter) – competitive advantage • Earn profit • Develop/further strategic relationships with key subs • Develop internal capabilities • Enhance reputation
Booth Mechanical/Berg Electric	• Enhance reputation with Sutter • Enhance reputation with RQ • Earn fair profit • Reduce risk on their projects
Regulatory Agencies (OSHPD / Yuba City)	• Minimal project changes • Delivery time – get income from tax, hospital operation • What does the inspector want?

(*b*)

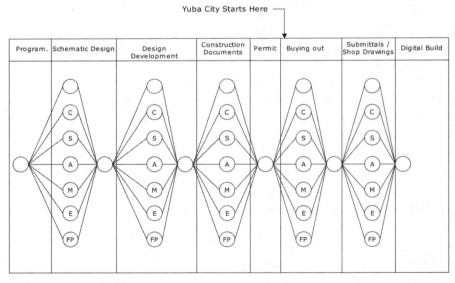

How best to coordinate, integrate, and validate? (Key areas of focus: intersections, connections, transitions and terminations)

(*c*)

- RQC made decision to pay Graphisoft to model the construction documents (architectural and structural only, no MEPS systems).
- A meeting was held with all MEPS trades to determine their 3D modeling capabilities and the coordination processes they currently use.

Figure 5.2.1
(*Continued*)

Questions

- How best to coordinate, integrate and validate?

- Who is going to do it?

- What systems are we going to use?

- What does the inspector want?

(*d*)

The Vision: Modeling Strategy

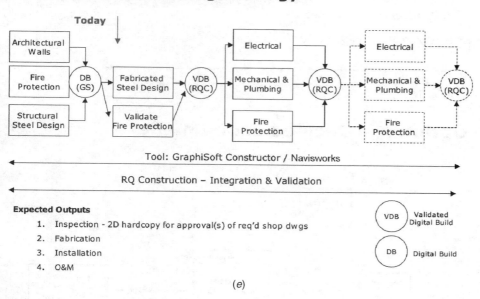

(*e*)

- An agreement was made with the MEPS trades that RQC would provide the model builds from .dwg files supplied by each trade. The final contract coordination was still the responsibility of the mechanical/plumbing vendor (Frank M. Booth).

The *design* and the MEPS coordination planning were based on the following decisions:

Systems to coordinate:

- *HVAC ducting.* FMB (Frank M. Booth, mechanical/plumbing vendor)
- *Mechanical equipment.* FMB
- *Plumbing (waste).* FMB

Figure 5.2.1
(*Continued*)

Next Steps (from 9-Jun-06)

1. Compile modeling strategy into a single document – living document **DONE** (This pp doc)

2. Map 3D capabilities (IT, people) in the value stream (steel, M&P, electrical, fire protection, etc.) **DONE**

3. Determine stakeholders' deliverable requirements

4. Validate proposed 'modeling strategy' against capabilities in the value stream

5. Finalize modeling strategy

6. Implement modeling strategy

7. Capture lessons learned

8. Create RQ standard modeling practice

(*f*)

Option A – Decided action model

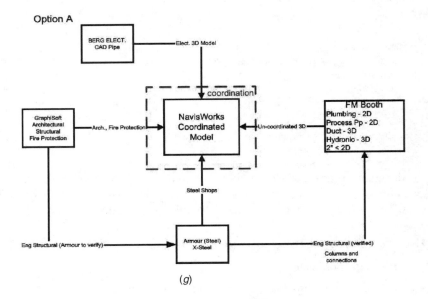

(*g*)

- *Pressure piping.* FMB
- *Hydronic piping.* FMB
- *Electrical conduits and cable trays.* BergElectric
- *Fire sprinkler.* Pro-Tech
- *Steel frame.* Armour Steel
- *Architectural (modeled prior to coordination process).* CFP Group (architects)

Organized team:

- *FMB.* Mechanical, plumbing, piping, equipment
- *BergElectric.* Electrical
- *Pro-Tech Fire Systems.* Fire sprinkler system
- *Armour Steel.* Structural steel

Note: Did not include architect or EOR (engineer of record); no reason was given, just didn't think they were necessary.

Cocreated coordination process:

- All MEPS systems are laid out in 3D space.
- Combine all models using NavisWorks Roamer.
- Post weekly model files to the share data file management (DFM) site. See Fig. 5.2.2.

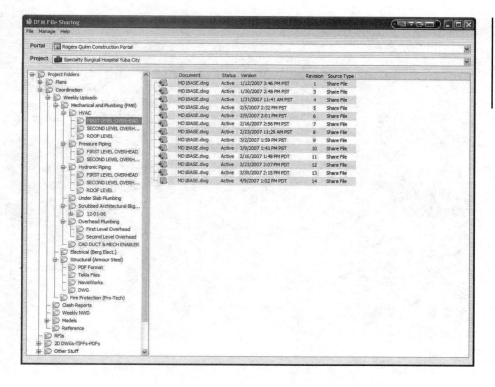

Figure 5.2.2

Data File Management protocol. (*Image courtesy of RQ Construction.*)

- Carry out weekly review and conflict resolution.
- Match coordination sequence and layout to construction sequence planning.
- Map team member 3D software compatibility (resulting in a matrix showing compatibility of file format and items modeled).
- Cocreate a coordination schedule (3D coordination work stream diagram).

During the *building* phase (including the coordination) the following was noted:

- Underslab systems were not part of the "design" coordination, so we modeled it with Graphisoft, 3D Pipe (BergElectric undergraduate), and SketchUp. See Fig. 5.2.3.
- FMB detailing team couldn't (didn't) start when planned due to resource short-fall (the detailing team was still working on other projects).
- Structural steel (Armour) model software (X-steel) was five versions behind current supported version and had difficulty exporting a structural model that could be imported and was compatible with NavisWorks or any other software used by the team (FMB). See Fig. 5.2.4.
- Armour Steel attempted to contract their detailing to India, but this failed due to undisclosed reasons. I think it was for nontechnical reasons (opinion, not fact).
- FMB detailing team started detailing layouts 2 months later than originally planned. They requested to use their tried-and-true light-table overlay process for coordination in lieu of detailing in 3D space for coordination. They still said they will detail

Figure 5.2.3
Underslab bearing zones—plumbing and electrical. (*Image courtesy of RQ Construction.*) See also color insert Fig. 2.6.

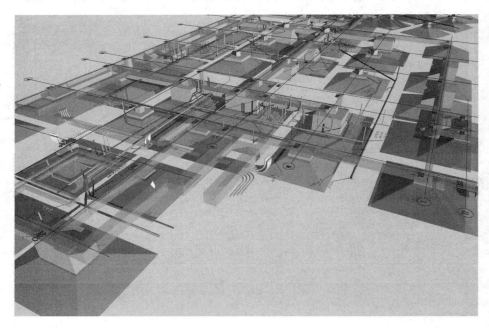

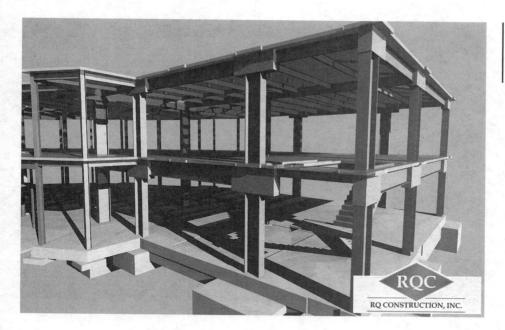

Figure 5.2.4
*Structural frame.
(Image courtesy of
RQ Construction.)*

in 3D—after coordination. I okayed this request to reduce the possible delay to the overall project build schedule. I still requested FMB detail in 3D space during the coordination process so I could run 3D coordination in parallel with their 2D light-table overlay process. See Figs. 5.2.5a and b.

- The system layout and coordination took twice as long as planned due to the unexpected high degree of system complexity. If the original design had been done in 3D space, this discovery would have been part of the define step.

- After the first area that was coordinated with the light-table overlay process was "signed off" and the "coordinated" 3D files were received and input into NavisWorks Clash, many conflicts were discovered. It was initially assumed that I had received pre-coordinated files and had discovered conflicts that were already resolved. This turned out not to be the case; what I had discovered was the level of conflicts that usually get "resolved" in the field.

- Step 7 was repeated 4 times for all the areas that needed coordination. Navisworks Clash was used as a final check in all these additional areas. FMB purchased and implemented Navisworks into their internal coordination because of the discoveries made in step 7.

- The fire sprinkler system was the only system not modeled in 3D during the coordination process because the vendor (Pro-Tech) did not have the internal capability. RQC hired a third-party modeler to model the "coordinated" fire sprinkler redesign with the intent of completing a final check of all systems prior to actual installation. The discovery is that a modeler is very similar to a subcontractor trade; if what they produce is of lower quality than required, all other systems may be affected—and

Figure 5.2.5

(*a*) Example of systems coordinated with light table—before (many conflicts). (*b*) Example of coordinated systems using 3D—after (conflicts resolved). (*Images courtesy of RQ Construction.*)

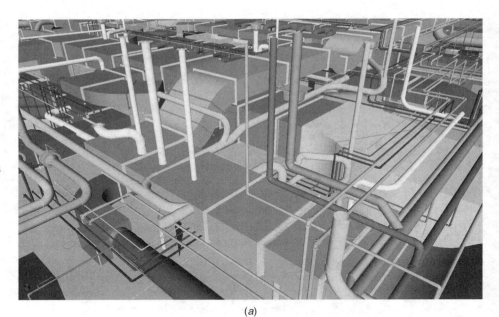

(*a*)

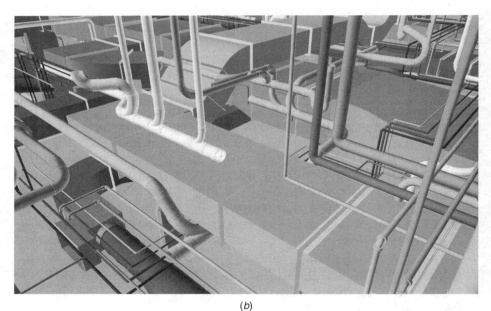

(*b*)

false-positive or false-negative discoveries and decisions can be made. This can be a *big* problem!

- Modeling of fixtures is done to verify support systems. See Fig. 5.2.6.
- The support hangers are added after MEPS coordination. See Figs. 5.2.7 and 5.2.8.

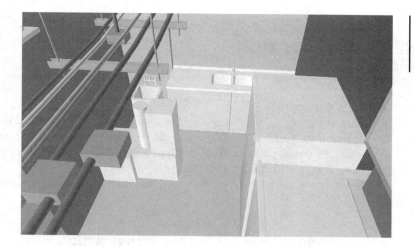

Figure 5.2.6
Fixture layout.
(*Image courtesy of RQ Construction.*)

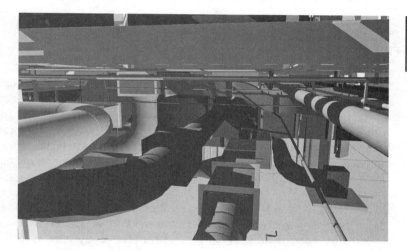

Figure 5.2.7
Duct coordination.
(*Image courtesy of RQ Construction.*)

Figure 5.2.8
View of overall coordination from above. (*Image courtesy of RQ Construction.*)

CASE 3: TURNER CONSTRUCTION, SEATTLE, WASHINGTON

Author's Comment

This case study is an almost diarylike account of the introduction to BIM for Turner Construction in Seattle, Washington. This represents a typical sequence of events leading up to the implementation of a new technology into the existing work environment. This honest discovery of the benefits of a new technology, and the immediate adoption of such a new process, is the hallmark of courage in the construction industry.

Introduction to BIM for Turner Construction, Seattle, Washington

by Renzo di Furia, Project Manager/Estimator,
Seattle Business Unit, Turner Construction

Background

Turner's German parent company, Hochtief, has been using 3D modeling in Europe for years with great success. In 2005, they offered Turner seed money to fund pilot projects to introduce virtual construction technology within the Turner Corporation. The initial pilot was focused on MEP coordination and clash detection. The systems developed as a result of this effort have been embraced with great enthusiasm, and to date, over $3 billion worth of Turner projects have used some form of BIM coordination.

In the spring of 2006 Hochtief offered additional funds to Turner to investigate model-based estimating systems. Turner's Seattle and Washington, D.C., business units were selected to spearhead this initiative, and because of my interest in modeling, I was invited to participate.

A committee was formed to discuss the many systems available and to determine a course of action. After several ideas were evaluated, it was decided to purchase one Graphisoft license and use it to reestimate a current Turner project to determine the practical use and possible pitfalls with this kind of estimating approach. Graphisoft was chosen since it appeared to have the most flexible estimating system. This plan was later modified to evaluate a current Turner self-performed concrete project.

The following questions were targeted:

1. What are the functions, features, and processes of the different model-based estimating applications? What are the inputs and outputs from these systems?

2. What skills are required to use these systems effectively? What training is required to reach a basic level of competency on these systems?

3. Are any special additional tools required to operate these systems? What are the administrative requirements to operate the systems?

4. Are there potential integration points for data exchange between these syste existing systems such as Timberline and Prolog? How open are the systems to evaluated toward integration with other systems and tools?

5. Is model-based estimating applicable to Turner's existing processes? If not, specifically why not?

6. Do the systems to be evaluated support the estimating process as the design evolves from a schematic sketch to construction documents? How do model-based technologies support the design process, and do these technologies have the potential to impact or alter Turner's role?

7. Is model-based estimating more cost-effective than the traditional estimating process?

8. What other benefits are created in the preconstruction phase or downstream in the project life cycle from performing model-based estimating; and how do these benefits impact the conclusions to question 7?

9. What are the coordination and interaction points with our subcontractors?

10. What changes would be required to our preconstruction methodology regarding roles, staffing, and process to achieve the maximum potential benefits of these systems? Are there viable alternatives to consider that achieve less benefit but incur less change to our existing processes and organization?

11. What are the inherent major risks of these systems that should be considered?

12. What are the hardware and software requirements for deploying these systems?

13. What is the potential impact that model-based preconstruction may have on Turner?

In the fall of 2006 one Graphisoft license was purchased, including Estimator and Control. My initial goal was to prove that using 3D modeling to capture quantities could be accomplished in relatively the same amount of time as using current take-off systems. To that end, the first step was to learn to model in ArchiCAD (Graphisoft's modeling engine). The pilot presented a challenge that consumed many nights and weekends, since I still had projects to complete and deadlines to meet. A fair amount of self-motivation was required to push through this challenging period. I began by modeling a medical office building that I was estimating at the time since I had the drawing's and permission to use them. Progress was slow due to the limited time available.

Project: Medical Office Building

This was a $90 million core and shell medical office building, 710,000 ft^2 and 15 stories. Structure: parking—post tensioned concrete, podium—CIP concrete, tower—structural steel with concrete decks. See Fig. 5.3.1.

One morning in early November, I showed one of our project executives the progress I was making with 3D modeling tools. He showed immediate enthusiasm and wondered if the 3D tools could be used to help solve some design detailing problems he was having on one of his projects. Even though this problem had nothing to do with estimating, it was a common field problem that could be solved using 3D technology. Based on that encounter, I was immediately given a new high-speed computer, a job number to charge time against, and direction to model the project during regular work hours. This sudden

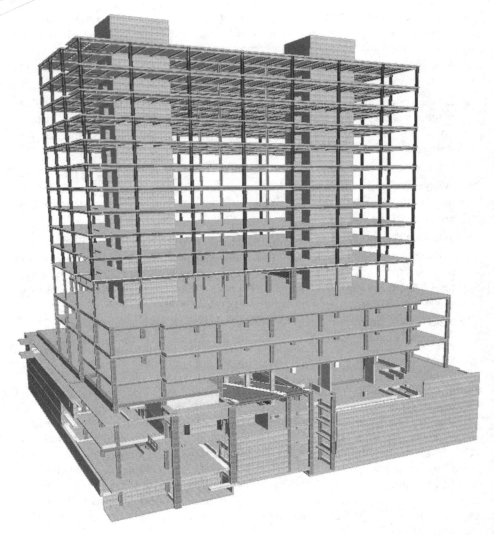

snell
aical office
building. (*Image courtesy of Turner Construction, Seattle, Washington.*)

shift of positive attention toward this work has not slackened, and I have since been working full-time on a long list of modeling projects.

The specific model request involved studying the building perimeter, specifically at sidewalk level in order to lay out and detail the brick corbeling, pony walls, planters, and precast panels at street level. The completed model was successfully used to coordinate these elements and communicate the results between the design and the construction team.

The $150 million residence is another concrete modeling example; by schematically modeling the structure only, a lot of estimating and coordination information can be visualized easily and provide big advantages over the traditional manual take-offs for the initial cost estimate.

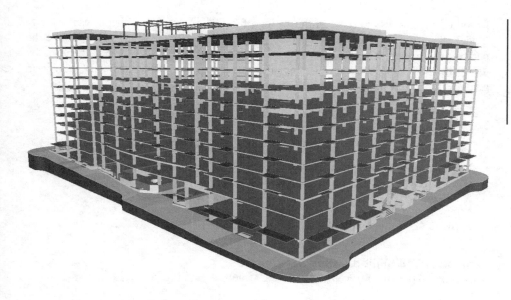

Figure 5.3.2
A $150 million residence. (*Image courtesy of Turner Construction, Seattle, Washington.*)

Project: $150 Million Residence

This project involves a 720,000-ft^2 12-level CIP concrete structure. See Fig. 5.3.2.

In December 2006, I received a request to estimate the drywall, CMU, and interior painting scopes for a new medical office building with underground parking. I made the decision to use model-based estimating tools for this exercise. The times required to complete these estimates were a bit longer than those using current methods, but the results were very accurate and provided a strong visual basis with which to scope these contracts. Accurately estimating walls in a parking structure with varying floor slopes and ceiling heights is difficult using 2D drawings. This is not so with a 3D model. In fact, the CMU subcontractor agreed to reduce his price significantly after reviewing the completed model and resulting quantities. See Fig. 5.3.3.

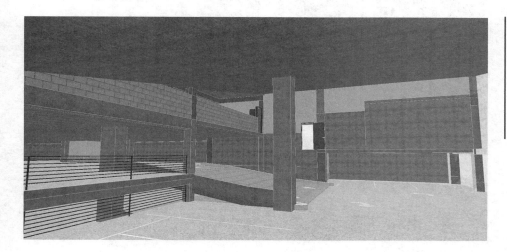

Figure 5.3.3
New MOB with underground parking. (*Image courtesy of Turner Construction, Seattle, Washington.*)

Based on the success to date, in the spring of 2007, an internal decision was made to model all self-performed Turner concrete projects. It was agreed that this would be the perfect way to beta-test new systems and at the same time reap immediate benefits by using the models to study specific logistic and sequencing challenges. The short-term goals were as follows:

- Estimate quantities using model.
- Tie quantities to database.
- Use model to qualify scope.
- Use model for subcontractor scope review.
- Use model to identify variance.
- Use model to aid value engineering review.
- Perform 4D sequencing.

Project: A $18 Million Office Building
This is a 120,000-ft^2, 8-level CIP concrete structure. See Fig. 5.3.4

Project: A $90 Million Core and Shell Medical Office Building
This is a 710,000-ft^2,– 15-story MOB. See Fig. 5.3.5

Project: A $100 Million Residence
This is a 380,000-ft^2, 38-level CIP concrete structure. See Figs. 5.3.6 to 5.3.10 which also show the related cost estimate database and quantitative model information.

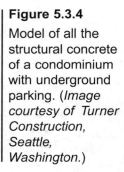

Figure 5.3.4

Model of all the structural concrete of a condominium with underground parking. (*Image courtesy of Turner Construction, Seattle, Washington.*)

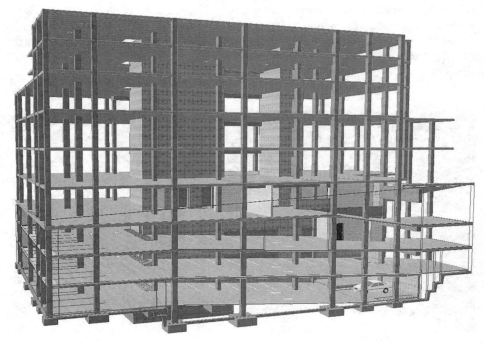

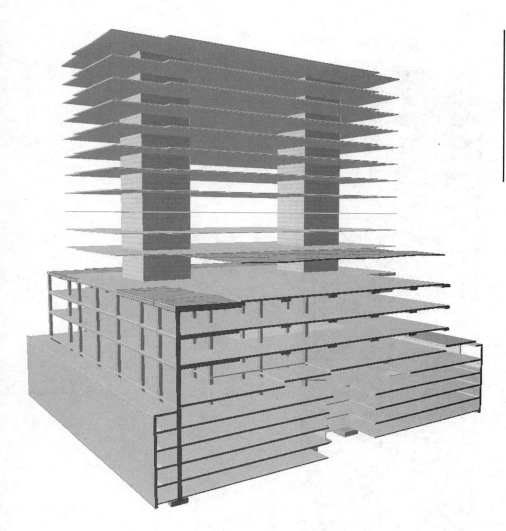

Figure 5.3.5
A 15-story con-
crete and struc-
tural steel frame
medical office
building. (*Image
courtesy of Turner
Construction,
Seattle,
Washinton.*)

Turner began taking the logical next step by using model-based estimating to capture building envelope quantities in May 2007. Not only is this approach quick and accurate, but also the model provides clear scope information (Figs. 5.3.7 to 5.3.10). This is particularly useful when multiple finishes and contractors are required. See Fig. 5.3.11.

Summary

Building information model (BIM) systems promise to enhance the quality and efficiency of the quantity takeoff and estimating process. These systems provide estimators with an enhanced ability to capture, define, and communicate the scope of an estimate while maintaining links to a cost database for pricing. By linking specifications and price data to specific building elements of a 3D representation of the project, estimators can produce a more comprehensive and accurate analysis of the project's quantities and constructability issues. Additionally, they can better manage scope changes and more

Figure 5.3.6

Model of all the structural concrete for a 38-story apartment build-ing. (*Image courtesy of Turner Construction, Seattle, Washington.*)

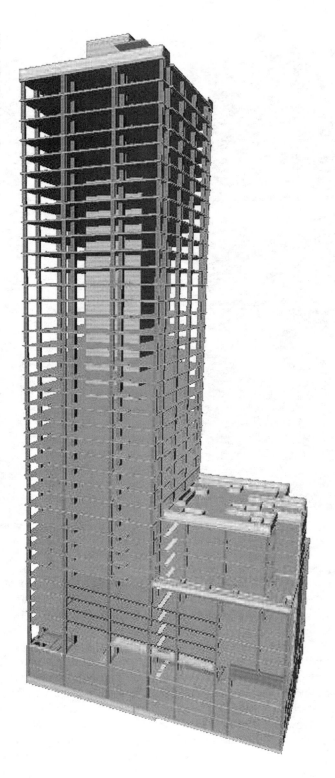

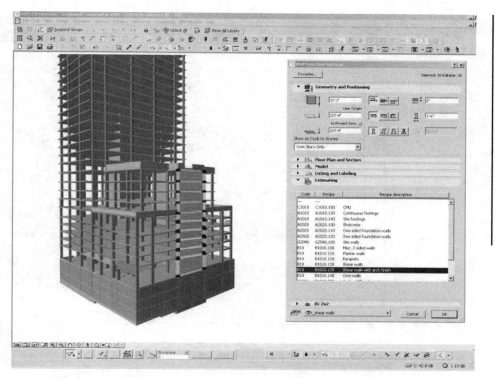

Figure 5.3.7
Model of the structural concrete of a 38-story apartment building, with the dialog box showing the link between a wall element and the Estimator recipe. (*Image courtesy of Turner Construction, Seattle, Washington.*)

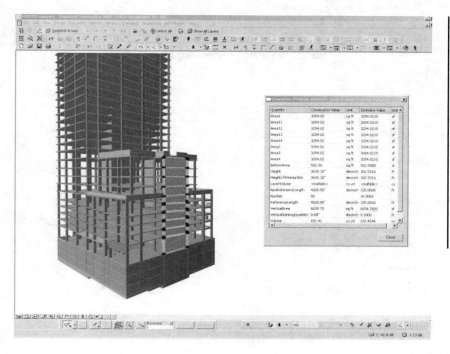

Figure 5.3.8
Model of the structural concrete of a 38-story apartment building, with the dialog box showing the quantitative information of a wall element in the Estimator recipe. (*Image courtesy of Turner Construction, Seattle, Washington.*)

Figure 5.3.9

The window in Estimator showing the recipe connected to the sample wall in the project estimate. (*Image courtesy of Turner Construction, Seattle, Washington.*)

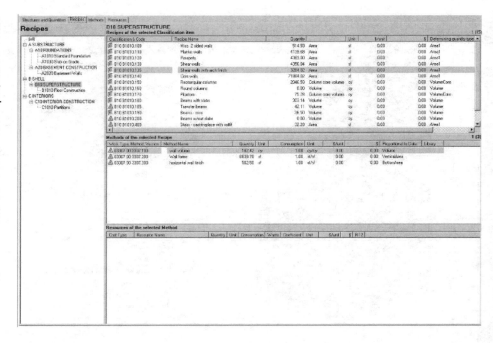

Figure 5.3.10

Another window in Estimator showing a different format for the project estimate listing of the sample wall. (*Image courtesy of Turner Construction, Seattle, Washington.*)

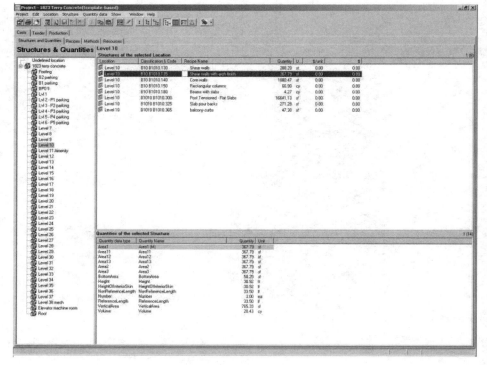

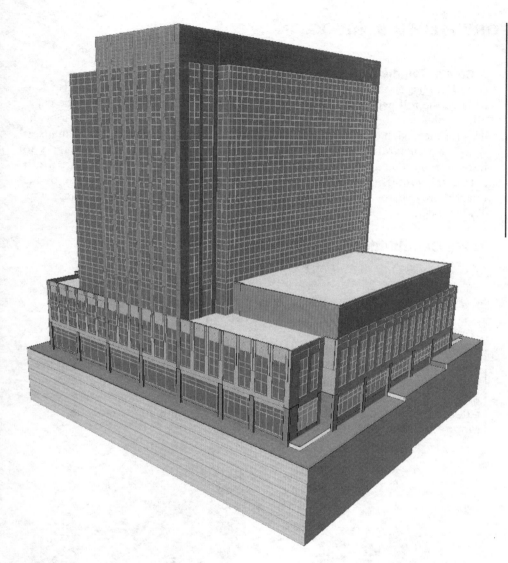

Figure 5.3.11
Exterior view of the 15-story medical office building. Just a little more modeling and the model can be used for a variety of other purposes. (*Image courtesy of Turner Construction, Seattle, Washington.*)

efficiently develop pricing for alternative scenarios. Visual queries and color coding functions of the 3D model allow quick and intuitive checks for the completeness and soundness of the estimate.

The initial big challenge of implementing these systems seems to lie in being able to find the time and energy to push through the initial learning curve required. It is intimidating, and people are very busy with schedules and deadlines. It is much easier to proceed with business as usual than to learn something new and seemingly complicated. The benefits, however, are huge and reward the individual willing to make the commitment required.

CASE 4: GREGORY P. LUTH & ASSOC., INC.

Author's Comment

Greg Luth has a structural engineering practice in Santa Clara, California. He contributed the following case study for a four-story steel structure to show the capabilities of Tekla software. Greg is dedicated to getting the most out of the tools he uses for the design and development of steel and concrete structures. He is an inspiration to structural engineers and fabricators, and has gone to great lengths to introduce and implement the state of the art technological advances that are available in this profession. Since a picture is worth a thousand words, please enjoy the images Greg shares of his creative approach to solving structural challenges with Tekla models.

Tekla Capabilities

by Gregory P. Luth, S.E., Ph.D.

See Figs. 5.4.1 to 5.4.6.

Figure 5.4.1

This is a Tekla model of a four-story building in a high seismic region at the end of design development. The building utilizes composite steel floors and an innovative energy-dissipating ductile in-filled concrete wall system on the exterior that provides a robust substrate for a Venetian stucco façade. (*Image courtesy of Gregory P. Luth & Assoc., Inc.*)

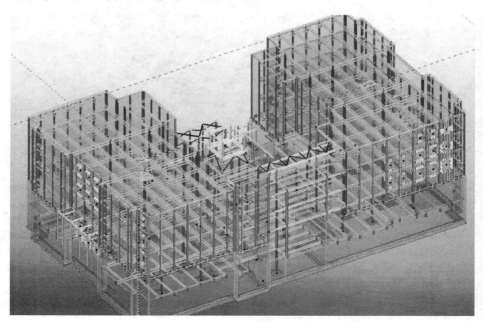

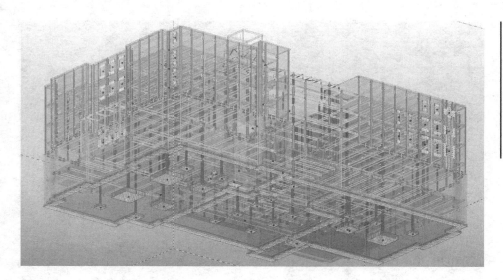

Figure 5.4.2
With Tekla we virtually build the building from the foundations up. (*Image courtesy of Gregory P. Luth & Assoc., Inc.*) See also color insert.

The 3D assembly drawings, such as the one showing the footing reinforcing, dowels, and wall reinforcing for the "L" footing and wall cast against the retention system, are much clearer than 2D placing drawings (which themselves have become rare) and can be used as placing diagrams for the rebar. Tekla will provide a complete bar list with

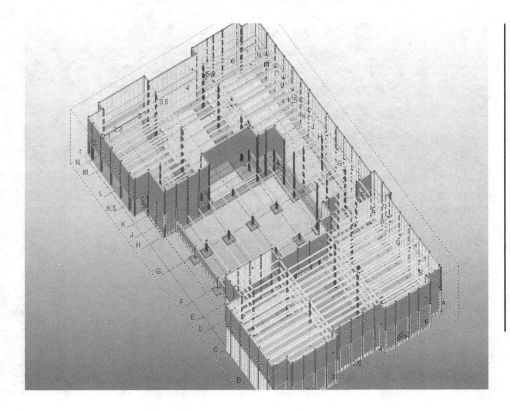

Figure 5.4.3
In this schematic design model we are not showing the concrete slabs and decks. Both the concrete and the deck—right down to the flutes—will be shown in the final model. At any point in the design we can pull off quantities of steel, concrete, and metal deck.
(*Image courtesy of Gregory P. Luth & Assoc., Inc.*)

Figure 5.4.4

(*a*) We can model all the reinforcing in Tekla such as the U bars around these windows. We can show recesses and inserts required to accommodate the stone trim in the façade. (*b*) With Tekla, we can model all the steel connections—either conceptually or for final detailing. We can hand off the model to the detailers or complete it ourselves. (*Images courtesy of Gregory P. Luth & Assoc., Inc.*) See also color insert for image b.

(*a*)

(*b*)

Figure 5.4.5

All details of the structure can be incorporated into the Tekla model. Unlike other 3D design tools, the Tekla model *is* the detailing model. Beam penetrations can be incorporated into the design model and integrated with 3D MEP shop drawing models for coordination purposes. (*Image courtesy of Gregory P. Luth & Assoc., Inc.*)

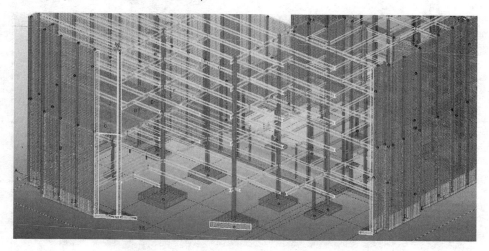

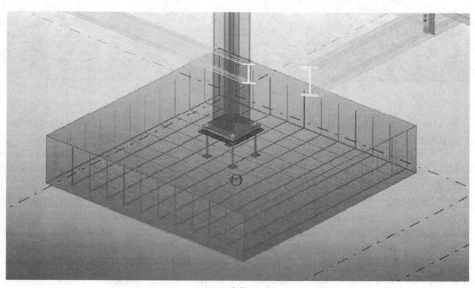

(*a*)

Figure 5.4.6

(*a*) Baseplates, anchor bolts, footings, and (*b*) foundation reinforcing are all part of the schematic design model. (*Images courtesy of Gregory P. Luth & Assoc., Inc.*)

Figure 5.4.6
(*Continued*)

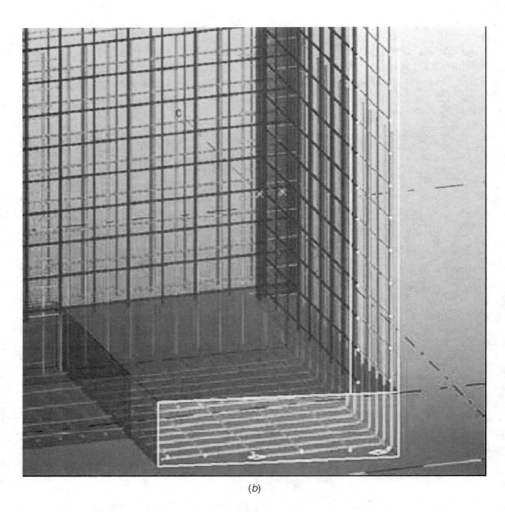

(*b*)

standard CRSI bending diagrams, making it possible to bid precise quantities of rebar and eliminating the waste and congestion that typify current practice.

The precast module for Tekla was completed several years ago and has become a standard in the precast industry. Tekla is focusing on adapting the rebar technology of its European products to accommodate U.S. practice. A task force of design practitioners is working with Tekla to develop a library of intelligent objects such as these posttensioned concrete beams, slabs, and columns. The goal is to model the building precisely as it is built to support downstream construction activities. This involves complex objects that reflect construction sequences such as the column rebar/lower column concrete/beam and slab rebar and concrete/and upper column concrete sequence implied in the above model.

The boundaries of the various material objects may be different, as with the two-story column rebar that traverses several concrete sequences and the beam/column joint that is functionally part of the column but is built with the beam. Tekla has the ability to do this because each of the materials is modeled explicitly. The modeling process is database-driven and parametric. The data are not stored as an extension of the graphics. The graphics are simply a visual report of the contents of the database. See Figs. 5.4.7, 5.4.9, and 5.4.10

Because of the ability to explicitly locate and define any sort of insert or penetration on the construction side, the model offers the opportunity to produce fully coordinated 3D lift drawings.

The following series of screen shots (Figs. 5.4.10 to 5.4.14) show the model when structural steel was complete and the model was turned over to the steel detailers to complete shop drawings. All beam penetrations for mechanical and miscellaneous supports for mechanical equipment were already coordinated and in the model.

The concrete was complete, and all window openings and mechanical penetrations were coordinated and in the model. Concrete slabs were in the model, but deck flutes were not incorporated to preserve model transparency. Consequently, the concrete quantities for the composite floors are off by the volume of the deck flutes.

Between design development and CDs, the design decision was made to shotcrete the walls. To facilitate that, the rebar cages between the columns will be fabricated in full-height panels. For erection, the rebar layout must be precisely coordinated with the embeds. The rebar has been removed from the global model with the exception of a typical solid and a typical window panel pending final coordination with the rebar sub. See Figs. 5.4.8 and 5.4.10.

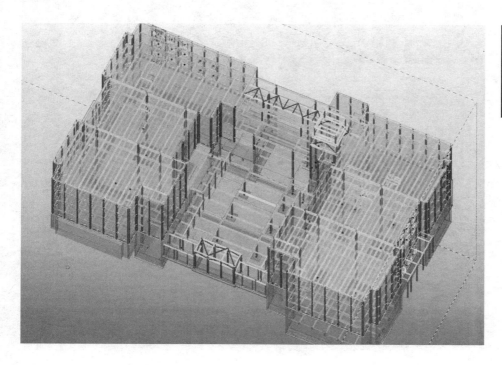

Figure 5.4.7
Model showing steel framing only. (*Image courtesy of Gregory P. Luth & Assoc., Inc.*)

Figure 5.4.8
Isometric detail of reinforcing in concrete wall panels. (*Image courtesy of Gregory P. Luth & Assoc., Inc.*)

Figure 5.4.9
Isometric view of concrete reinforcing for beams, slab and column connection. (*Image courtesy of Gregory P. Luth & Assoc., Inc.*)

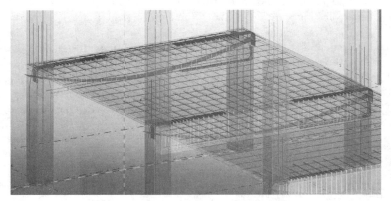

Figure 5.4.10
Isometric overview of concrete and steel frame structure, see detail in Fig. 5.4.8 (*Image courtesy of Gregory P. Luth & Assoc., Inc.*)

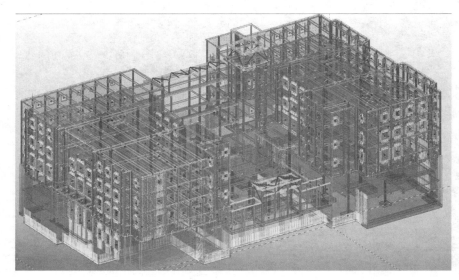

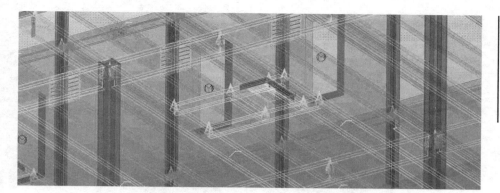

Figure 5.4.11
Miscellaneous framing for mechanical units. (*Image courtesy of Gregory P. Luth & Assoc., Inc.*)

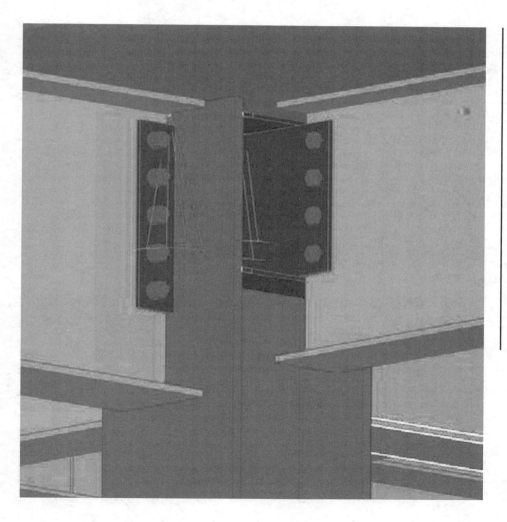

Figure 5.4.12
All connections are designed, but may be altered to suit the fabricator's preferences with relative ease prior to printing final shop drawings. Embedded plates and the connections to them are in the model. All material, including reinforcing at mechanical openings, is accounted for. (*Image courtesy of Gregory P. Luth & Assoc., Inc.*)

Figure 5.4.12
(*Continued*)

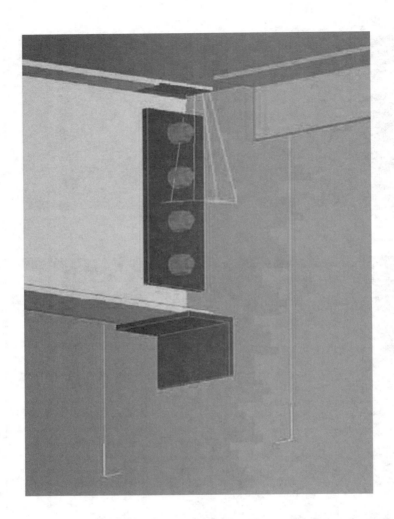

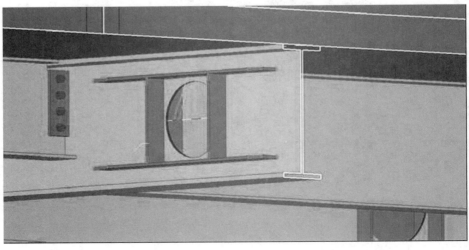

Figure 5.4.13
Wall subassembly extracted from the global model to facilitate coordination with the rebar subcontractor for fabrication and placing and with Tekla to automate the extraction of erection drawings and bar lists.
(*Image courtesy of Gregory P. Luth & Assoc., Inc.*)

(*a*)

Figure 5.4.14
(*a*) Lower section of wall panel showing (*b*) level of detail available for coordination with steel embeds.
(*Images courtesy of Gregory P. Luth & Assoc., Inc.*)

Figure 5.4.14
(*Continued*)

(*b*)

CASE 5: WEBCOR BUILDERS

Author's Comment

Modeling is playing an increasingly important role for self-performed work for general contractors. The advantages of working in 3D space are undeniable, and the rewards more than cover the cost of the modeling efforts. Webcor is on the forefront of BIM development and is dedicated to implement these processes company wide.

Implementation of Model-Based Estimating

by Jim Bedrick and Matt Ryan, Webcor Builders Inc.

History

Webcor's decision to launch an aggressive program of developing virtual design and construction (VDC) tools and integrating them into our standard processes was triggered by a meeting between our executives and those of Revit Technologies in January 2002. While Revit was demonstrating the process of building a model by tracing over an underlay 2D plan, we observed that the activity was almost identical to that of moving a digitizer over paper drawings (or a cursor over on-screen 2D CAD drawings) to generate a quantity takeoff. Two points quickly became obvious:

- A quantity takeoff generated by constructing a model is much more reliable than one generated by traditional methods, which rely on the estimator marking paper with felt pens (or CAD drawings with textures) to indicate what has and has not been counted. With appropriate infrastructure and standards in place, the model-based approach is much more "what you see is what you get"—if you see it in the model, it's counted; if you don't, it's not.

- The time spent creating a model replaces the time spent taking off quantities from 2D drawings. We subsequently found that with appropriate infrastructure, standards, and training in place, creating a model was at least as fast as generating a takeoff via 2D processes. Thus the model, which can be leveraged for other purposes such as schedule development and management and building system coordination, is essentially free.

We launched our VDC program with three thrusts: 3D quality control (constructability and coordination), 4D scheduling, and 5D cost estimating. At the outset we decided to lead with estimating, and this has worked well for us. This decision was based primarily on two points.

- *Timeliness.* The first thing we do with a project, once we decide to pursue it, is to generate a cost estimate, so the model-based estimating process gives us a model from the outset. This model is extremely useful in the project interviews as well as for 4D and 3D purposes such as design and construction progress.

- *Collaboration.* On most of our major projects, we are brought on early in the design phase to provide preconstruction services, and cost estimating is the majority of the effort. BIM is an invaluable collaboration tool during this effort, being extremely effective at helping all stakeholders visualize the project accurately and thus propose cost-saving measures that support the architect's design intent.

In March 2004, the executive leadership of Graphisoft came to us with an aggressive plan to develop a version of their ArchiCAD modeling program specifically for the construction industry. At that point Webcor and several other major contractors formed informal partnerships with Graphisoft, providing the real-world projects and domain expertise they needed to develop effective construction tools.

While we have major 3D and 4D implementations underway as well, the remainder of this study will focus on our implementation of 5D cost estimating. While our own program has developed with Graphisoft Constructor (now Vico Constructor after a management buyout in 2006), the study will remain as "application agnostic" as possible.

Implementation Approach

Webcor executives were convinced from the beginning that BIM-based processes would be advantageous for us, so we didn't expend much effort on ROI studies. Rather, our pilot projects were designed to develop processes, standards, and infrastructure, and to validate the results to generate confidence in the new approach. In many cases we found that the best approach was to simply provide additional resources to an existing project to run the BIM processes in parallel with the traditional until we had proved that the new processes were reliable.

The following discussion describes, at a high level, the processes, standards, and infrastructure we developed. While it is not a complete manual, it can be viewed as a checklist of the issues that must be considered in implementing a BIM-based estimating process.

Processes

Our usual project process is to work with the design team during preconstruction, providing several estimates of increasing precision, culminating in a guaranteed maximum price (GMP) at the conclusion of CDs. Because of this, we needed a system that would handle data of varying precision. For the most part this need does not exist on a hard-bid project, where the design information is at a high level of precision when the estimator begins.

The map in Fig. 5.5.1 shows our standard estimating process flow. This map was developed in collaboration with Graphisoft Construction Services.

Process Details

- *Set up locations.* We use the term *location* to denote building use type. For example, a mixed-use building might have garage, retail, and residential locations.
- *Create content plan.* The content plan contains information defining project-specific library objects and their supplemental data in the cost database.
- *Create project database (DB).* The project DB is partial copy of the corporate standard DB, initially created during project setup. Subsequently data are copied to the project DB from the standard DB as required by objects placed in the model.

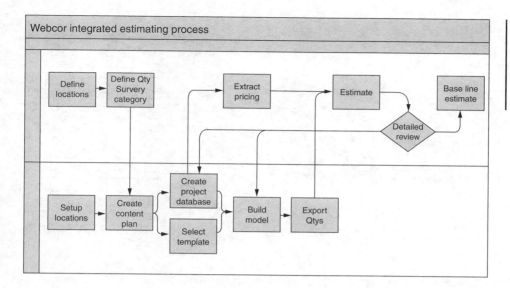

Figure 5.5.1
Estimating
process flow
diagram. (*Image
courtesy of
Webcor Builders.*)

- *Select template.* In most BIM tools, templates can be created that contain information common to a building type.

- *Extract pricing.* A report showing the estimate line items available in the project DB is extracted for review by the estimator. This is to ensure that the database contains complete and accurate information for the project.

- *Build model.* To date, Webcor has built all the models we use for estimating (early on we outsourced some models to Graphisoft Construction Services). As more architects adopt BIM design processes, we hope to leverage the architect's model to greatly speed up the cost feedback.

- *Export quantities.* This is a totally automated process in which the quantities from the model are exported along with cost information from the project DB in a spreadsheetlike format.

- *Estimate.* This is the traditional process where the estimator analyzes the estimate item by item, adjusting unit costs for project-specific circumstances.

- *Detailed review.* The estimate is compared, at a location and building system level, to recent similar projects as a reality check.

Progressive Estimates   As mentioned above, preconstruction work requires multiple estimates at increasing precision.

Data Progression   Early in the design, the estimate is usually limited to costs for each location and building system based on a cost per floor square foot. As the design progresses, line items are broken out from the location/system rollups and can be measured in any of the following ways:

- *Conceptual.* Cost per floor square foot
- *Unit.* Cost per hotel key, condominium unit, hospital bed, etc.

Figure 5.5.2

Conceptual model and estimate with quantities. (*Image courtesy of Webcor Builders.*)

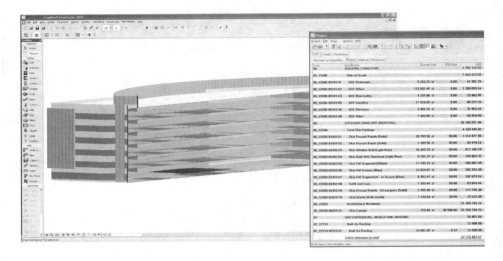

- *Measured.* Unit cost times actual quantity of the assembly
- *Lump sum.* Usually from a subcontract price for a specific work package

In the model, conceptual and unit prices are linked to zone elements. As line items are broken out and moved to a measured quantity, they are removed from the zone and their corresponding model elements are linked to the appropriate information in the project DB. As the project is bought out, line items in the spreadsheet view are replaced with lump-sum prices which are imported back into the project DB. See Figs. 5.5.2 and 5.5.3.

Variance Estimating As the design progresses, the level of precision can vary widely from one line item to another. Thus, stating that the entire project estimate has a precision of ±10 percent is not very useful. The structure might have ±2 percent and the interior construction ±20 percent.

Figure 5.5.3

More detailed model (3D section view) and estimate with quantities. (*Image courtesy of Webcor Builders.*)

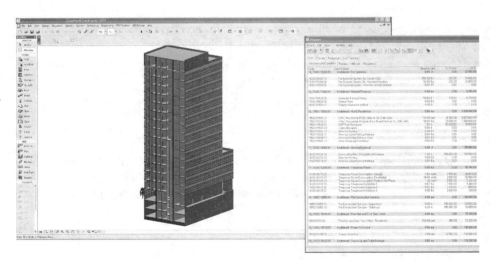

At our suggestion, Graphisoft added the capability to enter either a precise cost or a range of cost for each item in the database. This allows us to produce reports like the one in Fig. 5.5.4 (this example is rolled up to the location/system level, but the information is available at the line-item level).

This report clearly shows the architect where there is room to affect the budget and where there is not. As the design is further developed, we narrow the cost range on the items as more precise information becomes available, so each subsequent estimate will accurately show what we don't know as well as what we do.

Change Management   In progressing from one estimate to the next, there is often a question of whether it is best to begin the model from scratch or modify the model from the previous estimate. The problem is to accurately identify the changes that have been made from one drawing release to the next. If this can't be done reliably, we have no choice but to create a new model.

There are several tools available now (we use Graphisoft's Change Manager) that compare drawing sets and highlight changes, much as a word processor can compare documents. Note that the effectiveness of these tools depends heavily on the architect's adherence to some form of drawing standards. See Fig. 5.5.5.

Effective Collaboration   The best that a project team can usually expect from traditional processes is an estimate at the middle and end of each of the three design phases, and each of these takes on the order of three weeks. A lot of work goes on between the time a design decision is made and the time its cost implications are known. This process necessitates a lot of rework and usually results in so-called value engineering efforts in which scope and/or quality is reduced, often with negative impacts to the design intent.

The model-based estimating approach produces more useful cost information. Effective change management dramatically reduces the time needed to produce an estimate,

---

100% SD

21   RESIDENTIAL   236,841 gsf

System		Cost/sf		Total Cost		
		Min.	Max.	Min.	Max.	Variance
1	GENERAL CONDITIONS	12.00	14.00	2,842,092	3,315,774	473,682
2	BUILDING PAD, EARTHWORK, SITEWORK	1.00	3.00	236,841	710,523	473,682
3	LANDSCAPE & IRRIGATION					
4	FOUNDATIONS	3.00	5.00	710,523	1,184,205	473,682
5	BUILDING STRUCTURE	47.38	55.62	11,221,527	13,173,096	1,951,570
6	EXTERIOR ENVELOPE (VERTICAL)	32.96	48.41	7,806,279	11,465,473	3,659,193
7	WATERPROOFING, INSULATION, ROOFING	4.00	6.00	947,364	1,421,046	473,682
8	INTERIOR CONSTRUCTION	41.20	61.80	9,757,849	14,636,774	4,878,925
9	SPECIALTIES	1.00	2.00	7,806,279	11,465,473	3,659,193
10	BUILDING EQUIPMENT	5.00	7.00	1,184,205	1,657,887	473,682
11	FURNISHINGS					
12	SPECIAL CONSTRUCTION					
13	CONVEYING SYSTEMS	4.12	6.18	975,785	1,463,677	487,892
14	FIRE PROTECTION	2.70	3.20	639,471	757,891	118,421
15	PLUMBING	17.00	23.00	4,026,297	5,447,343	1,421,046
16	HVAC	17.50	21.50	4,144,718	5,092,082	947,364
17	ELECTRICAL	21.00	29.00	4,973,661	6,868,389	1,894,728
18	MISCELLANEOUS EXPENSES	2.50	4.25	592,103	1,006,574	414,472
19	CONTINGENCY	4.00	6.00	947,364	1,421,046	473,682
20	JOB EQUIPMENT	6.50	8.50	1,539,467	2,013,149	473,682
	Totals	254.82	350.87	60,351,824	83,100,402	22,748,578

Figure 5.5.4
Cost report from model with systems square foot costs and variances. (*Image courtesy of Webcor Builders.*)

Figure 5.5.5

Change Manager (Graphisoft) indicating changes in new drawings. (*Image courtesy of Webcor Builders.*)

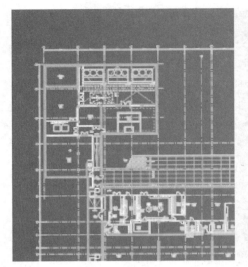 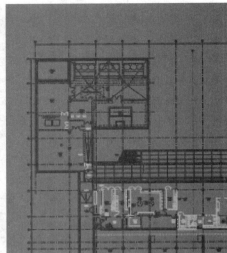

allowing this information to be produced faster and more often. This process produces information that the architect can use to guide the design rather than to fix it after it's broken.

Standards

We've mentioned more than once in this discussion that the effectiveness of these processes depends on having the necessary standards and infrastructure in place. Standards are mainly put in place for two reasons: to avoid redoing work that can be leveraged for multiple projects and to facilitate communications and information exchange. However, standardization and flexibility can both be beneficial—these tend to be opposing goals, so a balance must be struck. Since these processes are so new and it's obvious we have a lot to learn, we tend to aim for the minimum standardization necessary.

There are, of course, universal standards issues that have been well developed through 20+ years of experience with CAD—file naming conventions, data structures, layer naming, etc. This case study will skip these fundamentals and focus on two examples of standards we've adopted that are specific to the BIM environment.

Level of Detail   This is one of the most important standards to work out—too low a level can render the model useless, too high a level can waste a huge amount of modeling time. The appropriate level is determined by the intended use of the model—this can change as the project progresses, and there can be multiple uses at any given point.

In our case the model begins as an estimating tool. As the project progresses, it soon becomes a 4D scheduling tool and then a 3D system coordination tool as well. We'll focus on the estimating function for this study.

As discussed in the "Process" section above, any given element will progress through several levels of detail, and it may be broken down into an increasing number of line items. For example, the rebar in a pad footing progresses as follows:

Conceptual. At this level, the footing is not actually modeled. Its cost is derived from a dollars per square foot entry in the database linked to a zone in the model defining the footprint. The rebar cost is embedded in that number.

Schematic/design development. Here the footing itself is modeled as a simple block, whose dimensions are refined as the design progresses. The concrete quantity is determined from the volume of the block, and the rebar quantity is now broken out as a separate line item defined as a number of pounds of rebar per cubic yard of concrete. This is the highest level to which we'll take concrete elements in an estimating model.

Shop drawing. At this level, the rebar itself is modeled, and the quantity of various bar sizes is extracted from the model. It is usually only specialty subcontractors that find this level useful.

Model Progression Specification   Since various elements can progress to different levels of detail at different points in the design process, keeping track of what information is extractable from the model in what form and at what precision can become extremely confusing. Graphisoft developed an approach they call the Model Progression Specification (MPS) that we've found very useful. See Fig. 5.5.6.

Assemblies can have up to six levels of detail, from conceptual to shop drawing. Each level for each element in the model is specified in the MPS, and then these levels are mapped against the design phases to give a complete picture of the precision of the model at any point in the process. We are currently working with Graphisoft to develop our own MPS, but in the future the MPS will likely become a published standard.

Pad Footing	LoD 100	LoD 200	LoD 300 …
Model	N/A		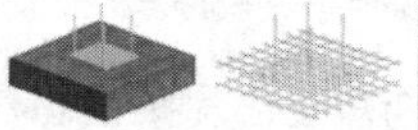
Estimating	Recipe based takeoff Foundation Conceptual ls or $/ sf	Model based takeoff •Formwork •Concrete Reinforcing •4000 psi Concrete	Model based takeoff •Formwork # of form uses •Grade of steel •# of rebar mats •Mat bar size •Bar spacing •Accelerator
Scheduling	Master Task Foundations	Master Tasks •Form Pad Footing •Reinforce Pad Footing •Pour Pad Footing	Micro Management •Prep •Set Anchor Bolts/Embeds •Formwork •Reinforcement •Place & Finish
Procurement	N/A	Purchase Order Subcontracts	Purchase Order Subcontracts
Fabrication	N/A	Tolerance	•Formwork design •Anchor bolts and embeds •Reinforcing Steel

Figure 5.5.6

Model progression specification by Graphisoft. LoD means level of detail and refers to the detail in the model components. (*Image courtesy of Webcor Builders.*)

Figure 5.5.7

Views of the beam and slab connection. (*Image courtesy of Webcor Builders.*)

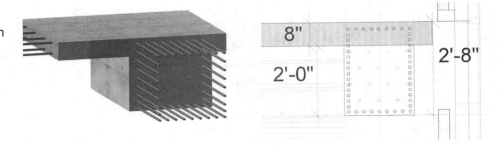

Specific Quantity Issues   Since Webcor self-performs a lot of work, our estimating needs run beyond that of a GC to the level of detail needed by specialty subcontractors. At this level, specific modeling practices can have significant effects on the accuracy of the quantity information extracted form the model.

A good example is the intersection between a slab and a beam shown in Fig. 5.5.7.

The question here is whether to model the beam as 2 ft 0 in deep or as 2 ft 8 in deep. It's generally best to model the slab as a monolithic piece, so that would point to modeling the beam 2 ft 0 in deep so as not to count the concrete in the intersection twice. However, the rebar is designed for a 2-ft 8-in deep beam. Since our practice is to determine rebar quantity as pounds per cubic yard of concrete, modeling the beam at 2 ft 0 in would miss a lot of rebar. Our solution to this type of problem is to apply a consumption factor (our cost database has a field for this). In this case the beam is modeled at 2 in deep and the rebar cage is 32 in deep, so the consumption factor is 1.33. Thus if the normal rebar content for beams is 400 lb/yd^3, for this beam it would be 532 lb/yd^3.

The point here is that using a model to generate a quantity takeoff is not simply a matter of pushing a button. Standards must be carefully set up and models audited for compliance in order to have them generate accurate numbers.

Infrastructure

Object Libraries   Most BIM tools support the creation of standard objects (ArchiCAD "favorites," Revit "families," etc.) that can be used to represent common building components. In our system, we're able to link these objects with their appropriate information in the estimating DB. For example, we have multiple wall types in our library, all modeled with the same "wall" tool but each attached to a different "recipe" of materials and costs in the estimating DB.

Templates   A lot of information is identical from one project to another, especially within a given building type. Most BIM tools have the capability of embedding this type of information in a template that can be used to start a project with a lot of information already immediately available.

We create templates for the project types we do repeatedly (office tower, high-rise residential, etc.) and include information such as the following:

Library objects for standard components.

Materials and colors to be applied to standard objects.

Elements to be split. This is for downstream 4D use. For example, a slab will initially be modeled as a single object for an entire floor, but if it will be poured in multiple stages, it will have to be split later on in order to support useful 4D schedule animation.

Layer standards.

Equipment (crane, human lift, concrete pump, etc).

Cost Database   Our implementation relies on a database of costs and other data that exist outside the model. As described in "Process Details" above, elements or "recipes" from the standard DB are copied to a project DB and linked to the model as required. Since costs are constantly changing, it's necessary to update the data frequently. It's important, though, that these updates be carefully controlled for accuracy, and that an update to the standard DB not change costs for a project estimate already underway without the knowledge of the project estimator. See Fig. 5.5.8.

Favorite is a term used in Constructor modeling, indicating the settings for a parametric tool that specifically applies to a given project model. It will generate an element with the chosen settings automatically when clicked. *Recipe* refers to the data in Estimator that are linked to a given model element in order to generate costs for that element.

Data Storage   Over the past years the cost of data storage has fallen dramatically, so this has tended to become less of an issue. However, BIMs are huge (ours average over 0.5 GB apiece) compared to other files, so the implementation of a program that results in people creating a lot of BIMs can quickly overload a firm's capacity. There's usually benefit in keeping a trail of the different versions of a model, but a carefully enforced archiving program is vital.

File Locations   Because of the size of the models, it's important to consider where they should be physically located. In our setup, we have a dedicated DS3 (45-MΩ) line between our Hayward and San Mateo offices. However, even with that kind of bandwidth, it takes an estimator in San Mateo 45 seconds longer to load a 0.5-GB model from a server in Hayward than from one in San Mateo. This doesn't seem like much at first glance, but it's annoying to estimators and disrupts their work, and it ties up network resources. We find it worthwhile to locate models on servers as close to the primary user as possible.

The location of corporate standard cost database, though, is not as critical. There is not a huge amount of traffic between the standard DB and the project DBs. We've located ours at our corporate data center, and it efficiently serves offices from central to southern California.

Conclusions

Because we chose to aggressively implement BIM-based processes so early, it's taken us longer than we'd have liked. At the outset of our program, BIM tools designed to support construction were in their infancy, and efficient processes to leverage these tools were hardly even thought of. Thus much of our time and effort went into helping

Figure 5.5.8

Data management diagram between the server and a local machine. (*Image courtesy of Webcor Builders.*)

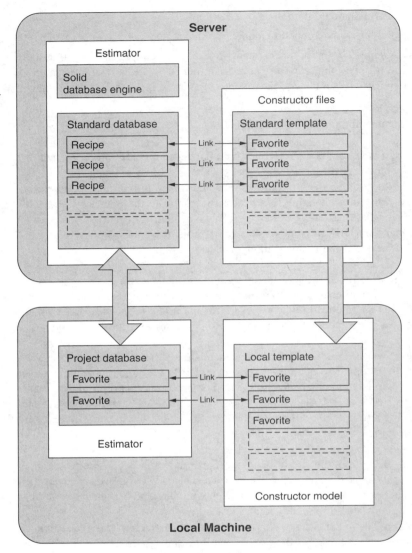

software developers create and hone tools that would work for contractors, and into developing new processes that would take advantage of these tools. The outlook is not as scary for contractors starting implementation programs now—the tools and processes have been developed and proved.

Despite the challenges we faced due to our early adoption, we've never looked back. In many areas, BIM-based processes are now our standard way of doing business.

CASE 6: TURNER CONSTRUCTION, SACRAMENTO, CALIFORNIA

Author's Comment

Laser scanning and point cloud modeling are very effective means to record existing situations and import the 3D information into an existing BIM for further use. Laser scanning can be compared to a combination of 3D photography and surveying. The result is a point cloud (the 3D image of the survey) that is a composite of several readings at different locations. Each of the readings (laser scans) is registered to known common points so that they can be interpreted together and allow more points to be tied into the overall image. The surfaces (that is what is being surveyed) that are not visible have to be interpreted when the point cloud is translated into a 3D model (backs of ducts, etc.). The resulting model is then inserted into the planning model of the project as the existing situation. This technology could conceivably also be used to develop (and check) as-built situations of new construction where tolerances were a critical issue. Turner Construction is already using laser scanning to "reverse engineer" existing facility modifications. Turner, the subcontractors, and the design teams use the laser scan to design and coordinate new structure, mechanical, and electrical systems into the exact positions in the 3D model. Turner Cnstruction is a pioneer in this area of BIM.

Laser Scanning in Medical Renovation Work

by Lev Kaganovich and George Zettel, Turner Construction Company, Sacramento

Project: Sutter General Hospital Renovation

Total structure square footage: 419,094 ft^2

Renovated square footage: Approx 340,000 ft^2

This hospital is a fully operational 24 hours per day, 7 days per week. At no one time will any part of the hospital be shut down until construction starts. This greatly limits the amount of investigation we are allowed to perform. Along with limited investigation abilities, there are not any reliable as-built drawings to refer to. To create less of an impact to the hospital and to save time and money in the end, Turner has purchased a laser scanner. With this scanner, we have the ability to scan above ceilings, creating point clouds which we then convert into 3D objects and create a true as-built drawing, or model, in 3D space. With this 3D model we can then have our contractors coordinate in the new work around existing systems without having the contractors ever stepping foot into the hospital.

All images in Figs. 5.6.1 to 5.6.6 are of Sutter General Hospital, a portion of basement level.

Figure 5.6.1
Sheet 2.M1.60.1C existing mechanical ducting. (*Image courtesy of Turner Construction, Sacramento, California.*)

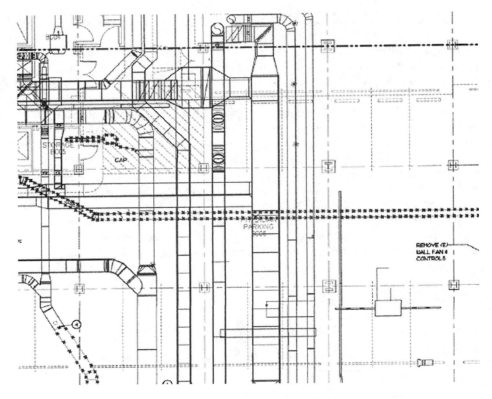

Figure 5.6.2
Sheet 2.P1.60.1C existing plumbing. (*Image courtesy of Turner Construction, Sacramento, California.*)

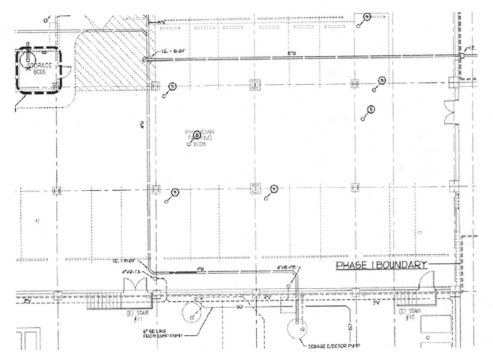

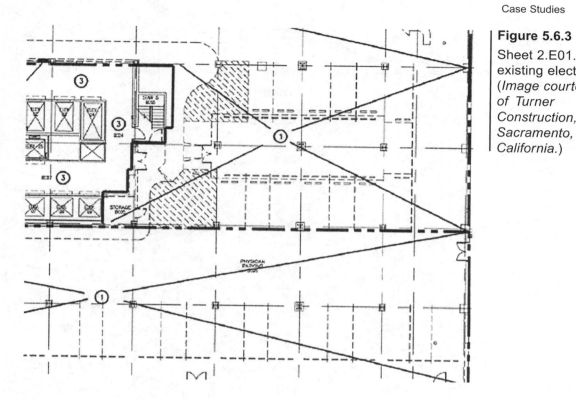

Figure 5.6.3
Sheet 2.E01.00.1 existing electrical. (*Image courtesy of Turner Construction, Sacramento, California.*)

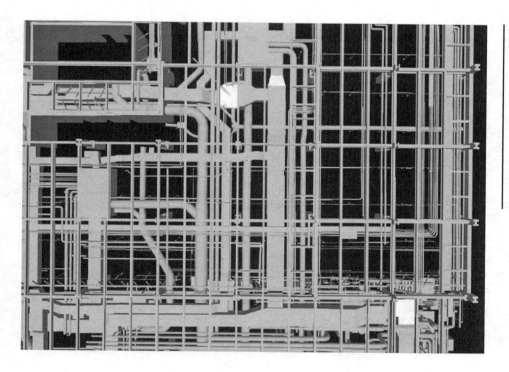

Figure 5.6.4
Scanned area of actual existing systems—modeled from a point cloud (area scanned with a laser scanner). (*Image courtesy of Turner Construction, Sacramento, California.*)

Figure 5.6.5
New design per mechanical contract drawings. (*Image courtesy of Turner Construction, Sacramento, California.*)

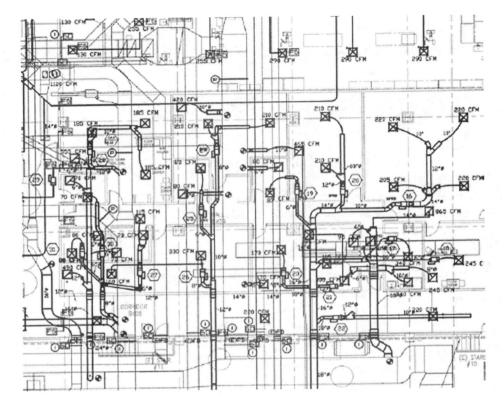

Figure 5.6.6
Fully coordinated mechanical design. Scanned area with all new MEP included and fully coordinated. (*Image courtesy of Turner Construction, Sacramento, California.*)

Glossary

Words shown in boldface in the text can be found in this Glossary. (Not all words in the Glossary are in all cases indicated by boldface in the text, however.)

Abstraction

An *abstraction* is a general symbol or diagram representing a specific object or idea. The dictionary describes it as "the forming of general ideas or concepts from specific examples" (Encarta *World English Dictionary*) or "formation of an idea, as of the qualities or properties of a thing, by mental separation from particular instances or material objects" (Webster's *New World College Dictionary*). A computer model can be seen as an abstraction of the project it represents; it conveys the sense of the building, and permits the user to imagine many features, without many of the realistic details. Humans have a great capacity to understand and use abstractions as shortcuts to communicate understanding.

Analysis

"A separating or breaking up of any whole into its parts, especially with an examination of these parts to find out their nature, proportion, function, interrelationship, etc." (Webster's *New World College Dictionary*). It is the analysis of the project that generates the understanding to be able to construct a model of the project; and it is the analysis of the model that generates the understanding to improve our methods of actualizing the project.

Architecture

The meaning of this term when it relates to software products refers to the structure of the organization of the tool, in other words the way the parts relate to each other. The architecture of a software tool determines the way in which it can be used to organize and process its data.

Automatic

This word has so many meanings attached to it that it only needs a warning in the context of its use in connection with building information modeling. There is very little that is truly automatic, so it will be worthwhile to find out just exactly what is meant in any specific context. There will be instances where *automatic* may still involve an extraordinary amount of manual input; it is good to be prepared for situations like this. It may also be possible that the automatically created results will not be usable as anticipated, and this also may create much anticipated work on behalf of the user. In general, to run a test prior to committing to a specific approach is well worth it; just be sure that the test includes all aspects of the complete process.

Big Room

The *big room* concept was developed to a large extent by CIFE (Center for Integrated Facilities Engineering) at Stanford University. It originates from manufacturing industries, and its focus is on facilitating collaborative communication, problem solving, and decision processes. The big room refers to a physical or virtual space where various project team members view and discuss project issues and develop solutions in real time. This often includes a Smart Board or other projected image that can be viewed by several persons at the same time so that communication can be facilitated. Not all discussion participants need to be in the same physical space, some may be connected via other forms of communication channels such as the Internet and phone. The purpose is to have the participants communicate directly face to face as effectively as possible. This avoids the waste of multitasking. Sharing the same physical space at the same time would be the most traditional solution to this challenge, and the introduction of more sophisticated technology will further aid this goal. It is understandable that if all project team members spent their working hours in the same space together, all helping one another to solve their problems, meetings would be unnecessary; the entire experience could be considered a working meeting. Project team members do not need to "go back to the office to work on it." The big room concept increases the amount of time that team members spend together solving project problems as a group, and reduces turnaround time from one project review to the next (response time to RFIs between members), thus accelerating the design development significantly. This approach significantly reduces the number of RFIs on a project as well.

BIM

- *Building information model* is a virtual representation of a building, potentially containing all the information required to construct the building, using computers and software. The term generally refers both to the model(s) representing the physical characteristics of the project and to all the information contained in and attached to components of these models. When BIM is used in a sentence, it will depend on the context whether it means building information model or building information modeling. A BIM may include any of or all the 2D, 3D, 4D (time element—scheduling), 5D (cost information), or nD (energy, sustainability, facilities management, etc., information) representations of a project.

- *Building information modeling* is the act of creating and/or using a BIM.

The term has been widely accepted as including almost anything that may be found in this text. There is a widespread dissatisfaction with the use of this term among the practitioners in the field; numerous other terms are regularly introduced to describe the general approach to this field, yet most individuals continue to use BIM due to lack of agreement on any other name. This book will not dwell on definitions of the name, but focus on the concepts, tools, and processes that are connected to this broad area.

Charrette

See Design Charrette

CIFE

The Center for Integrated Facility Engineering is located in the department of civil and environmental engineering of Stanford University. This research institution develops processes and methods for the construction industry. http://cife.stanford.edu. The phrase **VDC** which stands for Virtual Design and Construction was coined at CIFE.

Collaboration

Collaboration means working together cooperatively, as a team. This assumes that all persons who collaborate have the same goals in relation to the work that needs to be performed. True collaboration requires all participants to have a similar understanding of these goals so that their efforts can be supportive and complementary of one another.

Good examples of successful collaboration are the efforts of members of a sports team who are attempting to win a competition, or members of a musical ensemble who are performing. Clearly in these examples there is not much room for any member of the group to become too independent; all efforts need to be accurate, well timed, and supportive of the goals of the whole group to achieve success. One important aspect of successful collaboration in these examples is the need for practice, discipline, and strategic planning.

Common Sense

"A sense common to humans (in general)." The expression "Common sense is not so common" refers to the tendency of humans to disregard the obvious, often for personal reasons and often without realizing it.

Communication

This is the transfer or exchange of information, generally between individuals or groups. Communication takes place when information is both provided and received; a form of confirmation that information was in fact transmitted and received is important. It is notable that communication does not necessarily imply understanding, on the part of either the provider or the receiver of the information, although this understanding is often presupposed and can thus easily lead to misunderstandings.

Component

The word *component* may refer to an element in a 3D model, or it may also indicate an individual part of a BIM, e.g., the mechanical model or the structural model. It will be necessary to derive the specific meaning from the context.

Composite Model

A model consisting of several component models, e.g. the **integration** of an architectural, structural and MEP model.

Conceptual

Conceptual relates to the initial stages where an idea or thought is the beginning element for a process of development.

Constructability

This term refers to the analysis of the ability to construct. In the early phases of a project, such analysis can provide valuable input for the practicality of the assembly process of a project. Constructability analysis can take place on various scales, depending on the phase of the project and the level of detail available about the construction process.

Construction Budget

The project owner will generally determine the construction budget. It is the task of the project team to deliver a finished project to the owner that maximizes project value within the budget.

Construction Project

This is synonymous with building project, and it refers to the planning, preparation, and construction of a building. Projects typically are performed by individuals who use methods to achieve certain results. Figure G.1 outlines this relationship and will be the basis for most discussions in this book.

Figure G.1
The structure of a construction project.

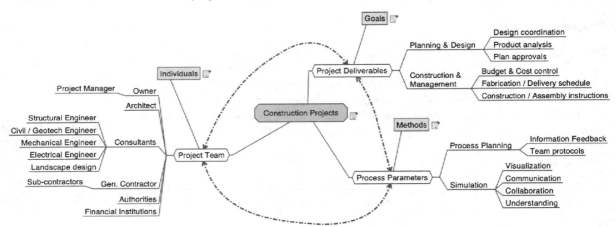

Coordination

"To bring into proper order, arranging, harmonious adjustment" (Webster's *New World College Dictionary*). Coordination is an essential activity in a construction project where multiple disciplines are sharing the same space for their components.

Cost Analysis

The analysis of cost can refer both to the construction cost and to the life cycle cost of a project or component of a project.

Cost Estimate

In traditional design-bid-build project delivery methods (see Delivery system), the architect establishes cost estimates for construction projects in the early phases of project planning. Once a building contractor becomes part of the project team, the projected construction cost will also become the contractor's primary concern. Historically the estimates generated by the builder are much more reliable than those generated by the designers. Alternative project delivery methods have been developed to include the contractor in the project planning process.

Database—Centralized and Federated

A database is a "large collection of data in a computer, organized so that it can be expanded, updated and retrieved rapidly for various uses" (Webster's *New World College Dictionary*). The terms *centralized* and *federated* are used by Bentley systems to describe the nature of the organization of the information in a BIM. A centralized database implies all the data in a single—centralized—location and managed all together by a single entity. Federated means "united by common agreement under a central authority" (Webster's *New World College Dictionary*). A federated database consists of various databases managed by different entities that have agreed upon a system of working together to permit access to each of those databases. A single entity can then oversee the management of the various databases, without having to manage them in detail. In the real world, centralized databases are generally either small and controlled or quite challenging to manage due to their size and complexity. It is thus more realistic to plan on intentionally federating the databases for a large complex construction project than to hope to manage them in a centralized format.

Delivery Method

Also known as *project delivery method or system*. The contracts describing the relationships and responsibilities of the project team members to the construction project and to one another define the project delivery method. The nature of such contractual relationships typically describes the assumption of project risk by the signers.

Deployment

The word *deployment* is defined as "to station or place (forces, equipment, etc.) in accordance with a plan" (Webster's *New World College Dictionary*). This refers to the preparations required to implement the BIM process; in this context to *implement* means "to carry into effect, to fulfill, to accomplish" (Webster's *New World College Dictionary*). In some cases it may be helpful to distinguish between these two easily confusable concepts. Deployment refers to the establishing of the conditions and circumstances that will enable implementation (action) to take place.

Design Charette

A design charette is a collaborative meeting/workshop of the designers of a project with others who have an interest in the project, i.e., owners, facility end users, contractors, etc. During a charette the discussions will focus on various design-related issues important to the group, and the designers will propose solutions that address these concerns. Such an event generally results in a number of quick sketch studies incorporating the ideas and requests from such input; these sketches are then used to indicate the direction for the project design. Such workshops are typically iterative in nature; i.e., each meeting will bring the group a little closer to a solution that reflects the owner's expected facility performance and project value. The general feeling of a design charrette is one of communication and collaboration between the designers and persons who are concerned about the outcome of the project.

Dimensionality—2D, 3D, 4D, 5D, *n*D

The common convention referring to the "geometric dimensions of some physical or abstract system" (Webster's *New World College Dictionary*), where 2D space is a flat plane; 3D space is three-dimensional space, e.g., length, width, and height; 4D space adds time as a dimension; 5D space will generally refer to cost; and *n*D will refer to any other yet undetermined quantity added to the mix, e.g., energy analysis, sustainable design, or facilities management information.

Documentation

This refers to the documents required to construct a building project, usually drawings, specifications, and contracts.

Element

An element is very similar to a component of a 3D model; the two words may be used interchangeably.

Elimination

Elimination will be used with respect to the removal of the unnecessary components, processes, etc. from a project or procedure. This term specifically relates to and supports the fundamental concepts of **Lean Construction** Practices.

Field

The *field* is a term usually referring to the physical construction site when it is used in a discussion of construction topics.

File Format

The file format refers to the nature of the computer files extension, i.e., the three letters after the period in a file name that indicate the software it is authored by, or intended for. Software tools create files in their native file format and often permit the translation of these files into other file formats that make the information available to other software tools. This is at the core of interoperability, the free (and complete) interchange of information among various files of different file formats.

Human Nature

Human nature is "the typical character that all human beings share, often seen as being imperfect" (Encarta *World English Dictionary*). This also refers to the characteristics of humans that cause certain actions or inclinations.

IFC

IFC means *industry foundation class*; it is a term coined by the International Alliance for Interoperability. The IFC is a standard file format for 3D models that will permit information to be exchanged among all models that can be translated into this file format. It is an attempt to bring about standards for a common language between the various model authoring and analyzing software tools. The website www.iai-international.org will provide more information on these concepts and standards.

Implementation (BIM)

Implementation refers to the actualization and utilization of tools and processes related to BIM technology. Also see *Deployment*.

Input—Graphical, Numeric

I*nput* refers to the information given to a software tool that describes an action to be taken. *Graphical* input refers to graphically—with the mouse—establishing the size and/or location of elements in a model. *Numeric* input provides this information with the keyboard, i.e., numbers. Both ways can provide accurate information to the computer, but care has to be taken to avoid unintended errors when providing input. Strict adherence to accuracy in modeling and information input can make life in the BIM world far more manageable.

Integration

Integration refers to the combining of components or information from various sources. Interoperability is a critical factor in the ability to integrate.

Interface

The interface of software is what we see on the screen. It is the visual impression of the software and affects the possibilities for interaction on the part of the user. A software tool is evaluated both by its interface and by its ability to process data.

Interoperability

Interoperability refers to the ability of different file formats to be integrated with one another and transfer relevant information among one another.

Lean Construction

Lean construction is a term coined in the 1990s by Glen Ballard and Greg Howell of the Lean Construction Institute. They adapted process and productivity improvements exhibited by the Toyota Production System in manufacturing industries over the last few decades for application by the construction industry. Toyota was heavily influenced after World War II by the U.S. Army consulting group "Training Within Industry" (TWI) and the quality teachings by Edward Deming.

Library Part

A library part is an object that has been preformulated for a 3D model, and can be placed multiple times into a virtual model. Each instance of the library part can be either unique or identical, as required; and each will have its unique internal ID number to distinguish it from all other instances of the same part, even though it may be identical in all other aspects (i.e., steel trusses). The use of library parts makes modeling easier and faster since many parts can be accessed through a library that has been built outside of the specific project model that uses it. Since library parts are external references to the model files, the model file will be able to be smaller than if it had to contain all these components. In other words, the components as we see them in the model are actually references to the actual components contained in the library. This principle is similar to that of linking to other external data, such as e-mails or invoices that can be linked to references in the model, and thus be accessible directly from the model.

Life Cycle Analysis, Cost

A *life cycle* refers to the entire life of a project; this includes from the earliest planning until its demolition and the recycling of materials. The energy consumption and maintenance costs of a project are important aspects of the life cycle cost.

Line of Balance Schedule

A line of balance is the representation of a particular task on a construction schedule by a line, whose vertical slope indicates the productivity of that task. The balancing of the various lines on such a schedule results in the fine-tuning of the tasks making up the project.

Link

A *link* is a connection between elements; these elements may be elements within a file or a file in its own right. Thus an icon (element) in a file can be linked to another document so that document becomes "attached" to the host file, and the information in that document is accessible through the host file by clicking on the icon.

Mapping

Mapping refers to the transfer of information from one format to another.

Method

"A way of doing anything; mode; procedure; process, esp., a regular, orderly, definite procedure or way of teaching, investigating, etc." (Webster's *New World College Dictionary*).

Model

A *model* is a representation of an object or an idea, usually with a certain degree of abstraction. A model is meant to represent reality—not to be reality. As the model takes more factors into consideration that bring it closer to representing reality, it can become more detailed and more complex. In this text the meaning of *level of detail* refers to the physical details that are represented in the model, i.e., how small the pieces of the object are that can be seen in the model. The *level of complexity* refers to the structure of the model and to the information that can be accessed through the model; e.g., the model components such as architectural, structural, mechanical, etc., will provide access to information that is contained in or attached to these models.

For a description of a solid model and a surface model, see Chap. 3 on software tools.

Object—Object Based, Object Model

The use of objects in 3D models renders them more usable and efficient in the BIM process. An object generally represents a physical entity (although nonphysical entities, e.g., events such as inspections, can also be represented by objects) in the project and is able to contain information relevant to the project. Objects are often composed of many parts that would be much more burdensome to the project model if treated as separate parts. See also *Library Part*.

Parametric

A parametric object or component is an object (or component) that permits a (usually limited) choice of values for defined parameters. A parameter is a variable value (as in a mathematical equation) that, when it changes, gives a different but related characteristic to the original object. An example is a steel beam in a 3D model that can have the size of the beam as one of its parameters. This means that the specific beam in the model needs to have its size specified, and it will thus reflect its physical size and weight accurately in the model. The chosen values for the parameters generate parametric information. In the case of the steel beam, the size of the beam implies a variety of information that will be determined by its size, e.g., its width, thickness, total weight (resulting from the length), etc.

Planning

"To devise a scheme for doing, making, or arranging" (Webster's *New World College Dictionary*). The BIM processes largely improve the planning activities of construction projects to reduce risk and waste and to increase quality and profitability.

Prefabrication

Prefabrication is challenging when the assembly takes place in the field. The use of BIM permits the coordination of various project parameters so that it becomes more likely that prefabrication is planned and implemented successfully.

Process

There is the BIM process, and there are the processes that produce specific results within the BIM. This book treats building information modeling as a process—as a tool to plan and manage projects through simulations. Within this overall project scaled process there are many other processes that relate to specific functions within the overall BIM process. These processes are also discussed in detail in this text. The context of the discussions will make it clear to which scale the word *process* applies.

Project Team

All the persons directly involved (on a more than occasional or one-time basis) with the planning and realization of the construction project. See Fig. G.1.

Quality Control

Quality control is difficult to address in the BIM field. Even an as-built model will rarely reflect imperfections. Construction tolerance control is an area being researched currently, and how this will be integrated into the BIM approach still remains to be seen.

Quantity Takeoff

The quantity takeoff for a project is the list of materials required to construct that particular project. The 3D model is a very effective means to generate such a list, since the list will automatically update itself with changes made to the model. This information will become the basis for the cost estimate for the project.

Real Time

This refers to events happening simultaneously; e.g., a real-time model view indicates that the view of the model represents its actual state. It does not need to be changed into a different format to be viewed, and therefore we can look at the original model and not a copy of it. *Real time* is also used when referring to communications among project team members; it indicates that discussions take place among members at the same time, not by e-mail, where the system creates a lag between the messages. See also *Big Room*.

Risk

"The chance of injury, damage, or loss" (Webster's *New World College Dictionary*). Risk is an important consideration in construction projects; ultimately the owner of a project will generally assume the majority of the risk for a project. It is, however, in the interest of all the project team members to reduce risk to a minimum.

Schedule

The project schedule is the time line for the events related to the project planning and construction. A construction schedule may also address the resources required to accomplish the tasks as well as the dependencies of the tasks on one another.

Schematic

Project planning traditionally is arranged in phases. The first phase is schematic design, followed by design development, then the construction documentation phase is completed before the bidding phase begins, and the last phase is the construction of the project. The schematic phase includes all preliminary planning for the project, and BIM models with a low level of detail are proving very beneficial at this stage of the work.

Sequence

A *sequence* refers to the order in which the tasks for a construction project are completed. The BIM may include a series of images (movie) showing the order in which a project is assembled, and this is called a sequence analysis; it is a visual way to show the construction schedule.

Simulation

This means "the reproduction of the essential features of something, for example, as an aid to study or training" or "the construction of a mathematical model to reproduce the characteristics of a phenomenon, system, or process, often using a computer, in order to infer information or solve problems" (Encarta *World English Dictionary*). In our sense of the word it will refer to the computer representations of objects and processes related to construction projects. Also see *Virtual*.

Target Value Design

This means the setting of a target value to try to achieve with the design process of a project. The target value will include both a budget and certain goals that are to be reached within the budget. The word *value* here implies getting what it is worth, maximizing the value for the cost, and minimizing the waste in the process.

Tolerance

Tolerance is the allowable deviation from a design specification. In construction, tolerances are an important concept; the building components have to fit together, and the building has to be tight against air and water infiltration. Many of the materials require a larger tolerance in their placement, i.e., cast-in-place concrete or masonry construction, while other manufactured components, such as steel and curtain wall components, rely on much smaller tolerances. It is clearly a challenge to represent and analyze tolerances in a computer model.

Transitioning

This term will generally refer to the change from traditional project management methods to the use of building information modeling in a construction company.

Understanding

Understanding is the "the ability to perceive and explain the meaning or the nature of something" (Encarta *World English Dictionary*). Understanding is typically a result of knowledge and experience. It develops in degrees, and it is often difficult to communicate with someone whose understanding in a given subject area is too different from our own. Simply gathering knowledge does not create understanding; and a teacher can only help students to make the necessary effort to develop their personal understanding.

VDC

VDC is a term coined at Stanford University's CIFE (Center for Integrated Facilities Engineering) that means *virtual design and construction*. Since the term *BIM* has been coined, its use and definition seem to be evolving. VDC is an attempt to introduce a name that is more descriptive of the actual process in its entirety, because the name includes the planning and design phase of a project as well as its construction phase more explicitly.

Virtual Construction

Virtual means *not real*, and this refers to the processes taking place in the computer. *Virtual construction* is a term used by CIFE and Graphisoft to describe the use of a 3D computer model to simulate not only the design of a structure but also its assembly, the construction process. Virtual construction will likely include the analysis of the construction time and costs of the project through the use of a cost database connection and a link to scheduling software. See *Simulation*.

Visualization

Visualization is "the creation of a clear picture of something in the mind, or a clear picture of something created in the mind" (Encarta *World English Dictionary*). A 3D model is a symbolic representation of an object that is designed to aid in the visualization of that object. This word is closely tied to understanding and communication; it is necessary in a construction project to transfer the visualization of one individual to others so that the group can make progress on the same basis in the project. As was noted under Communication, visualization does not necessarily imply correct understanding either. It is, however, required to have a correct visualization to generate correct understanding of a subject or object.

Waste

Waste is what lean construction attempts to eliminate from a project. The idea of exactly what waste includes will depend on the viewpoint taken, but it is a generally productive way to analyze any process. Waste is unnecessary and should therefore be eliminated.

X-Ref

X-Ref is a term used in AutoCAD that means cross-reference. It is a file that exists outside of the actual project file, but is referenced in the project file so that it actually appears to be part of it. The advantage of an X-Ref is that since it exists in its own right, it can be modified independently and used in multiple host files. Thus updating an X-Ref will update all projects using that particular file. The concept is very similar to that of library part or module in other software tools. An X-Ref can be an entire project in its own right, and several layers of embedded X-Refs are not uncommon in complex projects.

Index

Abstractions, 47–48
    defined, 249
    models as, 95
    with solid models, 100–105
    with surface models, 98–99
Accuracy of models, 144
Actualization, in 3D space, 12
AGC (*see* Associated General
    Contractors of America)
American Institute of Architects
    (AIA), 8–9, 18, 21
Analysis, 37, 249
Anticipating problems, 14
ArchiCAD, 128, 129
Architects:
    contract issues for, 19
    evolution in role of, 5
    as project coordinators, 6
Architectural models, 108
    in DPR Construction case study,
        179, 180
    level of detail for, 186
Architecture:
    defined, 249
    incorporating BIM in education for,
        170
Archived file versions, 106
As-built models/drawings, 46
    specifying models, 75–76
    updated BIM as, 150
Assembly instructions, 42
Assembly sequences, 61, 113
Associated General Contractors of
    America (AGC), 8–9, 18
Autodesk, 36, 124–128
Automatic, defined, 249–250
Automatic links, 35

Ballard, Glen, 14, 15
Bea Campus, San Jose, 122–123
Bedrick, Jim, 235
Bentley, 36, 122–124
Best practices, 152

Big room, 40, 90, 192, 193, 250
Billing controls, 62
BIM (*see* Building information
    modeling)
BIM facilitators, 86–87, 147, 148,
    151–152
BIM implementation, 84–92
    BIM specialists' training for, 152
    continual evaluation in, 26
    defined, 255
    defining/scheduling of deliverables,
        90–92
    developing BIM processes, 87–90
    legal aspects of, 17–23
    planning for, 81–84
    project team selection, 85–87
    skills for, 137
BIM managers, 86, 147–148, 151–152
BIM operators, 86, 147, 148, 151–152
BIM project planning, 52–84
    in construction phase, 58–64
    fundamental questions for, 52
    for implementation, 81–84
    in planning and preconstruction
        phase, 53–64
    in postconstruction phase, 65
    in preconstruction phase, 37–43
    as process, 88
    specifying the model, 65–81
Borzage, Michael, 10
Building, as part of human
    experience, 1
Building contractors, 5, 150
Building information modeling
    (BIM), 25–53
    benefits of, 46–52
    course of construction in, 43–45
    defined, 250–251
    implementation of (*see* BIM
        implementation)
    misunderstanding of, 20
    in postconstruction phase, 45–46
    preconstruction planning in, 37–43
    processes of, 37–47

Building information modeling
    (BIM) (*Cont.*):
    as project as well as process, 25
    and project documentation, 7–8
    project information in, 36–37
    and project management, 4–6
    project models in, 28–35
    project planning in (*see* BIM
        project planning)
    psychological approach for, 3
    as a tool, 3
    and transparency of management
        process, 3
Building projects:
    social context of, 1
    tasks related to, 4
Building system controls, 46
Bundled software, 109

California Academy of Sciences,
    San Francisco, California, 54
California State University, Chico,
    44, 50, 140, 149
Camino Medical Group project (*see*
    DPR Construction case study)
Carlyle project, 116–117
Cash flow analysis, 62, 113
CATIA, 94*n*
CDs (*see* Construction documents)
Center for Integrated Facility
    Engineering (CIFE), 16,
    89–90, 251
Centralized databases, 36,123–124, 253
Change orders, 12
Charettes (*see* Design charettes)
CIFE (*see* Center for Integrated
    Facility Engineering)
Civil engineering, incorporating BIM
    in education for, 170
Clash detection, 38, 84
    as BIM application, 110, 112
    with NavisWorks, 122
    for resolving conflicts, 193, 194

Clash detection (*Cont.*):
  with 3D model, 40, 41, 55–56
  as tool for virtual coordination,
    146–147
CMAA (Construction Management
  Association of America), 9
CMs (*see* Construction managers)
Collaboration, 1
  as BIM benefit, 47, 51
  in construction projects, 2
  of consultants, 55
  in contractual relationships, 12
  defined, 251
  Fruchter's program addressing, 60
  in human action/interaction, 3–4
  human characteristics helping/
    hindering, 2–3
  in Integrated Agreement, 23
  in learning, 141–142
  for problem solving, 47
  promoting, 86
  for risk reduction, 14
  team roles involving, 147
Commercial projects, VDC for (*see*
  DPR Construction case study)
Common sense, defined, 251
Communication:
  as BIM process, 88
  and complexity of projects, 12
  defined, 251
  forms of, 49
  Fruchter's program addressing, 60
  in human action/interaction, 3–4
  illustrations and movies for, 110–111
  for integrated project teams, 23
  planning channels of, 59
  in project management, 5
  on project teams, 85–86
  for risk reduction, 13–14
  skill set for, 146
  with 3D models, 28
  through 2D documents, 7, 8, 28
  for true collaboration, 51
  2D methods for, 12
  as two-way exchange, 48, 49
Competition, among team members, 12
Component information, 76–77
Components:
  defined, 251
  linking of time-related information
    to, 36

Composite models, 31, 34, 252
Conceptual, defined, 252
Conceptual design and marketing,
  53–54
Conceptualization, of installation
  requirements, 43–45
Conceptual models:
  for project visualization, 143–144
  specifying, 69–71
Conceptual phase, cost assessment in,
  41–43
Conflicts, elimination of, 51–52
Confucius, 139
Constructability:
  defined, 252
  study of, 49–50
  visualizing, 41
Constructability analysis, 57, 110, 112
Construction, skills and interests
  required for, 1
Construction budget, 38
  cost buckets in, 62
  creation of, 54
  defined, 252
Construction contracts, incentive for
  change in, 21–23
Construction cost estimates, 113
Construction documents (CDs):
  in design-bid-build method, 10
  evolution of, 5
  model linked to, 38
Construction industry:
  contractual incentives for change
    in, 21–23
  current practice in, 8
  delivery systems in, 8–11
  goals for process improvement in,
    13–17
  inefficiency of, 6
  transition to model-based contracts
    in, 18–21
  and weaknesses of planning and
    construction process, 11–13
Construction management:
  approaches to, 6
  BIM simulation of, 43–45
  BIM specialists in, 151–152
  incorporating BIM in education for,
    166–171
  processes enabling, 37
  use of BIM for, 59–60

Construction Management Association
  of America (CMAA), 9
Construction managers (CMs), 8–9
Construction models, specifying, 72
Construction phase, project management in, 58–64
Construction process management,
  61–64
Construction projects:
  benefits of BIM for, 46
  collaboration in, 2
  defined, 252
  different BIM for phases of, 37
  (*See also specific phases*)
  goals for, 3
Construction schedule, 57
  analysis of, 61
  in construction phase, 61–62
  defined, 259
  improving, 16
  optimization of, 59
  sequential analysis for, 113
Construction sequence, simulation of,
  57
Construction sequence analysis,
  43–45, 52, 61
Construction Simulation Lab, 10
Construction tolerances, 95
Constructor, 128–131
Consultants:
  collaboration by, 55
  models produced by, 108
Contract authors, 8
Contracts for construction, 5
  access to BIM information in, 21
  architect's responsibilities in, 19
  contingency clause in, 20
  delivery systems used in, 8–11
  with model-based project manage-
    ment, 18–21
  standard of care clause in, 20
Contractual issues with BIM, 150
Contractual responsibilities, 9
Coordination:
  as BIM process, 88
  defined, 252
  of installation, 199–201
  management of process, 185,
    189–194
  of MEP/FP systems, 175–176
  of modeling, 194–195

Coordination (*Cont.*):
  in preconstruction phase, 40
  of project team work, 59
  pull coordination schedule, 195–197
  skill set for, 146–147
  in 3D visualization, 50
Cost analysis:
  at conceptual design stage, 53–54
  defined, 253
  links for, 58
  with solid modeling, 106
Cost buckets, 62
Cost databases, 41–43, 58, 243
Cost estimates, 31
  defined, 253
  deriving, 41–42
  planning for, 53
  quantitative analysis for, 113
  (*See also* Webcor Builders case
    study)
Cost reductions, 14–16

Daily stand-up meetings, 198–199
Databases:
  centralized, 36, 123–124, 253
  cost, 41–42, 58, 243
  defined, 253
  federated, 36, 123–124, 253
Data control, 65
Data storage, 243
DD (design development) documents,
  71
DDE (*see* Direct digital exchange)
Deadlines, 142
Deliverables, 59
  choosing methods for, 82–84
  defining/scheduling, 90–92
  processes necessary to generate, 88
  understanding, 81–82
Delivering the BIM, 88
Delivery methods/systems, 8–11
  defined, 253
  just-in-time, 15
  lean, 14–15
  and risk for architects, 19
  shifting of risks with, 46–47
  standard vs. BIM, 145
Deployment, 253
Design-assist method, 9, 10
Design-bid-build method, 8–10

Design-build method, 9–11
Design charettes, 16, 254
Design development (DD)
  documents, 71
Design models, specifying, 69–71
Design to Build, 131–133
Detailing models, specifying, 73–75
Di Furia, Renzo, 214
Digital Data Licensing Agreement
  (AIA C106-2007), 21
Digital Data Protocol Exhibit
  (AIA E201-2007), 21
Dimensionality, 49, 254
Dimensions, in model intelligence,
  29, 30
Direct digital exchange (DDE), 62, 101
Documentation:
  conflicts among, 7–8
  defined, 254
  2D, 28
DPR Construction case study,
  173–203
  architectural model in, 179, 180
  benefits of VDC in, 201–203
  coordination of MEP/FP systems
    in, 175–176
  daily stand-up meetings for,
    198–199
  electrical model in, 183
  general and specialty contractors'
    roles in, 177–178
  installation coordination in, 199–201
  levels of detail for models in,
    184–188
  management of coordination
    process in, 185, 189–194
  mechanical model in, 181–182
  modeling coordination schedule for,
    194–195
  plumbing model in, 183–184
  prefabrication with 3D MEP/FP
    models, 178
  pull coordination schedule for,
    195–197
  selecting elements/systems to
    model, 178–179
  sprinkler model in, 184, 185
  structural model in, 179–181
  use of Last Planner System in, 198
  weekly coordination meeting
    agenda for, 197–198

Drawings:
  computerized, 7
  misunderstandings with use of, 7
  responsibility for, 19
  shop, 62
  2-D, 5

Edges, in surface modeling, 99
EDI (electronic data interchange), 62
Educating in BIM (*see* Learning of
  BIM)
Electrical models:
  in DPR Construction case study, 183
  level of detail for, 187–188
Electronic data interchange (EDI), 62
Elements, 35
  defined, 254
  installation sequence for, 42
Elimination:
  as BIM benefit, 47, 51–52
  defined, 254
Energy analysis, 110
Energy performance:
  as preconstruction phase issue, 55
  simulating/evaluating, 42
Energy-related components, return on
  investment in, 55
Energy use, improving, 17
Engineering, incorporating BIM in
  education for, 170
Equipment maintenance schedules, 46
Estimates (*see* Cost estimates)
Evaluation, 26, 49, 55
Expectations of participants, 20
External information, 79
Extreme Collaboration (XC)
  approach, 193

Fabrication, 62–64, 73, 74, 104–105
Facilitated coordination meeting, 45
Facilities management (FM), 65
Federated databases, 36, 123–124,
  253
Field:
  avoiding problems in, 27
  defined, 254
File formats, 31
  defined, 254–255
  and model linking, 35

Files:
   registration, 109
   working vs. archived, 106
Fire protection (FP) models, 108
   (*See also* DPR Construction case
      study)
5D models, 49, 254
   for conceptual design and
      marketing, 53–54
   schematic, 58
FM (facilities management), 65
Forecasting project, 58
Fort Bliss Headquarters, 29, 30
4D models, 49, 199–201, 254
FP (fire protection) models, 108
Fruchter, Renate, 55, 60, 61,86, 90

Gehry, Frank, 94*n*
General contractors, in VDC process,
      177
General Motors (GM), 10–11
GMP (guaranteed maximum price), 9
Goals:
   for process improvement, 13–17
   of projects, 3
   of project team members, 3
   for simulations, 53
Goethe, Johann von, 140
Google, 121–123
Government Services Administration
      (GSA), 46, 128, 152
Graphical input, 255
Graphisoft, 128, 241
Graphisoft Construction Services, 236
Gregory P. Luth & Assoc., Inc. case
      study, 224–234
GSA (*see* Government Services
      Administration)
Guaranteed maximum price (GMP), 9

Hochtief, 214
Howell, Greg, 14, 15
Human action/interaction, basic
      concepts of, 3–4
Human nature:
   defined, 255
   helping and hindering collaboration,
      2–3
   and learning, 137
   as obstacle to communication, 12

IAI (International Alliance for
      Interoperability), 35
IFC (industry foundation class), 255
IFC (international foundation class)
      format, 35
Implementation of BIM (*see* BIM
      implementation)
Industry foundation class (IFC),
      255
Information:
   access to and flow of, 49
   communication of, 48, 49
   project (*see* Project information)
Information feedback loop, 26,
      27, 51
   as BIM process, 88
   in model contents development,
      55
   monitoring of model specifications
      in, 90
Information management, 87–88
   skill set for, 146
   with solid modeling tools, 106
Input, defined, 255
Installation coordination, 199–201
Installation requirements, visualization/
      conceptualization of, 43–45
Integrated Agreement (Sutter Health),
      22–23
Integrated Project Delivery (IPD)
      Team, 22–23
Integrated project teams, 21–23
Integration, 255
Intelligent objects, 81
Interface, 255
International Alliance for
      Interoperability (IAI), 35
International foundation class (IFC)
      format, 35
Interoperability:
   defined, 255
   with model-to-model links, 35
   with NavisWorks, 109
   of software tools, 35, 94
   with virtual catalog parts, 107
IPD Team (*see* Integrated Project
      Delivery Team)
i-room, 89–90
Iterative analysis of BIM, 83

Just-in-time (JIT) delivery, 15

Kaganovich, Lev, 245
Khanzode, Atul, 173
Knowledge, understanding vs., 26, 27

LAP (look ahead plan), 197
Laser scan process, 46, 75–76
   (*See also* Turner Construction
      (Sacramento, California) case
      study)
Last Planner System (LPS), 15, 196,
      199
Layers (in modeling), 105
LCI (*see* Lean Construction Institute)
Leadership in Energy and
      Environmental Design (LEED®,
      16, 17
Lean construction, 14–15, 47,
      52, 256
Lean Construction Institute (LCI),
      14, 15
Lean project delivery, 21–22
Lean Project Delivery System (LPDS),
      175
Learning of BIM, 137–170
   by BIM specialists, 151–152
   ease of use and learning curves in, 83
   by incorporating BIM in existing
      classes, 166–171
   learner characteristics for, 149
   methods for, 138–142
   motivation for, 138–139
   obstacles to, 139–140
   by project owners, 149–150
   skill sets in, 143–148
   steps for success in, 140–142
   by university students, 152–168
LEED® (*see* Leadership in Energy
      and Environmental Design)
Legal aspects of BIM implementation,
      17–23
Library parts, 242
   defined, 256
   as information link, 80–81
   in solid modeling, 106–107
   in surface modeling, 99
Lichtig, William, 18–19, 21–22
Life cycle analysis, 256
Life cycle cost, 256
Life-cycle cost, 42
Life cycle cost analysis, 113
Life cycle management, 150

Life-cycle performance improvement, 17
Lighting, simulating/evaluating, 42
Light tables, 7, 38, 40
Lines of balance schedule, 57, 150, 256
Link, defined, 256
Linked information, 78
Linking, 35, 36
  for cost data, 41–42, 58
  embedded, 49
  to postconstruction databases, 46
  in project models, 35
  for visualization, 48
Litigation, 13, 17
Location conflicts, 52
Look ahead plan (LAP), 197
LPDS (Lean Project Delivery System), 175
LPS (*see* Last Planner System)
Luth, Greg, 224

Maintainability of components, improving, 17
Maintenance, return on investment in, 55
Management of process, in BIM implementation planning, 83–84
Management processes, 3
  (*See also* Construction management; Operations management)
Mapping, 256
Marketing:
  illustrations and movies for, 110–111
  models for, 53–54
Master builders, 4–5
Mathematical models, 95
Mechanical, electrical, plumbing (MEP) models, 108
  (*See also individual case studies*)
Mechanical models:
  in DPR Construction case study, 181–182
  level of detail for, 186–187
MEP (mechanical, electrical, plumbing) models, 108
  (*See also individual case studies*)
Methods:
  defined, 257
  delivery (*see* Delivery methods/systems)
  for determining interoperability, 257

MicroStation TriForma, 122–124
Model analysis, 109–117
  qualitative, 110–112
  quantitative, 113–117
  sequential, 113
Model-based contracts, 18–21
Model-based estimating (*see* Webcor Builders case study)
Model-cost data link, 41–42
Modeling:
  object-based, 31
  selecting elements/systems for, 178–179
  software tools for, 95–107
  (*See also* Building information modeling)
Modeling coordination schedule, 194–195
Model intelligence, 29–34,38, 46
Model production:
  by BIM specialists, 151
  software tools for, 107–109
Model Progression Specification (MPS), 241–242
Models:
  components of, 36
  composite, 31, 34
  defined, 257
  object-oriented, 53
  outsourcing of, 34, 108
  project, 28–35
  responsibility for, 19
  smart, 29, 31
  solid, 29
  surface, 29
  virtual, 38–42
  (*See also* DPR Construction case study; *specific types of models*)
Model-to-information links, 35, 36, 79–81
Model-to-model links, 35
Motivation to learn, 138–139
MPS (*see* Model Progression Specification)
Multicultural experiences, 61

NavisWorks, 97, 98, 109, 119–121
*N*D, 254
Non-3D element modelers, 95–99
Numeric input, 255

Object based, defined, 257
Object-based modeling, 31
Object libraries, 242
Object model-based management, 65
Object models, 257
Object-oriented models, 53
Objects, 53
  defined, 257
  intelligent, 81
Object tools, 106
Obstacles to learning, 139–140
On-site superintendents, 5
Operations and maintenance models, specifying, 76
Operations control, 65
Operations management, 37, 65
Organization of models:
  solid models, 105–106
  surface models, 99
Outsourcing of models, 34, 108
Owners:
  benefits of BIM for, 150
  goals of, 3, 53
  learning of BIM by, 149–150
  reporting progress to, 59
  risk assumed by, 9
  unrealistic expectations of, 20
Ownership of BIM model, 150

Parametric, defined, 257
Parametric information, 30–33, 77–78
  for objects, 35
  with solid modelers, 107
Partnering, 19
PBL (*see* Problem-, Project-, Product-, Process-, People-Based Learning; Project Based learning Lab)
Perseverance, 142
Peters, Frank, 205
Planes, in surface modeling, 99
Planning, 4
  in BIM, 25
  (*See also* BIM project planning)
  BIM specialists in, 151
  defined, 257
Planning and construction process:
  BIM's similarity to, 25
  weaknesses of, 11–13

Planning and design phase (*see* Preconstruction phase)
Plumbing models:
  in DPR Construction case study, 183–184
  level of detail for, 188
Point cloud, 75
Postconstruction phase, BIM project planning for, 45–46
Post-design constructability reviews, 18
Preconstruction phase:
  BIM processes in, 37–43
  improving, 16
  project management in, 58–64
Prefabrication, 16, 105
  defined, 258
  with 3D MEP/FP models, 178
Preparation for BIM, 142
Problem-, Project-, Product-, Process-, People-Based Learning (PBL), 60–61
Problem solving:
  collaboration for, 47
  in construction phase, 43–45
Process controls, 65
Process(es), 37–46
  BIM as, 258
  (*See also* BIM implementation; BIM project planning)
  BIM specialists' training with, 151–152
  in course of construction, 43–45
  defined, 258
  developing, 87–90
  in postconstruction phase, 45–46
  in preconstruction planning, 37–43
Process improvement, goals for, 13–17
Process modeling, 95–98
Process-related skills, 145–147
Production rate information, 57
Productivity, 6
Professional disciplines, 5
Progressive estimates, 237–240
Project, BIM as, 25
Project Based learning Lab (PBL), 60, 90
Project coordinators, 5–6
Project costs, forecasting/tracking, 58
Project design:
  improving, 16
  processes enabling, 37

Project development:
  defining all aspects of, 52
  processes enabling, 37
Project information:
  in BIM, 36–37
  in BIM implementation planning, 83
  feedback loop for, 26, 27
  in specifying models, 76–80
  in visualization, 48
Project information processing, 87–90
Project management:
  evolution of, 4–6
  in preconstruction and construction phases, 58–64
Project models, 28–35
  linking in, 35
  model intelligence, 29–34
  sources for, 31, 34
  virtual, 29
Project quality improvement, 16–17
Project schedule, 259
Project team management, 59–61
Project teams:
  assembling, 2–3
  BIM specialists on, 151
  collaboration in, 51
  competition among members, 12
  defined, 258
  defining members and skills for, 84
  dynamics of, 85–86
  goals of, 53
  integrated, 21–23
  interpretation of goals by, 3
  litigation among, 17
  roles on, 86–87
  selection of, 85–87
  in simulation production, 47
  working processes established by, 7
Project templates, 152
Property management phase (*see* Postconstruction phase)
Pull coordination schedule, 195–197
Purchasing software, 115–118

Qualitative model analysis, 112–113
Quality control, 258
Quality improvement, 16–17
Quantitative model analysis, 113–117
Quantity takeoff, 113, 258

Real time, defined, 258
Real time communication, 60
Reed, Dean, 173
Registration, 144
Registration files, 109
Reporting protocol, 59
Requests for Information (RFIs), 8, 11–12
Return on investment, 55, 176–177
Revit, 101, 103, 105, 113, 124–128
RFIs (*see* Requests for Information)
Risk:
  assessment of, 9
  defined, 258–259
  elimination of, 51, 52
  with integrated project teams, 23
  shifting, 12, 19, 47
Risk reduction, 13–14, 46–47, 149, 150
Ritz Carlton project, 112, 114–115
Role-related skills, 147–148
RQ Construction case study, 205–213
  building phase in, 210–213
  definition phase of, 205–208
  design and MEPS coordination planning in, 208–210
Ryan, Matt, 235

Safety, improving, 14
Schedule analysis, 61
Schedules:
  construction (*see* Construction schedule)
  defined, 259
  for deliverables, 90–92
  modeling coordination, 194–195
  pull coordination, 195–197
Scheduling advantages, with use of BIM, 150
Scheduling conflicts, 52
Schematic, defined, 259
Schematic models, 54
  as basis for design work, 55
  5D, 58
  production of, 108
  specifying, 69–71
SCOP (sequential composite overlay process), 175
Sequence, defined, 259

Sequence analysis, 105
  (*See also* Construction sequence
    analysis)
Sequential composite overlay process
    (SCOP), 175
Sequential model analysis, 113
Shop drawings, 62
Simulations, 25, 95
  advantages of, 27
  BIM (*see* Building information
    modeling)
  defined, 25, 259
  structuring, 145
  (*See also* Models)
Site models, 108
SketchUp, 99, 121–123
Smart models, 29, 31
Software industry, 93
Software tools, 93–136
  ArchiCAD, 128, 129
  from Autodesk, 124–128
  from Bentley, 122–124
  Constructor, 128–131
  Design to Build, 131–133
  ease of use and learning curves for,
    83
  gaining control over, 144
  from Google, 121–123
  for intelligent models, 46
  interoperability of, 35, 94
  links with, 35
  management of, 88–90
  MicroStation TriForma, 122–124
  for model analysis, 109–117
  for modeling, 95–107
  for model production, 107–109
  NavisWorks, 119–121
  non-3D element modelers, 95–99
  preparing for purchase of,
    115–118
  Revit, 124–128
  SketchUp, 121–123
  solid modelers, 100–107
  Tekla, 133–136
  from Vico, 128–131
  for virtual design and construction,
    38–42
Solid modelers, 100–107
Solid models, 29
Space studies, 61
Space utilization, use of BIM for, 46

Specialty contractors:
  managing handoffs with, 190–192
  in VDC process, 178
Specialty fields, 5
Specialty models, 108
Specifications, computerized, 7
Specifying models, 65–81
  as-built models, 75–76
  conceptual or schematic models,
    69–71
  construction models, 72
  design models, 69–71
  detailing models, 73–75
  and function of object in project, 67
  links between models and informa-
    tion in, 79–81
  matrices for, 65–67
  nature of information for, 76–79
  operations and maintenance
    models, 76
  physical parameters of objects, 67
  shop drawing models, 73, 74
  stories of, 67, 68
  for temporary unseen work, 68–69
Sprinkler models:
  in DPR Construction case study,
    184, 185
  level of detail for, 188
Standard of care, 20
Standards, 240–242
Stanford University, 60, 61, 90
Structural models, 108
  in DPR Construction case study,
    179–181
  level of detail for, 186
Surface modelers, 29, 95–99
Sutter General Hospital renovation
    project, 245–248
Sutter Health, 17, 21–22
Sutter Surgical Hospital North Valley,
    56, 58, 71, 72, 75
  (*See also* RQ Construction case
    study)
Symbols, 47
Systems coordination, 110

Target value design, 23, 38, 41–42
  in conceptual design stage, 54
  defined, 58, 259
Team information processing, 85–87

Technical logistics, 185, 189
Tekla, 101, 104, 133–136
  (*See also* Gregory P. Luth &
    Assoc., Inc. case study)
Templates, 242–243
3D models, 49, 254
  for conceptual design and
    marketing, 53–54
  development of, 55–59
  in fabrication, 62–64
  for project models, 28
  and project team management, 59
  for project visualization, 143–144
Time reductions, 16
Timing of model production, 96–97
Tolerances, 95, 144, 259
Tool management, 88–90
Tool-related skills, 143–145
Tools, 2, 151–152
  (*See also* Software tools)
Toyota Motor Company, 14, 15
Toyota production system (TPS), 15
Tracking projects, 58, 88
Training:
  of BIM specialists, 151–152
  for software operators, 89, 94
  (*See also* Learning of BIM)
Transitioning, 260
Transparency:
  of BIM process, 82
  of management process, 3
Turner Construction (Sacramento,
    California) case study, 245–248
Turner Construction (Seattle,
    Washington) case study, 214–223
  background of projects, 214–215
  medical office building project,
    215–216
  $90 million core and shell medical
    office building, 218, 219
  $18 million office building project,
    218
  $100 million residence, 218–223
  $150 million residence project,
    217–218
2D, 49, 254

Understanding:
  of BIM deliverables, 81–82
  of BIM processes, 25

Understanding (*Cont.*):
  defined, 260
  in human action/interaction, 3–4
  knowledge vs., 26, 27
  of need for reevaluation, 26
  processes enabling, 37
  in 3D space, 12
  visualization and, 47
University BIM programs, 152–168
  faculty preparation for, 170–171
  first-semester, 156–160
  fourth-semester, 161–166
  introduction class, 153–156
  overview of, 153
  second-semester, 158–160
  third-semester, 160–161
University of California Santa
  Barbara Student Resource
  Center, 50, 91–92
Updating of BIM, 59, 88, 106

Value engineering, 18, 54, 57
VDC (*see* Virtual design and
  construction)
Vico, 36, 101, 103, 128–133

Vico Project control, 113
Victorville City Hall, 29, 30
Virtual catalog parts, 106–107
Virtual construction:
  with BIM, 27
  defined, 260
Virtual design and construction (VDC):
  on commercial projects (*see* DPR
    Construction case study)
  defined, 260
  development of (*see* Webcor
    Builders case study)
  software tools for, 38–42
Virtual models, 29, 38–42
Visualization:
  as BIM benefit, 47–50
  as BIM skill, 143–144
  of constructability, 41
  defined, 260
  in human action/interaction, 3–4
  incorrect, 11
  of installation requirements, 43–45
  for problem solving, 43–45
  surface modelers for, 29
  with 3D models, 28
  in 3D space, 12

Waste, 15
  defined, 260
  elimination of, 51, 52
  in lean construction, 52
  in starting model over, 36–37
Waste reduction, 47, 149–150
Webcor Builders case study, 235–244
  history of project, 235–236
  implementation approach in, 236,
    237
  infrastructure in, 242–244
  processes in, 236–240
  standards in, 240–242
Weekly coordination meetings,
  197–198

XC (Extreme Collaboration) approach,
  193
X-refs, 81, 261

Yoakum, Sue, 20, 21

Zettel, George, 245